W9-AFC-870

Gumercindo and Aparicio Saravia

JOHN CHARLES CHASTEEN

HEROES

A LIFE AND TIMES

ON

OF THE LAST

HORSEBACK

GAUCHO CAUDILLOS

UNIVERSITY OF NEW MEXICO PRESS ALBUQUERQUE

Library of Congress Cataloging-in-Publication Data

Chasteen, John Charles, 1955–
Heroes on horseback : a life and times of the last gaucho caudillos /
John Charles Chasteen. — 1st ed.   p.   cm.
Includes bibliographical references and index.
ISBN 0-8263-1597-6. — ISBN 0-8263-1598-4 (pbk.)
1. Saravia, Aparicio, 1856–1904.   2. Saraiva, Gumersindo, 1852–1894.
3. Uruguay—History—1875–1904.   4. Rio Grande do Sul (Brazil)—History—
Federalist Revolution, 1893–1895.   5. Caudillos—Uruguay—History.
6. Caudillos—Brazil—Rio Grande do Sul—History   I. Title.
F2726.S26C43   1995   94-18720   CIP
981'.05—dc20

Frontispieces courtesy the Biblioteca Nacional Montevideo, Uruguay

Designed by Linda M. Tratachaud

A SERIES OF COURSE ADOPTION BOOKS ON LATIN AMERICA:

Independence in Spanish America: Civil Wars, Revolutions, and Underdevelopment—Jay Kinsbruner, Queens College

Heroes on Horseback: A Life and Times of the Last Gaucho Caudillos—John Chasteen, University of North Carolina at Chapel Hill

Series senior advisory editor is Lyman L. Johnson, University of North Carolina at Charlotte

CONTENTS

ACKNOWLEDGMENTS

In the beginning was the dissertation. My grateful acknowledgement to the Social Science Research Council, the U. S. Department of Education, and the Institute for the Arts and the Humanities of the University of North Carolina at Chapel Hill for funding the various stages of its creation and its transformation into the present book.

I also want to thank many who helped in other, no less vital, ways. My mentors Joseph Tulchin, Gilbert Joseph, and José Pedro Barrán guided my wobbly first steps. Many others read and commented on the manuscript, contributed an annecdote or a citation, offered encouragement, or otherwise aided and abetted this undertaking: Ambar Joffre Abelar, Carlos Benavídez, Rachel Bowman, Sarah Chambers, Juan Pivel Devoto, Germán Gil Villaamil, Tim Henderson, David Holtby, Víctor Gannello, Sandra Jatahy Pesavento, Lyman Johnson, Sharon Kellum, Josie McNeil, Ricardo Marletti Strada, Enrique Mena Segarra, Sharon Mújica, Gervásio Neves, Franklin Parker, Júlio Petersen, Michael Pratt, Juan Rial, Bill Schell, Lars Schoultz, Tarcisco da Costa Taborda, Allen Wells, and Barbara Weinstein.

Nor can I forget to acknowledge the Uruguayans and the Rio Grandenses who fetched out relics of various kinds in archives, libraries, museums, ministries, churches, banks, and ranch houses. They also shared *mate*, roasted *churrascos*, recited *El gaucho Martín Fierro*, showed how one judges cattle or throws a *taba*, patiently demonstrated the strum to *lundu* and *milonga,* and suffered their horses to be ridden by a complete *maturrango.*

Thanks, also, to my father, who taught me that the past is never dead; to my mother, who taught me her love for the written word; to my children, who kept this book in perspective by scarcely noticing it; to Carmen, who generously tolerated it for more than a decade; and to all my friends who offered an embrace, or a cold beer, or whatever, and who (not being scholars, for the most part) preserve a healthy appreciation of what is boring and what is not.

To readers like them, I dedicate this book.

HEROES ON HORSEBACK

1

CAUDILLOS

"Viva el General Saravia!" A shout went up invariably when his men saw him on horseback in battle, but Aparicio Saravia's famous white poncho made him a clear target for enemy sharp shooters as he rode in front of his line of soldiers to encourage them. Always he had laughed—"But they can't hit me!"—at the concern expressed by his officers. This time, at dusk on 1 September 1904, the massed fire came from only two hundred yards away. Two bullets hit Saravia's horse, staggering it, and his sons Nepomuceno and Mauro went toward him, but before they arrived a third bullet hit the general, who slumped forward onto his horse's withers, and a shudder went through the insurgent army. Having watched a lot of bullets do their work, these tough fighters knew to expect the worst when Nepomuceno opened his father's shirt to staunch the welling blood. It was a stomach wound, bringing high risk of fatal infection. Aparicio tried to smile, but he looked pale and wan as darkness settled over the Brazilian–Uruguayan borderland. The moon rose, and the congealing frost seemed to glow dully on the trampled grass. "Don't let the men know I'm wounded," he said as they carried him away, but the army already knew.[1]

During that day of fighting along the Brazilian border, Saravia's Uruguayan insurgents had stood firm against a strong force of Uruguayan government troops. They also possessed the advantage of superior reserves for the next day. Had they stayed to fight, they might well have won. Instead, the astonished government forces awoke to see the insurgents streaming away across the border in a disorganized rout. Without their hero to give them unity, they had lost all cohesion. The insurgent officers refused to obey the formal second-in-command, and their men seemed altogether to have lost the will to fight. During the next few days, Nepomuceno found the archive of his father's general staff abandoned in a shed near the battlefield, while not far away, in a ranch house just across the Brazilian border, Aparicio Saravia's raging fever signaled the onset of peritonitis, and then, of pneumonia. As the cold wind of a southern hemisphere winter howled outside, Aparicio sank into delirium, directing past battles and ordering imaginary attacks, but even before he died, the army he commanded had ceased to exist. Thus ended the Uruguayan civil war of 1904, the last of so many to convulse that small country in the three generations since independence.[2]

This military collapse recalled the similar loss of an irreplaceable leader during the Brazilian civil war of 1893–1895. Here the fallen hero was Gumercindo Saravia, Aparicio's older brother. Following Gumercindo's death in August 1894, his followers had agreed unanimously that the best path to follow was the quickest one out of Brazil, but they found themselves too far from the border to escape with the body of their slain leader, whom they buried in a nearby church yard. What happened next, recounted in a dozen different versions by the tellers of this tale, shows the special importance attached to the person of the leader by friend and foe alike. The pursuing government forces found Gumercindo's grave, exhumed his corpse, and sprawled it by the roadside. The government commander marched his troops past it so everyone would see that this rather small man—the subject of some very tall tales in the past year—was truly dead. Then the government forces forbid anyone to bury Gumercindo, and when an old woman reburied him anyway, they exhumed him again. Finally, a government officer cut off Gumercindo's head, alleging that the cranium of this misguided military prodigy merited scientific study, just as was done to the body of millenarian leader Antonio Conselheiro a few years later in the backlands of northeastern Brazil.[3]

The brothers Gumercindo and Aparicio Saravia were *caudillos*, leaders capable of inspiring intense devotion among a loyal personal following independent of any formal institution, leaders who became generals *after* acquiring an army of followers rather than the other way around. In many ways, the Saravias' mounted guerrillas of the 1890s resembled the "gaucho hordes" who had struck terror in the heart of city-dwelling writer Domingo Faustino Sarmiento half a century earlier, leading him to begin the Spanish American polemic on the phenomenon of *caudillismo* with his *Facundo, or Civilization and Barbarism* (1845). By the 1890s, the impromptu light cavalry of the southern plains was no longer a match for government armies, now equipped with Mauser rifles and Krupp artillery, coordinated by telegraph and transported by rail, and the insurgents could do little more than gallop through the grasslands with government troops in hot pursuit, rarely capturing towns and never holding them for long. If Facundo was among the first "gaucho" caudillos, the Saravias were among the last.[4]

Occurring on the eve of the twentieth century, the Saravias' rebellions were much better recorded than those of the 1830s and 1840s. Daily newspapers in modernized capital cities sent reporters, a number of well-educated participants produced numerous accounts of their own, and, in contrast to earlier condemnations by observers like Sarmiento, many chroniclers of the 1890s—particularly in Uruguay— celebrated the rustic qualities of these "barbarous" caudillos and their "gaucho" followers, thereby displaying the same creole nativist spirit evident in the Argentine pulp novels of the period. The Saravias' appeal as nativist symbols led Manuel Gálvez, the conservative Argentine literary nationalist of the early twentieth century, to write a *Life of Aparicio Saravia* (1942), and an Uruguayan historical and literary tradition has continued to surround Aparicio with tribute in prose and verse since the last years of the nineteenth century. Interestingly, however, the image of the older brother Gumercindo, once famous throughout Brazil, has faded practically into oblivion. Today, an equestrian statue of Aparicio towers over a busy intersection in Montevideo, the capital of Uruguay, while no statue of Gumercindo can be found in Brazil—yet, of the two, Gumercindo was the better general.[5]

The Saravias' contrasting careers as culture heroes provide a metaphor for general Spanish American and Brazilian patterns of nineteenth-century political history. Caudillos stand in the path of any narrative of Spanish American history, enigmatic and unavoidable.

One encounters the most famous of them—Rosas, Morazán, Santa Anna, Alvarez, Artigas, Páez, Obando, Castilla, Flores, and so on and on—somewhere between independence and the onset of export-oriented economic growth after 1870. The list of national-level caudillos alone includes hundreds of names, especially if one adds all the leaders to whom the term has been applied in the twentieth century. Almost invariably, their rise occurred in a "revolution," or at least, in a civil war or barracks revolt that they termed such. Narratives of Brazilian national history, on the other hand, offer few equivalents. A different Brazilian pattern is clear in the career of one of that country's best remembered military leaders, the Duque de Caxias, who put down provincial rebellions and fought foreign wars but never turned his arms against the government. Why do such heroes on horseback dominate the pages of Spanish American, but not Brazilian, history in the nineteenth century?[6]

This book will suggest an answer to that question by using the careers of Gumercindo and Aparicio Saravia to make an argument that departs significantly from the conventional wisdom concerning Spanish American *caudillismo*. Current interpretations all privilege the logic of political economy. Since Sarmiento, historians have observed the close relationship between landowning and political power in the nineteenth century, a relationship naturally central to Marxian renderings. Tulio Halperín Donghi has pointed out the militarization of rural society, resulting inevitably from the long and hard-fought Spanish American wars of independence, and John Lynch has described how caudillos distributed the spoils of war and then became the "prime protectors" of the propertied classes in the 1830s. E. Bradford Burns has argued that some caudillos gained a following by defending the interests of ordinary folk. All these historians, however, present economic interests as the driving force of Spanish American caudillismo, and they say little about the leaders as heroes, attractive figures who occasionally prompted idealistic emulation as well as pragmatic obedience among their followers. It is this last element—the caudillo as culture hero—that will be emphasized here. By concentrating on what the Saravias' followers thought about them, I hope to show how backlands caudillos could thrill and inspire, whether or not they defended the material interests of their followers.[7]

The undeniable attraction exercised by many caudillos over their followers is usually termed a matter of "charisma," or personal magnetism, but the notion of charismatic leadership seldom receives close attention from historians. Beginning from the premise that leadership must be analyzed less in terms of a leader's personal qualities than as a relationship between leader and followers, I will argue that, like beauty in the proverb, the charisma of the Saravia brothers was in the eye of the beholder. It was intensely personal but also dependent on a collective assessment and therefore accessible to reconstruction. Leaders who exercise an unusual attraction must embody something of transcendental significance for those who respond to them charismatically. What the Saravias represented to their followers, I believe, was a collective identity that elicited reactions similar to those associated with the appeal of nationalism. The twentieth-century cult of Aparicio Saravia has powerful overtones of romantic nationalism that will surprise anyone who thinks of caudillos as mere providers of spoils, protection, and patronage. I thought at first that the heroic tints of the Saravias' portraits had been added after their deaths, but in the course of my research I found, to the contrary, that the cult of exemplary heroes already exerted a powerful attraction for nineteenth-century borderlanders and that it contributed to the meteoric political rise of Aparicio, especially.[8]

This conceptualization of caudillo charisma might be described as Durkheimian. That is, the leader gains the group's allegiance by personifying it and facilitating (for some of its members) the powerful experience of self-transcendence. Rather than a small, tightly-knit community like a peasant village, the Saravias' followers were a large and diffuse "imagined community" of people who recognized each other through symbols of a common heritage and destiny. To study caudillos as culture heroes and symbols of collective identity, one must piece together in detail the outlook of their followers, seeking to recover the material textures of their daily lives and trace the constellations of meaning embedded in their particular historical experience. Next, one must pay careful attention to narrative representations of the leader and try—by zigzagging back and forth between text and context—to identify the qualities that resonated most strongly among their followers. That, at any rate, is the method adopted here.[9]

Consequently, this book is organized into two separate streams of chapters, braided together. The first stream is composed of short narrative chapters following the Saravias' careers as political and war leaders of the 1890s. These chapters (introduced by dates) necessarily echo previous tellings of the Saravias' campaigns in oral tradition, newspapers, pamphlets, and a string of partisan biographies. The second stream of chapters (introduced by thematic titles) alternates with the first stream and provides a context or gloss for the narrative. These longer, thematic chapters describe basic characteristics of borderland society, explore the political impact of the border itself, and trace the gradual onset of hard times toward the end of the nineteenth century. Because relatively little documentation about the Saravia family has survived from the time before their rise to fame, one must reconstruct the social origins of the caudillos through a detailed re-creation of the rural milieu in which they lived. The reconstruction draws on such sources as census data, tax rolls, local newspapers, judicial records, and the reports of local administrators from both sides of the Brazilian-Uruguayan border.

Throughout, the story of the Saravia brothers guides the presentation, and an initial "plot summary" may provide useful orientation for the reader.[10] Gumercindo Saravia's career fits the conventional profile of most nineteenth-century caudillos. This Saravia brother began as a local strongman, a rich landowner with a powerful presence and the habit of dominating those around him. He was a fighter and a killer—sometimes chief of police, at other times the armed rival of the police, a leader in his neighborhood one way or the other. Gumercindo fought his way to leadership of a Brazilian insurgent army and became the focus of a personal cult with messianic overtones. Anecdotes about Gumercindo echo Sarmiento's famous descriptions of Facundo Quiroga's mesmerizing gaze and the fanatical devotion of Facundo's followers. Younger brother Aparicio Saravia, on the other hand, was remembered by his neighbors mostly for his sense of humor, and seemed destined to remain a rancher like the rest until he accompanied Gumercindo in the Brazilian war of 1893 and inherited command of the army at his brother's death. Aparicio, too, knew how to fight, but—more skilled at leading a charge than at deciding what the army should do next—he was soon surrounded by urban men who used his military experience (and political inexperience) to further their own ends. The political power of this Saravia brother lay partly in the nativist image of him disseminated by the print media. The photographs and pamphlets presenting Aparicio as a patriotic "Countryman in Arms," reincarnation of heroic caudillos past, produced an enthusiastic response among his party's rank and file, catapulting Saravia over the heads of hundreds of more experienced leaders to make him, at the turn of the century, the second most powerful man in Uruguay.

Now to set the scene. The Saravia family lived on the rolling prairie that stretches for hundreds of miles between Uruguay and Brazil's southernmost state, Rio Grande do Sul. The family's ranches lay in the southeastern part of this borderland, the most active meeting place between Spanish Americans and Brazilians since the eighteenth century. Here the Spanish and Portuguese empires had fought for control of the Río de la Plata, and Brazilian armies repeatedly occupied the area after independence. Large numbers of Brazilian ranchers migrated south into Uruguay in the wake of these invasions, the Saravia family among them. Life on this rough cattle frontier gave borderland males all the skills needed to become irregular light cavalry—collectively, a *montonera*—at a moment's notice. In December of 1892, about four hundred horsemen gathered around Gumercindo to form a montonera much like those of the independence era. Hammer blows rang on steel as borderlanders prepared for war in the manner of their fathers and grandfathers, breaking apart heavy sheep shears and lashing the broad blades atop cane poles to make lances, their principal weapon.

2
JANUARY 1893

W hile Gumercindo Saravia's men waited to invade Brazil, they concealed themselves in the low trees that line the stream beds of the borderland, green and sweltering in the southern hemisphere summer. This year there were violent thunderstorms and people laughed about "atmospheric revolutions." Around the cooking fires, Saravia's men gathered to talk in a Portuguese heavily laced with Spanish terms while they passed a gourd of bitter *mate* (Paraguayan tea) from hand to hand, carefully lifting the kettle with rough hands to pour water into the gourd over the packed leaves and then drain the brew through a metal straw. Each of the men had brought several horses, the sheep-fleece which served as saddle and sleeping gear, and little else. Although some of these three to four hundred men had firearms (generally of some antique variety), most carried only a lance and a long knife. Rather surprisingly, given the size and capability of the Brazilian army just seven years before the turn of the twentieth century, the plan of this montonera was to invade the Brazilian subcontinent and force its government to its knees.[1]

Gumercindo Saravia's montonera presents us with an interpretive problem. Inevitably, one wonders: Were these men crazy? Why did they start a bloody civil war against a vastly superior force? How were they able to march six hundred miles north through the Brazilian states of Rio Grande do Sul, Santa Catarina, and Paraná, to threaten—if only for a moment—the country's political and economic

9

heartland? More difficult than explaining their fleeting success (for, though not professional soldiers, these men were impressive military athletes) is explaining their motivation and, above all, their resolve to fight on for thirty long months, animated only by the most far-fetched hopes. At the outset, I wish to renounce the goal of certainty in this explanation. Surely we can never really know the hearts of people distant from us in time and circumstance, especially when they left so little record. We can only hope to make reasonable inferences about their interior lives, drawing on a knowledge of external circumstances and using a bit of imagination.

Almost all of the horsemen who joined Gumercindo Saravia's invasion of Brazil were rural men, inhabitants of the ranches—called *estancias*—that covered the borderland of Uruguay and Rio Grande do Sul. From various descriptions, one can guess their social circumstances. Some were the owners of considerable property, as indicated by the fine quality of their woolen ponchos lined with cotton, by their wide pants and high black riding boots, and by the silver inlay on their spurs and on their horses' bridles. Others among them owned modest properties hardly big enough to be called estancias, but they held their heads high because their relative poverty seemed less important in the rowdy male society of the camp. Many in the rough crowd of men who sat drinking mate, sharpening their weapons, and remarking on each other's horses during this steamy January were not landowners at all, but day laborers or *agregados* who cared little what party ruled in Porto Alegre, the state capital of Rio Grande do Sul. (Agregados lived on someone else's land and grazed horses and cattle of their own in return for occasional services to the landowner. Many of the agregados and day laborers were black and mulatto men.) And finally, there were ragged drifters—black, indigenous, white, and anywhere in between—the last generation of real gauchos. They wore headbands to hold back their long hair, and, in lieu of pants, the Guaraní chiripá, a long woolen loin cloth secured around the waist by a very broad belt, and most carried their foot-long blades thrust diagonally under that belt at the small of their backs. Some still knew the Indian language, Guaraní, spoken by most of the first gauchos. A fuller description of these men (there were no women among them, yet) will emerge in the chapters ahead.[2]

Why had they gathered around Gumercindo Saravia? The answer

surely varied from man to man, depending on his personal, social, and economic circumstances. The matter might appear most clear cut in the case of the agregados, who owed various services to their landowning patrons, since going to war was traditionally one such service in the borderland. As for the day laborers, many had joined the group in hope of getting enough to eat, for times were hard in the borderland, and most day laborers did not find work every day or even every week. Such men could take a gaucho's proverbial solace in the "free air and fat meat" of a mounted guerrilla war. Finally, the owners of estancias had certain economic interests of their own—especially involving the taxation of goods and animals crossing the border. These matters, too, will be discussed in due time. Let us proceed, for now, to the matters that the borderlanders themselves seem to have invoked most often when going to war.

Asked to justify their involvement in an insurgency, most of these men would have mentioned personal relationships of one kind or another. In fact, personal loyalty to Gumercindo (or to one of Gumercindo's allies) accounted for the presence of some insurgent volunteers who had no connection at all to Brazil. While the majority of Gumercindo's followers were Brazilians or, at least, Uruguayans of Brazilian extraction who retained strong cross-border ties, perhaps a hundred of the riders who gathered on Saravia lands spoke only Spanish and lacked those ties altogether. These men were from a more southern part of Uruguay called San José. Their links to Gumercindo probably dated to the late 1870s or early 1880s when he and Aparicio had worked driving borderland cattle to market in the south. The men from San José called themselves Maragatos, a nickname associated with the early settlers of their locality. The presence of these Spanish speakers in Gumercindo's montonera led to the entire group's being called the Maragatos after they arrived in Brazil, first by their scornful enemies and later by their supporters as well.[3]

Personal relationships would have been featured prominently in the frequent stories of atrocities told in the montonera. Gumercindo's cousin Cesáreo Saravia, for example, had joined the invading force strictly to avenge the death of his brother Terencio. Republican partisans had recently captured Terencio, tortured him, and hung him in a tree for target practice, while his watch, knife, boots, spurs, and other clothing were divided up among his killers. Cesáreo lived in

Uruguay, and his life was not greatly affected by the political order north of the border. Had it not been for the imperatives of revenge, he would probably not have joined Gumercindo.[4]

Family ties did not always bind. Gumercindo's brother Aparicio became second in command of the montonera, but his other brothers declined to join because of responsibilities that kept them at home in Uruguay. Basilicio, the second oldest brother after Gumercindo, had a business to tend. Antonio Floricio (whom everyone called Chiquito), the third oldest, was needed to protect family interests as police comisario in the Saravias' rural neighborhood. But Aparicio, who was four years younger than Gumercindo, committed himself whole-heartedly to the enterprise, allowing four hundred men—who could eat several cows or forty sheep at a single meal—to camp on his ranch for weeks. Numerous stories circulate about why Aparicio went to the war as Gumercindo's second-in-command, since he frankly disclaimed any interest in Brazilian politics. He seems to have gone partly for the adventure, partly out of a sense of family obligation, and partly from personal friendship. He could not help admiring the domineering figure of his older brother, with whom he had been close since the years when the two worked as drovers, taking borderland cattle to market. And, who knows? As a boy, Aparicio may really have dreamed of becoming a general as the oral tradition has it.[5]

Gumercindo Saravia's recorded explanations of his own decision to revolt also turned on questions of personal loyalty. Consider what happened when the Rio Grandense Republican party tried to recruit Gumercindo in the early 1890s. During these years, Gumercindo was a local strongman who held sway in an isolated cattle county called Santa Vitória do Palmar, a sandy finger of land interrupted by marshes and dotted with palm groves, reaching down the Atlantic coast toward the Río de la Plata at the southernmost tip of Brazil. As chief of police in Santa Vitória during the last days of the Brazilian Empire, he had raised a lot of eyebrows by affording his protection to a public meeting of Republican youth, attending a Republican banquet, and providing his own sons a tutor with well-known Republican sympathies. At least in theory, Gumercindo believed in republics—it was the local Republicans whom he did not like.[6]

When local Republicans visited Gumercindo Saravia's ranch to ask him to join them, Gumercindo arranged for the gentlemen from town to find him napping outside on his saddle blanket under a centenarian fig tree. At the time, Gumercindo was almost forty years old, and his short build remained athletic. His face was framed by a high forehead above and a full beard below. As a younger man, he had worn his hair long and oiled in mid-nineteenth-century fashion, but now it was cropped short and thinning on top. Gumercindo was a man of few words, and his heavy-lidded eyes had a hard glint that inspired respect. Rising to greet his visitors, he explained that sleeping on the ground was a way of toughening his body for a military campaign. Why had he resolved to fight? Gumercindo thought the question absurd: The Republicans had exiled Dr. Gaspar Silveira Martins, Gumercindo's political patron and friend. What kind of man would he be to forget that? Then, when a emissary from the state capital went so far as to offer Gumercindo leadership of the local Republican party, Saravia declined again, saying that he would never join a party that harbored disloyal opportunists like the Republicans of Santa Vitória. "Your discourse has impressed me greatly," he added for the benefit of the distinguished emissary, "but I like revolutions more than politics."[7]

Clearly, Gumercindo wanted to be known as a steadfast friend and a dangerous enemy. Most borderlanders placed a high value on that kind of reputation, and naturally so, since everything in their lives, from ranch work to politics, depended on face-to-face alliances between individuals. The people involved could be social equals (like two landowners), but often (like landowner and agregado) one was clearly dominant, the patrón—and the other, his client. The idiom of friendship applied to equal and unequal alliances alike. Reciprocity of some kind always played a part, as in an exchange of gifts between equals or an exchange of a client's service for a patron's largesse, but these were not coldly contractual relationships. Instead, they formed part of the warp and woof of people's emotional lives, as one can easily tell by observing the bitter accusations of "ingratitude" leveled at those who failed in their reciprocal obligations. If the logic of patronage and clientele is essential to understanding a political conflict like the Rio Grandense civil war about to begin, and if Gumercindo explained himself by reference to Silveira Martins, let us examine his relationship to Silveira Martins.[8]

Together, the exiled Silveira Martins and Gumercindo exemplified a particular sort of patron–client relationship highly characteristic of nineteenth-century Brazil. Silveira Martins was a doctor of laws (a *bacharel*, plural: *bacharéis*) who supplied governmental patronage—especially in the form of public employment—to Saravia and his other clients. Saravia was a local strongman (a *coronel*, plural: *coronéis*) who reciprocated by delivering votes for Silveira Martins from the county of Santa Vitória do Palmar. Gumercindo's influence in the county came partly from the henchmen who surrounded him constantly, partly from his connection with Silveira Martins, and partly from the fifteen thousand hectares of pasture land and thousands of cattle and horses that the Saravias owned in Santa Vitória. As long as the party of Silveira Martins controlled the government of Rio Grande do Sul, Gumercindo prospered, but when his enemies grasped the levers of power in the provincial capital of Porto Alegre, it seemed that Gumercindo was permanently at the center of a police investigation. The alliance between the two was so important to Silveira Martins that, as the edifice of monarchical rule began to show dangerous cracks in its last months, Gumercindo's influential patron even offered him a title, Baron of Santa Vitória do Palmar, to insure his continued loyalty. Gumercindo refused the title but stayed loyal anyway.[9]

In November 1889, the fall of the Brazilian empire suddenly truncated the political career of Silveira Martins. Gumercindo's patron had been one of the most influential public men of the late empire, an opposition firebrand in his youth (when he won the name of Tribune for his anti-authoritarian attitudes and for the oratorical pyrotechnics of his parliamentary style), a pillar of the monarchy by the height of his career in the 1880s. Silveira Martins belonged to an extremely wealthy borderland family with landholdings not far from those of Gumercindo's family. Unlike most landowners' sons in the borderland, he had gone away to law school in the 1850s, then followed—at an accelerated pace—the political trajectory typical of a successful bacharel, beginning with a prestigious municipal judgeship at the seat of the imperial court in Rio de Janeiro, followed by a deputy's seat in the provincial assembly and then by a place in the national assembly a few years later.[10] Silveira Martins left the borderland permanently to become a cosmopolitan urbanite, and, despite the gauchesque poses that he struck for admirers in the salons of the imperial court, he became much more comfortable there than on a borderland estancia. By 1889, rotund, bewhiskered, and booming, Silveira Martins had been cabinet minister, governor of Rio Grande do Sul, councilor of the emperor, and imperial senator with life tenure. So powerful was his hold on the Liberal party of Rio Grande do Sul that it was said to obey him "like a regiment of Fredrick the Great" and so strong was the party's hold on the province that, after 1872, the Liberal party often retained a majority in the provincial assembly and continued control of local governments even under Conservative ministries—a rare feat, indeed, in the imperial system where influence from above generally determined electoral outcomes. In the final hours before the emperor's abdication, the imperial prime-minister even suggested putting Silveira Martins at the head of a last-ditch effort to save the monarchy, and for this reason Gumercindo's patron was one of the few Brazilians exiled after the Republican coup.[11]

Gumercindo's life, in contrast to that of Silveira Martins, had never taken him far from the cattle lands, and the weapons that he brandished were not rhetorical ones. In fact, Gumercindo was quite uneasy when called upon to speak Portuguese in public situations. Although his parents were Brazilian, and although Portuguese had been the language of the household in which Gumercindo grew up, he felt surer of himself speaking Spanish, the language in which he had a few years of schooling. The Saravias' estancia household was quite rustic by the standards of the urbane Silveira Martins. Long after his patron had become well accustomed to a frock coat of English wool, Gumercindo wore a winter poncho of bull hide scraped and cured at home. Countless hours of boyhood practice had given him an agility on horseback that no man from the city could hope to equal. Gumercindo had first joined a montonera at the age of eighteen, and he had been, by turns, a war captain, a police comisario, and a trail boss driving borderland herds to slaughter. Since the longhorns often crossed the border on their way to market, his experience as trail boss gave Gumercindo an extensive knowledge of the countryside in both Uruguay and Rio Grande do Sul. Though he had lived his first thirty years in Uruguay, he moved to Brazil to escape prosecution in 1883. For Gumercindo, the advent of the Brazilian republic in 1889 brought the mentioned invitations to join the Republican party and then, when he declined to do so, it brought renewed official curiosity regarding unmarked graves on his property in Santa Vitória do Palmar.[12]

In the early 1890s, committed young Republicans who had agitated unsuccessfully against the monarchy for years finally had their day in Porto Alegre, and they then moved with impressive swiftness to consolidate their control over the state. They gave particular attention to replacing the national guard with a refashioned paramilitary police force that harbored no lingering loyalties toward the old regime. The triumphant Rio Grandense Republican party accepted all properly penitent monarchist converts as long as they accepted a subordinate role, but this neither Silveira Martins nor many borderland coronéis like Gumercindo were disposed to do. After all, their personal networks of patronage and clientele still extended across Rio Grande do Sul and included many of the most powerful men in the state. Because of their military experience and resources (and thanks to the tactical advantages offered by the border itself), the masters of the old order believed themselves capable of resisting their subjugation by the insolent young Republicans. After all, during the last imperial election, the Republicans had failed to win a single seat in the provincial assembly. The leader of the Rio Grandense Republicans, Júlio de Castilhos, was a mere upstart in the eyes of the old guard. A man of integrity, Castilhos was an indefatigable political organizer and partisan journalist—a doctrinaire disciple of Auguste Comte, who struggled not to stutter at the podium, but whose pen dripped lethal venom for the enemies of the republic (a category that, for Castilhos, encompassed anyone who did not endorse his own positivist vision and his personal leadership of the new Rio Grande do Sul).[13]

In November 1891, totally shut out of the elections for the state's constitutional convention (just as they had formerly excluded the Republicans), the disgruntled former lords of the borderland made their first attempt to turn back the clock. They saw their chance when Brazil's first Republican ruler, the harried, old, and rigid military president Deodoro da Fonseca, closed the national congress in a fit of pique, diminishing the new regime's aura of legitimacy. Montoneras quickly formed all over the southeastern part of Rio Grande do Sul, including a party of one hundred lancers commanded by Gumercindo. Taken by surprise, Castilhos abandoned the governorship without a fight, leaving his regime cleanly decapitated. A fragile alliance of Castilhos's enemies, involving some dissident Republicans as well as old monarchists, now took over the reins of state government. Gumercindo Saravia returned in triumph to Santa Vitória do Palmar, where he forcibly ejected his enemies, cleared himself of the criminal charges pending against him, and happily telegraphed the interim governor: "Free of persecutions, awaiting orders." The success of the Rio Grandense uprising then inspired a naval revolt in Rio de Janeiro that forced the offending chief executive of Brazil to resign in favor of his military vice-president, the tougher and more resilient Floriano Peixoto, with whom Castilhos had, as of yet, no working relationship.[14]

Elated at this easy victory, Silveira Martins returned from exile and summoned his devotees from all over Rio Grande do Sul to a meeting in April 1892 at the borderland town of Bagé, home of both Silveira Martins and another graybearded leader of imperial days, Gen. João Nunes da Silva Tavares. The resulting political alignments grafted the patronage networks of the now-defunct monarchical Liberals and Conservatives to create a single force of borderland reaction, the "Federalist party." The Federalists took that name, apparently, to deflect the predictable accusations of monarchism that the ousted Republicans immediately hurled and to associate themselves with Rio Grandense traditions of borderland independence. Gumercindo did not attend the meeting, being content to let others do the talking. At Bagé, the Federalists adopted a vaguely libertarian program that they seldom mentioned afterward because their complaints against Castilhista authoritarianism and their collective loyalties to Silveira Martins and General Tavares were the real principles of their group cohesion. Since their common enemy, Júlio de Castilhos, had already been toppled, the Federalists turned their attention to parceling out the public employment that had always constituted the most important spoils of political power in Brazil.[15]

Meanwhile, Júlio de Castilhos took advantage of his earlier refurbishment of the state's paramilitary police, who had remained sympathetic to his cause, and whom he persuaded to overturn the Federalists and recapture the governor's palace for him in July 1892. As his last official act, the ousted interim governor telegraphed General Tavares in Bagé to make him provisional head of the tottering Federalist government. Tavares again called out his partisans, but

Castilhos had by now reached an understanding with President Peixoto that gave him control of regular army units as well as the state police and montoneras led by his own coronéis. The national government quickly endorsed the Castilhos coup, and Republican partisans led by personal enemies of Tavares descended on Bagé to squash the Federalist resistance. After securing assurances that there would be no looting in Bagé, Tavares fled across the border into Uruguay with about five hundred supporters. The promise to spare Federalist lives and property was not kept, however. During the second half of 1892, there were dozens, and then scores of political murders, most of them perpetrated by vengeful Republican partisans. By the time that Gumercindo began to gather his montonera in December 1892, ten thousand Federalists had sought refuge in Uruguay, and, having recovered from its brief reversal, the Republican party had entrenched itself in power with every intention of staying, whether borderland Federalists liked it or not.[16]

In January 1893, at the camp of Gumercindo's montonera, the Saravias moved between the cooking fires of Brazilians and Uruguayans with the ease of people perfectly in their element. They had friends and relations on both sides of the border and spoke the two languages equally well (or equally badly, as many borderlanders joked). The Saravias had thrived in the borderland partly because of the strength of their family—their mother's success in bearing and raising, and their father's in disciplining and providing for, no fewer than thirteen offspring. Virtually all were now grown and lived nearby, and many surely visited the encampment in January 1893. The sheer size of the family gave it advantages in a society where most activities, including political ones, were structured through networks of personal relationships. Although only a few of Gumercindo's kin had actually signed up for his invasion of Brazil, he could draw, at least to some extent, on family resources from a dozen estancias in supplying his war party.[17]

The Saravias had seen all this before: the fabrication of lances from bamboo and sheep shears, the agglomeration of hundreds of obstreperous horsemen, the swearing of revenge for injuries done to friends and family. In their experience, political conflict meant war more often than not, and in many ways, this montonera differed little from those that had been formed on countless occasions in the borderland during its long and tumultuous nineteenth century. In fact, outsiders often remarked that traveling into the borderland from Porto Alegre or Montevideo was like going back in time. One could watch from the train window for hours, it seemed, without spying a human habitation—only birds, scattered wild dogs and scrawny sheep, darting groups of flightless rheas, herds of untamed horses, and above all, thousands upon thousands of cattle, descendants of the free-roaming herds of Iberian longhorns that had attracted the ancestors of Gumercindo and Aparicio to this wild frontier five generations earlier.

3

BORDERLANDERS

The borderland began as a no-man's-land separating the South American possessions of Spain from those of Portugal. Between the Spanish settlements of the Río de la Plata and the Portuguese settlements on the Brazilian plateau stretched a rolling, grassy plain, very sparsely peopled in the 1600s, and treeless except along the numerous streams and rivers. Unlike the great plains of North America, these fields are well watered, and today cattle and sheep graze side by side here, just as they do on the neighboring pampa of Argentina. Spanish horses and cattle escaped from early mission settlements and multiplied more rapidly than on the Argentine pampa (where a rougher ground cover originally took the place of grass). By the mid-eighteenth century millions of hooved animals roamed freely across the borderland's undulating sea of green, and the indigenous Charruas and Minuanos of the borderland (who lived in small, nomadic tribal groups) learned to ride the horses and to hunt the tough and agile longhorns. Guaraní Indians from the Jesuit missions also harvested the herds of the grasslands. Especially after a number of missions were destroyed in the middle of the eighteenth century, thousands of Guaraníes migrated permanently on to the plains and took up the roving way of life of the first gauchos. At that time, the only Iberian inhabitants east of the Uruguay River were those who dwelled in the various walled port citadels along the coast. The Portuguese outpost of Colônia do Sacramento was one of these, the Spanish base at Montevideo, another. During the more peaceful interludes, the Portuguese at Colônia traded and fraternized with the Spanish, and that must be how a certain militia captain at the Portuguese citadel, Antônio, came to marry a Spanish woman, Juana, in the 1730s. According to the work of careful genealogists who have traced bloodlines that the Saravias themselves did not seem to cherish particularly, Antônio and Juana were the great-great-great-grandparents of Gumercindo and Aparicio. It seems only fitting that such an international couple should be their earliest known ancestors on these plains where empires collided.[1]

Around 1737, Antônio and Juana became settlers at a new fortified outpost called Rio Grande de São Pedro. Located on a strategically important but desolate sandy spit of land, Rio Grande was the first permanent step toward the creation of the Brazil's southernmost province. Antônio died in an expedition against the Spanish, and Juana fled north with their children as part of a general Portuguese exodus when the Spanish captured Rio Grande in 1763. The family then spent a generation near Porto Alegre, which, owing to the Spanish occupation of Rio Grande, became the new center of Portugal's southern vanguard settlement. Before this point, the borderland had attracted Portuguese speakers mostly for the purpose of raising mules. Muleteers had driven long strings of the animals north to a yearly fair at Sorocaba in the province of São Paulo and, ultimately, to the gold mines of central Brazil. The São Paulo muleteers were always few, however, so the Portuguese monarchy buttressed its hold on Rio Grande do Sul by steadily and stealthily bringing families of militia colonists from its overpopulated Atlantic islands, the Azores, and in this manner it finally built enough demographic strength to expel the Spanish from Rio Grande. Several members of Juana's family served as militiamen in these wars against her Spanish compatriots, and some of her grandsons even became soldiers in Portuguese royal line battalions. In 1777, Portugal and Spain negotiated and began to survey a line to demarcate their claims in this southern region, and then, like the province of Rio Grande do Sul as a whole, Juana's family flourished. By 1800, her grandson Manuel presided over a clan wealthy enough to erect its own chapel and cemetery and prominent enough to give its name to a stream that tumbled south through the hills toward lower ground in Spanish territory only a few miles away. When not fighting the Spanish, Rio Grandenses like Manuel Saravia farmed wheat, which grew exuberantly in the climate of Rio Grande do Sul, but a blight that ravaged harvests in the early 1800s and chronic warfare in the independence period discouraged the cultivation of the grain.[2]

Raising cattle made more sense than planting wheat to early nineteenth-century Rio Grandenses. With a spontaneous reproductive rate of about 25 percent a year, and the habit of foraging for itself, livestock required less labor than crops (especially important when the men were away at war), and cattle could be evacuated more easily than grain fields in case of a Spanish invasion. By 1825 or so, the rolling landscape of the borderland consisted of one estancia after another, with substantial agriculture still practiced only on the small truck farms that ringed borderland towns. The estancias varied greatly in size but otherwise seemed exact copies of each other.

The imprint which the estancias made on the landscape was minimal. Streams and the unmarked crests of long, parallel ridges indicated property boundaries only for the initiated, and the dense scrub along the watercourses presented the sole barrier to the free movement of animals. The most frequent signs of human presence were the large brands burned into the hides of grazing horses and cattle. In the early years of the century, many longhorns still roamed unbranded, waiting for determined people to catch and tame them. These feral cattle abounded on the Spanish side of the borderland. Great tracts of Spanish territory had been monopolized by rapacious speculators whose scheme was not to settle them but to resell them at a profit, a circumstance which retarded effective settlement, and unremitting political turmoil further slowed the growth of a Spanish-speaking population after 1810. Until the 1880s, the eastern borderland of Rio Grande do Sul was about twice as populous as the adjacent region of Uruguay. For two generations of Rio Grandense borderlanders, the thinly-settled Spanish territory south of Brazil became a land of opportunity, particularly during the early 1820s, when Rio Grandenses occupied that territory militarily and briefly annexed it to the Portuguese crown.[3]

From their first contact through the rest of the nineteenth century, Spanish- and Portuguese-speaking borderlanders seem to have mingled easily despite the frequent conflicts between their governments. Intermarriage was common. On the other hand, willingness to live

Map 1   Formation of the Border, 1750–1801

together did not imply shared identity. The French naturalist Auguste de Saint Hilaire, who spent a year traveling on both sides of this border during the period of Portuguese occupation, found little difference in the land or the estancias, but he commented often on the contrasts ("très sensibles") between the Portuguese- and Spanish-speaking people, and remarked that Rio Grandenses and Uruguayans clashed even more rancorously than did their European-born cousins. The people south of the border seemed to him more frank and egalitarian, less devout, less patriarchal, and above all, less European racially—more apt to wear a Guaraní chiripá and the toeless boots that constituted the most surprising article of gaucho garb. Saint

Hilaire praised the circumspection of Portuguese rule south of the border but doubted it could transform the Uruguayans into loyal subjects of Lisbon. As soon as they had a chance, he wrote, the Spanish-speaking borderlanders would revert to a life of plunder and *"Viva la patria!"*[4]

The opportunity to accumulate unbranded cattle and cheap land in Spanish territory beckoned the sons of Manuel Saravia, among them, Gumercindo's grandfather, Francisco. The first documentary evidence of Francisco's presence south of the border comes from the Uruguayan district of Cerro Largo in the 1830s, when he rented an estancia in steep, rocky country that few have ever attempted to farm, but where longhorn cattle thrived. In Cerro Largo, Francisco and his wife Maria Angélica found themselves among people who were not recent European transplants like the Rio Grandense borderlanders. Rural Uruguayans descended from families who had inhabited the pastures of the Río de la Plata for centuries, and their gene pool and culture were profoundly mestizo. The migratory currents that populated rural Uruguay came mostly from neighboring provinces of the former Spanish viceroyalty—Santa Fe, Entre Ríos, Corrientes, Misiones, and Paraguay—and Guaraní blood from the former Jesuit missions flowed strongly in the veins of these plains people.[5]

Francisco and Maria Angélica had not previously associated with Guaraníes like Marcelino Nongoí and Jacinta Canuaní, a couple who grazed their own small herd to the west of the Saravia homestead. Marcelino and Jacinta had come from the Argentine province of Misiones during the wars of independence. Their children had little trouble finding other Guaraníes to marry in the Uruguayan countryside. During the eighteenth century, in fact, Guaraní had been the lingua franca of the borderland, as revealed by the frequency of place names in that language. The stream called Tupambaé, running near where Francisco and Maria Angélica lived, had a Guaraní name linking it to activities of the former Jesuit missions, though no one remembered how it had gotten that name. One traveler to the Uruguayan backlands described hearing a group of Guaraníes, missals in hand, sing a church service in Gregorian chant "with appropriate pauses and entonation." In the 1830s people whose ancestry was purely Guaraní or purely European were in the minority among Uruguayan borderlanders. Mixed blood had become so common that census takers had no separate category for it. Many of the borderland's earliest Spanish-speaking settlers came from Paraguay, one of the most thoroughly mestizo regions in Spanish America. The census takers classed the Saravias' Paraguayan neighbor, Pedro Pablo Cabrera, as white and his wife and children as Indians, but the family's multi-hued phenotype likely represented the result of many generations of blending rather than a "mixed marriage."[6]

The Uruguayans held fewer African slaves than the Rio Grandenses, but Francisco and Maria Angélica had plenty of free neighbors who descended from slaves. Usually, they too were people of mixed ancestry. The Uruguayan census takers described the African/European mix in a separate category called *pardo,* but they listed free pardos politely as "don" and "doña." For example, don José Domingo Zapata and doña María Mercedes had come from the province Entre Ríos and could boast a small herd of cattle and horses. However, like the Nongoí family, they probably rented their land, squatted on it without title, or lived as agregados of the owner. Such was usually the situation of couples like José Pablo and María Oribe, free Africans whom the census takers denied the title of "don" or "doña." The two ran a few horses and cows on an outlying area of the large Oribe estancia where they functioned as *puesteros* (operating an outpost called a *puesto*) and supervised the labors of a slave woman and two black hired hands. As their last name indicates, María and José Pablo had formerly been slaves of the Oribe family. Another former slave born in Africa was the paid overseer, Tomás Silveira, who slept at the main house of the Oribe estancia and directed four more hired hands, one of them white. Thus, large estancias owned by Uruguayans were frequently inhabited by diverse collections of people. The González estancia, not far from Oribe's, provides another example of diversity: an administrator, an overseer, and four hired hands from different parts of Uruguay, all classed as white; two puesteros from neighboring Argentine provinces with their families, classed as white and Indian, respectively; an Indian agregado with family and another without; two Indian hired hands; and three enslaved men from Africa.[7]

Rio Grandenses migrating south into Uruguay brought scores of slaves, and their households were more homogeneous. Within a few miles from Francisco and Maria Angélica, for example, lived the affluent Silva Moreira family with thirty-five slaves—more than twenty of working age and all but three of these male. That number of slaves paled beside the slaveholdings on coffee or sugar plantations in central Brazil, but it ostentatiously exceeded the small labor requirements of a borderland estancia. The number of slaves on estancias varied greatly. Old João da Silva Moreira had only two Uruguayan hired hands in his Portuguese-speaking extended household of forty-eight, because the rest of his workers, including his puesteros, were enslaved. More typical of Rio Grandense estancia families were neighbors like the Dias de Oliveiras, with eight slaves, or the Correias, whose two households in the Saravias' neighborhood counted only ten slaves each.

Poorer Rio Grandenses like Francisco and Maria Angélica, who rented from the Correias, might try to conduct their social life with other Brazilians (like the families of Francisco's brothers who had settled nearby), but they inevitably rubbed elbows with many Uruguayans as well. Such families could not afford a tutor, for one thing, and if their children were to have schooling, they would have to learn Spanish. Eventually, adaptation to the Uruguayan environment would become one of the Saravias' strengths, as we will see, contributing to augment their fortunes until, in later years, Gumercindo and Aparicio Saravia could court and marry Correia and Dias de Oliveira women. In the 1830s, though, the brothers' grandparents owned no more than two or three slaves and no land in Uruguay. Because of this relative lack of property to generate legal paperwork, ordinary frontier people like the Savarias left little trace in the written record.[8]

Our occasional glimpses of the Saravias' lives in this generation often resulted from a brush with the law. Thus, when one of the sons of Francisco and Maria Angélica stabbed a neighbor's slave in February 1842, during the preparations for branding, a neighborhood assistant to the justice of the peace took pen and paper to the Saravias' house where the slave Justino lay wounded on the temple and in the chest. Justino and several witnesses agreed on the essentials of the ruckus. Cándido and Cisério Saravia (Cisério was the father of Cesáreo Saravia, Gumercindo's cousin who joined his montonera in 1893), Justino, and other men had been rounding up and separating unbranded cattle when Justino saw an animal he thought did not belong in a group that Cisério Saravia was driving away. Justino cut the cow in question out of the bunch without consulting Saravia, who wheeled and charged back to claim it. Saravia pulled his knife and Justino defended himself with his *boleadora* (the three tethered balls that borderlanders used to hunt rheas and, occasionally, to brain their adversaries). Cándido Saravia then arrived to break up the fight. The official noted that the wounds were serious, and Justino's owner sued for damages—demanding restitution from Cisério's father for medical expenses and three pesos a day in lost wages.[9]

The incident reveals a certain lack of social distance often characteristic of frontier life. For the most part, slaves and free laborers did the same work, ate the same food, lived in the same places, and spent a lot of time in each other's company. Cisério Saravia, a slaveowner's son, was doing the same job as the slave Justino. They were, in fact, competing, which is the very reason for the fight, and despite the social inequality between them, Justino was not subservient. If he had been, no fight would have occurred. Unlike slaves in most of Brazil, borderland slaves often went armed and mounted, sometimes even crossing the border alone in the course of their work. Some wore the Guaraní chiripá. Through the middle years of the nineteenth century, labor was scarce and opportunities to escape omnipresent, so borderland ranchers tended to regard decent treatment of their slaves as the most economical policy, and freedmen—like several of the African-born men already mentioned—were often persuaded to stay on as agregados.[10]

Evidence of the Saravias disappears for a time in the early 1840s after Cisério's father died of an illness and the suit for damages was dropped. There follows a decade in which little can be said with certainty about the family. The widowed Maria Angélica, accompanied at least by the younger part of her large brood (which ranged from Manuel, twenty-one and already married, to little Plácido, aged eight) seems to have left Uruguay soon after her husband Francisco's untimely demise. She bought (or perhaps already possessed) a modest parcel in the district of Arroio Grande, just north of the border where her family lived. She no doubt felt especially inclined to return home because a decade-long civil war was finally ending in Rio Grande do Sul, a war which may have motivated the family's original move to Uruguay.[11]

Between 1800 and 1870, Rio Grandense and Uruguayan borderlanders often had to include war in their planning. They had so often gone to war by mid-century that doing so had become something of a habit, and it took very little to transform a group of ranch hands into irregular light cavalry. In the case of the Rio Grandense "revolution" of 1835–45, known as the Farrapo War, borderland ranchers and their slaves formed the backbone of the insurgent army. The Farrapos had raised the banner of republican liberties when imperial policies—particularly a tax on livestock sent to Brazil from Uruguayan estancias—struck them as intolerably onerous, and, as long as their supply of horses lasted, they easily outmaneuvered the imperial army, making their secessionist borderland republic the gravest challenge ever to the territorial unity of Brazil.[12]

As an added incentive for Maria Angélica Saravia and her younger children to return to Brazil, a decade of bitter struggle known as the Guerra Grande began between Uruguay's two parties, the Blancos and the Colorados, each with allies outside the country. The Colorados, supported by the French and British fleets, held the port city of Montevideo, while the Blancos controlled the rest of Uruguay with the help of Argentine dictator Juan Manuel de Rosas. This was a lawless epoch in the Uruguayan countryside, and when a band of marauding cutthroats—bandits, soldiers, deserters, or the police themselves—attacked an estancia house or herds, a landowner wanted true allies at his side.[13]

Agregados served this purpose much better than temporary hired hands. A hired hand might occasionally act as a personal retainer for his patrón, but he left nothing of value behind on the estancia if he preferred to vanish, while the agregado left his wife, his children, his animals, and his place on the land. Like wage workers, agregados watched over the landowner's herds and helped at round-ups and branding, but unlike hired hands, agregados did not have to be paid, receiving instead the right to pasture their own animals on the estancia. As long as the population remained sparse and land plentiful, such an arrangement had many advantages for the landowner. The agregado, in turn, could raise a small herd of his own, and perhaps use the profits to rent additional land or even to purchase some property himself. If any of Maria Angélica's sons remained in Uruguay after their father's death, they probably lived as agregados on an estancia belonging to a friend or relative. Rio Grandense landowners south of the border showed an early and enduring preference for Rio Grandense agregados.[14]

We can place one of Maria Angélica's sons, named Francisco like his father, working as a puestero in Cerro Largo (the part of Uruguay's eastern borderland where the Saravias lived ever after) during the 1850s. This Francisco—the father of Gumercindo and Aparicio—was fairly short like both of them, and he wore his long hair brushed straight back from the high forehead that all his children inherited. He had never gone to school and always needed someone else to scratch his name on the titles of his real estate purchases over the years. During the 1850s he did some shoeing of horses for more income, and his grandchildren later whispered of his gambling forays with a partner to the Brazilian bordertown of Jaguarão, where the two men apparently contrived to make sleight of hand triumph over the whimsies of chance. According to legend, at least, Francisco's winnings were the beginning of the fortune that he amassed gradually over the next forty years. He started modestly enough. In 1854, when his mother Maria Angélica finally opened the legal proceeding of her deceased husband's estate, the ambitious young puestero had received money enough for only a few dozen breeding stock, but soon he had to rent more pasture to accommodate his growing herd of longhorns. Sometime during these years, a young woman who lived near his mother's house in Arroio Grande attracted Francisco's admiring gaze. As he would learn in coming years, he could have found no better partner in all Rio Grande do Sul than Propícia da Rosa, the daughter of an estancia family much like his own. The lovers conducted their courtship in true borderland style, first flirting at dances or horse races, no doubt, and finally eloping. Propícia's parents awoke one morning to find her whisked away across the border to Cerro Largo, and they considered the matter settled. Francisco and Propícia did not formalize their union until a church ceremony years later in 1858.[15]

The couple's grandchildren later insisted that, at the age of nineteen, Propícia had actually helped to tend the livestock on horseback. That would have been quite unusual, though not unprecedented. Normally women had enough to do without riding and roping. They prepared the meals, cared for the children, made the clothes, and washed them on the banks of a nearby stream. A man would seldom do any of these things for himself, except when at war. In the winter months, when gray skies drizzled for days on end, the women sewed and fried batter cakes while the men fashioned halters, reins, bridles, and lassos of braided leather. Otherwise, the men's principal occupation on the estancia was working the stock—dangerous work, because the longhorn cattle were tough and agile, not the sedate products of English scientific husbandry. But hazards and demands of ranch work constituted attractions for most of the men, who vied with one another in displays of daring and dexterity. Except at periods of peak activity, the labors of estancia men left plenty of time for smoking cigarettes of black tobacco wrapped in corn husk, sipping mate or drinking cane liquor at a country store, and talking endlessly about horses.[16]

Borderlanders who spent so much of their time on isolated estancias relished social gatherings. Country stores vending liquor, tobacco, sugar, mate, and other daily necessities attracted groups of garrulous men any day of the week. Marriages, baptisms, and other important events of family life provided an excuse for the favorite assemblage of young people, a dance—one of their few opportunities to approach members of the opposite sex. On the night of the festivities, the scant furnishings of a rural house would be cleared away, leaving only ranks of straight-backed chairs around the walls where the participants would retire between songs, men on one side, women on the other. The people who flocked from surrounding estancias wore their best clothes, and those who did not dance entertained themselves with commentaries on those who did. Partners changed frequently, with women much in demand because invariably in the minority given the masculine skew of borderland demography. Early in the century, a single guitar player strummed the beat and the dances featured fancy footwork, often with an African twist in the movement of the body. By the 1880s, though, accordions had become popular—probably spreading from the German colonies in northern Rio Grande do Sul—along with couple dances like the waltz and polka. Some dances involved improvisation of rhymes by the dancers (an activity at which Aparicio later displayed particular skill). Horse races provided another occasion for collective fun. They were all-day affairs, bringing people from many miles around to pit their best steeds against each other in a series of one-on-one heats, and they involved heavy betting. On either side of the straight course, several hundred yards long, vendors offered food and spirits in makeshift tents, and between them, gold and silver coins shone on ponchos outspread on the ground to collect wagers for the next race. Contests of ability on horseback were frequent at all kinds of celebrations, from weddings to national holidays. Of the wedding frolics when Gumercindo and Amélia married in 1873, the family recalled how the groom's teenage brother José had stood on the back of a galloping horse.[17]

The wealth of the estancias consisted above all in animals. For example, when the widow Maria Angélica had the family's property in Arroio Grande inventoried for the distribution of her husband's estate, two hundred of the animals on her small estancia were worth more than fifty times the value of her thatch-roofed house. Breeding stock (which had a normal proportion of bulls, cows, and calves) was calculated at twelve Brazilian milréis or Uruguayan pesos a head. If the herd was semi-wild, as it often was early in the century, the animals brought less because they were unbranded and much more difficult to handle. Fattened steers ready for slaughter fetched about twice what breeding stock cost, and an ox used for pulling a cart was worth yet more. The price of horses varied widely. A saddle horse cost at least ten milréis or pesos, and a colt with potential went for five. Any kind of mare was undervalued—often at less than one peso— because riding a mare was considered preferable only to walking. (Anything was preferable to walking. One might see a man mount to go open a gate a few paces from the house.) In the early and middle years of the century, only a few sheep were kept for the domestic consumption of their flesh and wool.[18]

The estancia houses of the borderland generally stood on hilltops. In the rocky country where the Saravias lived, the walls were of stone, a couple of feet thick, and they extended rearward from each side of the house to form a square compound surrounded by outbuildings— the kitchen, storerooms, and quarters for the slaves and hired help. Such a house had a tile roof and might have a small second-story room from which to observe approaching riders. The front door was of massive planks with iron bolt and hinges, and iron grills protected the windows. In the patio was a well or a cistern that collected rainwater from the roof and often a clay oven shaped like a round bee hive. A high, vine-covered frame reminiscent of a grape arbor provided shade for saddled horses and summer gatherings—a popular place for guitar music and dancing—and near the house often rose an ombú tree, squat and huge, several trunks growing from its bulbous base many yards in diameter. Not far away one would find a round corral with walls of stone or earth and wood so thick that a man could walk around on top of the wall to use his lasso. The one built by the Saravias could hold two thousand cattle. Many an outnumbered war party made a stand inside such a corral.[19]

Poorer landowners and almost all landless families, on the other hand, lived not in sturdy houses like this but in *ranchos*. Ranchos were usually constructed of upright posts into which were woven slender branches or reeds and the whole covered with mud. Another kind of construction employed only squares of sod laid like bricks. The roof was always thatch and the floor packed earth. The house where Maria Angélica lived in 1854 was a rancho, and it was to a rancho that Francisco took Propícia when they eloped. One can get a feeling for these dwellings from the fact that Maria Angélica's rancho was assessed at one hundred milréis, while the rude kitchen structure out back was worth half that much itself.[20]

In the early years of their marriage, Propícia and Francisco ate and socialized in the kitchen, where an open fire blazed on an earthen platform slightly raised in the middle of the room. Coals were kept from day to day, so that the hearth might not have to be rekindled in years. Spits of beef, the fatter the better, were thrust into holes in the platform and leaned sizzling toward the flames. Above the fire dangled a sooty chain from which hung a pot of stew or a kettle for mate alongside chunks of meat curing in the smoke that billowed up to find its way out through the blackened thatch. Meat was essential at all meals, for all social classes. It might be prepared in various stews of corn, potatoes, carrots, *boniato* (another tuber), tomatoes, onions, rice, or *zapallo* (a large squash). Manioc flour brought from Brazil frequently accompanied the meat (to soak up the grease). One sampled carnivorous morsels from the spits by seizing a corner in one's teeth and cutting it loose from the roast with a knife. The method was not without its risks, and the contours of more than one nose were altered in the process.[21]

In the house, Propícia kept saints' images and prayed to them in time of need, for Rio Grandenses seemed more attentive to daily religious practice than were their Uruguayan neighbors. If she was like most women of the estancias, Propícia enjoyed pets: a small green parrot to enliven the long hours of housework, a little dog to warm the foot of the bed. She and Francisco also kept larger dogs fierce enough to keep any visitor on his horse until they were called off. Arriving at an estancia, a Spanish-speaking visitor would shout *"Ave María Purísima!"* (Hail Purest Mary!) and someone in the house would come out to look him over, then complete the formula—*"Sin pecado concebida!"* (Conceived without Sin!)—and control the dogs, inviting the visitor to dismount. Wild dogs of a wolfish appearance had taken over the ecological niche of the jaguars and pumas, which were already scarce by the early nineteenth century. Large packs attacked both stock and people, and they proliferated especially in wartime when there was a lot of carrion around. At the end of the Guerra Grande in 1852, twelve thousand wild dogs were exterminated in Cerro Largo.[22]

For Francisco and his growing sons, the most often performed job was rounding up the cattle and making sure none had strayed. When a herd was first tamed or relocated to a new pasture, watch had to be maintained around the clock until the animals developed an attachment to the place. Afterward the job of vigilance was much easier. Iberian longhorns have extremely varied markings designated by borderlanders in several dozen terms. Along with the animal's brand, age, sex, weight, shape of horns, and other characteristics, the distinctive color patterns allowed rural men to identify each animal individually. Gumercindo's brother José, for example, was said to notice the absence of a single steer among hundreds without counting them. Borderlanders rode their mounts very hard and each man exhausted several in a working day. If Francisco and Propícia had a hundred cattle, they probably had at least fifty horses, though only a few of these were saddle horses. At any given time, one of the men on the estancia, the *domador* by name, would be in the process of breaking new mounts. The job of the domador, often performed by a Guaraní or a slave, required special skill. It was also extremely dangerous, since the basic method was simply to clamber atop the furious animal and ride until it stopped bucking.[23]

In spring or fall, the men would brand and castrate the yearling cattle. Branding and castration required more hands than the estancia maintained at other times. Like all activities that brought together the inhabitants of scattered estancias, this was an important event. The men and boys of the agregado families would all be present, and others would come for wages or for sport, trusting that the landowner would provide food and drink in abundance for everyone. The walls of the corral would be lined with spectators as an animal was first deftly separated from the swirling herd, roped, toppled, castrated if male, and its flank charred with a very large iron brand. A single brand indicated original ownership; a second mark with both the old brand and a new one signified transfer of ownership. Eye-catching displays of expertise in roping or horsemanship brought appreciative cries from the onlookers and possibly a drink proffered personally by the patrón, but failure attracted ridicule. Music and dance often accompanied these activities, sometimes for several festive nights in a row, and fond recollections of branding time would become a staple of "gaucho" nostalgia in later years.[24]

When Gumercindo Saravia gathered his montonera in January 1893, surprisingly little had changed in the daily activities of borderlanders since the early nineteenth century. Armed retainers and fortresslike houses were still the norm. The skills of a man's work on the estancias of the 1890s—agility and endurance in the saddle and the ability to spill blood with a blade—were still exactly the skills needed for the light-cavalry operations of a montonera, and, with so few firearms, the montoneros' "guerra gaucha" of speed and maneuver was plainly what Gumercindo had in mind. As always, the border itself provided a refuge and a base of operations for insurgents. It is hardly puzzling that, in such circumstances, Saravia should consider "revolution" a political option of something more than last resort.

4
FEBRUARY 1893

A t last, on an evening of nearly full moon in early February 1893, Gumercindo Saravia readied the montonera to cross the border into Brazil. The Maragatos milled about with their horses in the moonlight, tightening cinches, drinking the last gourdfuls of mate brought out by the women of the estancia, and regaling each other with the raucous high spirits of the long-awaited moment. The Saravia women tried with uneven success to bid dry-eyed farewells. Their lives would be immeasurably more difficult during the war, and there was always the chance that their husbands would not return at all. Gumercindo's wife Amélia had six children to take care of, one of them a babe in arms, and she was pregnant as well. Aparicio's wife Cándida also had six children, but at least she could remain in her own house. (Amélia could never return to her house in Santa Vitória—the house she remembered as the scene of joyful dances at which her accordion playing and singing had made her the center of attention—since it was razed to the ground by Gumercindo's enemies.) Borderland ranchers like the Saravias were not absentee landlords, and the women they left behind would bear significant responsibility for administering their estancias, though the numerous relatives in the neighborhood would, of course, lend a hand. Finally, after issuing repeated admonitions to keep quiet during the ride north across the shadowy countryside, Gumercindo mounted and led the montonera away from the estancia, its three to four hundred lances pointing skyward.[1]

Gumercindo took the montonera north at night in order not to encounter the Uruguayan authorities, who also preferred to avoid a confrontation if given a chance to look the other way. The high road north ran right by his father's house, past the Uruguayan town of Melo, straight to the Brazilian line. In a land where the principal barriers to communication were swollen streams, this long ridge crest had for a century been the route of armies moving north or south through the heart of the Saravias' borderland. It was merely a larger version of many similar ridges (called *cuchillas* in Spanish and *coxilhas* in Portuguese) that together formed an undulating landscape, rather rougher here than in most of Uruguay. The road along this Cuchilla Grande ran high enough to provide quite a view of the surrounding moonlit hills, but its height also made a montonera conspicuous, and the high road saw considerable traffic—including stage coaches, herds of cattle on their way to market, and the large two-wheeled ox carts that still carried most of the freight in the borderland.[2]

Instead of taking the high road, Gumercindo led the Maragatos on a parallel route though the bottom lands of the Río Negro, the largest river in the borderland. In time of peace, the Río Negro presented a significant impediment to the movement of people, not only because its roaring torrent spread for miles beyond its banks at flood stage, but also because of the gauchos, deserters, and bandits who found excellent hiding places in its maze-like floodplain, densely-grown with bushes and low trees, where high points became islands in rainy weather. In wartime, however, the Río Negro became the natural habitat of a montonera. The river's headwaters rose on the Brazilian side of the border, and this upper stretch of the river bisecting the border became a hideaway to which the insurgents would return repeatedly during the revolutions of the 1890s. This area had been a hideaway for generations of insurgents. Half a century earlier, the rebellious Farrapos had resisted the forces of the Brazilian empire successfully for a decade thanks, in part, to logistical opportunities presented by this borderland redoubt. In this area, the Farrapos had proclaimed their secessionist republic in the flush of an early victory, and here they had withdrawn, exhausted, and finally capitulated to imperial forces.[3]

The town and surrounding countryside of Bagé—a center of the

Federalist insurgency now just as it had been of the Farrapo insurgency years before—was the most important settlement in this part of the Brazilian borderland. Like the town of Melo, south of the border, Bagé had grown up on the site of an army encampment squarely athwart the high road between Brazil and Uruguay, an advanced bastion of the Portuguese military presence in its late colonial thrust toward the Río de la Plata. With a population of almost twelve thousand in the 1890s, Bagé remained a garrison town, with saber-carrying officers in imperial uniform and unruly recruits much in evidence, the army barracks on the edge of town among its largest structures. The church, standing at one end of a long hill, was impressive by borderland standards and boasted fancy onion-shaped domes atop its twin steeples. The railroad station at the other end of town was also something to brag about in the borderland, where the railroad age had only just arrived on the tracks of the Southern Brazilian Railway. The town's main street, named for the date of Brazilian independence, stretched along the hill top to the market with its arcaded stalls, though many of the merchants whose shops lined that street were foreigners: Portuguese, Italian, Spanish, or French. There were several newspapers, a theater, primary and secondary schools, the offices of a few surgeons, dentists, lawyers and notaries, and a score of taverns. The principal thoroughfares were festooned with street lamps but mostly shadeless—though there were spacious gardens full of fruit trees inside the walls of many houses, particularly toward the edge of town. Almost all the houses were of one story with tile roofs and windows divided into small panes in Brazilian fashion.[4]

By early 1893, the situation in Bagé had become so tense that a late-night rumble at a shindig in the outskirts of town caused the mobilization of the panicky garrison, only too aware that most people in the town sided with the Federalists. For almost fifty years the town had been the political territory of the Silva Tavares family. Here, Gen. João Nunes da Silva Tavares (old "Joca," as he was generally called) had joined with Silveira Martins to form the Federalist party less than a year before. Bagé had been occupied by Republican irregulars after the collapse of the short-lived Federalist government, and Joca Tavares had sworn to avenge the mistreatment of his people there. Also on his mind was the killing of two of his nephews in a midnight police raid on their house in Porto Alegre only a few weeks earlier. As the head of a family that had gained its prominence principally through its military exploits, Tavares made an intimidating enemy. Joca had "covered himself with glory" during the Paraguayan war and then followed in his father's footsteps as national guard commander on the Jaguarão frontier, a sensitive vanguard region of the empire. During the 1870s and 1880s, when Silveira Martins was a rising star in national politics, the Tavares family was devoting itself to building patronage networks in the borderland around Bagé. The family's landholding north of town was among the largest anywhere around, of a scale that had not been common since the first half of the nineteenth century. Eventually, Joca, his father, and one of his brothers all received titles of nobility, and two of them occupied the governorship of Rio Grande do Sul. As a consequence of all this, the ex-colonels of the national guard who commanded the Federalist montoneras quite naturally accepted Joca as their military leader.[5]

When Gumercindo and his montonera rode north along the Río Negro in 1893, Tavares was at a ranch house near the headwaters of the river, just south of the Uruguayan line. No doubt Gumercindo conferred with him there before officially beginning the Federalist insurgency by crossing the border into Brazil on 2 February. Seventy-six years old, excessively corpulent, and in ill health, Joca Tavares hardly felt up to a major campaign, yet the insurgents had no other war captain of his stature. The thought of Silveira Martins at the head of a montonera would have made the staunchest borderland Federalist wince. The *guerra gaucha* was simply not for frock-coated bacharéis, so old Joca it had to be, and he crossed the border shortly after Gumercindo. Over the next two weeks, they were joined by other groups ranging in size from a few dozen to a few hundred horsemen, and soon there were almost three thousand in what the insurgents began to call the Liberating Army.[6]

Joca Tavares would have liked nothing better than to move immediately against the Republicans occupying his home town of Bagé, but the town's well-armed garrison presented a considerable deterrent. The town of Santana do Livramento, to the west of Bagé, seemed a more vulnerable initial target, farther from the Southern Brazilian rail line that could quickly bring government reinforcements from the coast, better as an insurgent headquarters because it was a true bordertown (separated from the Uruguayan town of Rivera by no more than a broad street). Furthermore, since Rivera was served by a rail connection with Montevideo, Silveira Martins could conveniently join them there to set up an insurgent government. Consequently the Federalists set out west toward Santana do Livramento, paralleling the border and only a few miles north of it.[7]

On the way to Santana do Livramento lay the much smaller town of Dom Pedrito (named a century earlier for a Spanish captain of borderland smuggling parties), which was destined to become the first conquest of the insurgency. In the predawn hours of 22 February 1893, the Liberating Army surrounded the ragged cluster of dark tile roofs and whitewashed walls around a dusty square, all its inhabitants numbering somewhat less than the besieging army. Hoping to take the little town by surprise, Tavares ordered an assault at first light, but the army garrison of 250 soldiers had already barricaded the four entrances to the square and met them with bullets. After two hours of inconsequential firing from windows and doorways and from behind the barricade, General Tavares signaled for a parley, made a ceremonious display of his forces, and called upon the defending officers to surrender all arms and any soldiers who should choose to join the insurgents, offering in return a guarantee of liberty for the captured officers and respect for the persons and property of the townspeople. The garrison commander seems to have been less than terrified by the show of insurgent force, because he declined to surrender and forced Tavares to resume the attack, using up the Federalists' paltry supply of ammunition. Gumercindo and three other coronéis each took about fifty men and went in shooting through the plots of beans and squash around the village. When the fighting stopped for the night, Gumercindo held one of the four corners of the town square, and the next morning the defenders waved a white flag.[8]

At the cost of a handful of dead and a few dozen wounded, the Liberating Army had won a small but heady victory. Among the heroes of the day—the men who, along with Gumercindo, had breached the defense of Dom Pedrito at nightfall—were a number of local landowners. Dom Pedrito lay not far from Bagé and well within the heartland of Federalist strength, so the insurgents received a warm welcome, and a good part of the town's garrison decided to join them, bringing along fifty carbines and three hundred pistols, a not insub-

stantial contribution to the firepower of the revolution. The vox pop-
uli of the countryside celebrated the outcome of this diminutive first
battle of the war in droll songs about the trouncing received by the
government forces and also began to echo the name of Gumercindo's
Spanish-speaking Maragatos, while the insurgents basked in their
triumph for a couple of days before setting out once more, in a
column miles long, toward Santana do Livramento.[9]

5

STATES AND NATIONS

The insurgents marched parallel to the border on their way to Santana do Livramento, far enough in Brazil to defy the government of their enemies but close enough to Uruguay so that they could escape if hard pressed. After all, only on Brazilian soil did their actions against the Republicans transcend conspiracy to become a "revolution." (They understood the word in the Lockean sense, as an effort to restore the legitimate political order, not an attempt to refashion the social order.) To make clear the claims of his montonera, parts of which might otherwise have been taken for the kind of bandit gang that often inhabited the headwaters of the Río Negro, Gumercindo Saravia had issued a formal proclamation of insurgent intent immediately after invading Brazil, and Joca Tavares had done the same. Gumercindo's proclamation asked especially that he not be viewed as a foreigner but as a patriotic Brazilian. If the protestation seems a bit surprising in a person who is known to have preferred Spanish to Portuguese, the intent is clear: nationals, not foreigners, were the proper protagonists of legitimate revolution. The Republicans, on the other hand, were careful to call the invaders "Uruguayan bandits," in a bid to deny them political legitimacy. Because nineteenth-century revolutions and their heroes on horseback often retarded the institutionalization of national states, many believe caudillismo antithetical to the idea of nation. Nothing could be farther from the truth, however, in the late-nineteenth-century borderland, where insurgents drew sustenance from the idea of nation even as they struggled against the agents of the state.[1]

How important could state and nation be in a land where the supposed dividing line between countries was so recent and so palpably artificial? The adjoining landscapes of Uruguay and Rio Grande do Sul could hardly show more social and economic continuity at the time of the Federalist insurgency. Outsiders in the company of the invading Maragatos might easily have missed seeing the border entirely. Although this southern limit of Brazil is defined by shallow, easily-forded rivers at its eastern and western ends, the middle—where the Maragatos crossed it to begin their "revolution"—stretched for over a hundred miles along a low ridge, with no indication that two national states divided there. Travelers working their way south from the mountains of Santa Catarina (just north of Rio Grande do Sul) frequently commented that the physical geography and rural settlement characteristic of Brazil ended well north of the border. "Physically, this is the southern extreme of Brazil," wrote a North American naturalist in the 1880s, referring to the place where the Brazilian plateau ends abruptly along the Jacuí River and the traveler can gaze over miles of plains stretching south toward the Río de la Plata. "The plants, animals, landscape, the very way of life of Brazil, industries and commerce, are left behind. Politically the Empire goes on for a few hundred kilometers, but socially the rest of the province gravitates toward the Platine Republics." This is a persuasive image, and it fits well with the attitude of other Brazilians toward Rio Grandenses, but it should not lead to the assumption that the border meant little to the people of the borderland themselves. However invisible on the ground, the border had a large impact on their lives and held an important place in their understanding of the political order. After all, the border had not been imposed on them, as its invisibility seemed to indicate. Rather, the borderlanders had imposed the border in wars with each other.[2]

The area later to become the Brazilian–Uruguayan borderland had been the most contested ground between the Spanish and Portuguese empires, the one place in the hemisphere where their competing plans for territorial expansion led to prolonged military conflict. Initially, there was little to attract the energies of the Iberian colonizers to windy grasslands lacking precious metals as well as a docile labor

Map 2   Chief Localities of the Saravias' Borderlands

force, and so, through the seventeenth and eighteenth centuries, Portuguese and Spanish imperialists continued to face each other across a no-man's-land that both claimed but neither tried to populate or control. Attempts to parley dividing lines in 1750 and 1777 led to considerable surveying and even, in the latter case, to the erection of some markers, but both agreements eventually broke down. The modern outlines of the border between Brazil and Uruguay were established by force of arms in the first quarter of the nineteenth century (though not formally confirmed by treaty until 1851). The native Charruas and Minuanos were gone by the 1850s, when Gumercindo and Aparicio were born, and as for the wandering gauchos, they recognized no king, no law, and no God—according to the expression of the time—but only the temporary supremacy of those stronger and better mounted than themselves. Until roughly the middle of the nineteenth century, Brazilian and Uruguayan mounted police squads and army detachments waged a losing battle against the parties of drifters, deserters, bandits, and smugglers who crisscrossed the countryside, living off the fat of the half-wild herds. In the 1880s, when an outbreak of cholera in Uruguay led Brazilian authorities to "close" the border, they still could hardly do more than block the habitual crossings.[3]

Various sorts of armies, militias, mounted police, and border garrisons could always be found in the borderland, however imperfect their pretensions to complete control, and the military authorities of each side normally maintained a formal correspondence with those across the border. Their presence made this a highly militarized society, where flags and uniforms abounded and emblems of nationalism acquired a heightened meaning from juxtaposition with those of the other state. Especially in Rio Grande do Sul, the distribution of land had gone hand in glove with armed conquest, and many Federalist families traced their social dominance to leadership in wars against the Spanish a century earlier. In the interim, Rio Grandense borderlanders had repeatedly served as military vanguard, bearing the brunt of the fighting in all the wars fought by the Brazilian empire, since virtually all took place on the borders of Rio Grande do Sul. Throughout the nineteenth century, there were far more regular line troops in Rio Grande do Sul than anywhere else in Brazil (from a quarter to a third of the whole imperial army), creating strong military traditions and a steady circulation of Brazilians from other provinces to remind Rio Grandenses of their participation in a sprawling empire. The Rio Grandense national guard saw more action and constituted a more effective force than any other in the country—and naturally so. At mid-century the national guardsmen of the province might be called up for years to campaign in Uruguay, Argentina, or Paraguay, or to assume patrol duties along the border while regular troops did the campaigning.[4]

Since the border was a good place for enemies of the government to gather and organize, the borderland showed an early and enduring vocation for insurgency, expressed most notably in Uruguay. The first of the innumerable rebellions to shake nineteenth-century Uruguay was launched from the Jaguarão River shortly after the country's first president took office, and ever thereafter the border region called Cerro Largo, home of the Saravia family, remained a stronghold of the perennially insurrectionary Blanco party. The function of the Uruguayan national guard was undercut by the Blanco militias that shadowed it or, in places, replaced it altogether. All Blanco partisans held military ranks because, having attained a given rank in one revolution, a Blanco officer always maintained his rank until the next. In either the national guard or the Blanco partisan militia, military rank signaled social position as well as battlefield courage. Therefore, the distribution of ranks had little to do with the number of captains or colonels actually required to command a given number of troops. In 1869, there were 118 "retired" colonels and lieutenant colonels on the payrolls of an Uruguayan army that had never, in its short history, numbered more than a few thousand soldiers altogether. Official recognition of rank, implying reincorporation into the hierarchy of paid "retired" or reserve officers, sometimes figured specifically among the rebel demands for a negotiated peace. The Blanco party also called itself the *Partido nacional* and its partisans always carried the national flag. Although Brazilians and Uruguayans occasionally participated in each other's partisan struggles, most revolutionaries marched as soldiers of a specific nationality.[5]

Like Gumercindo himself, many Rio Grandense borderlanders could be Uruguayan or Brazilian "depending on the circumstances" (as one disgusted police chief reported from Melo in 1870), but they were never at a loss for a nationality. Brazilian residents of Uruguay frequently invoked their foreign status to stay neutral in a Blanco revolution or to avoid being impressed into the Uruguayan army, and they often carted their children to Brazil for baptism. According to one European traveler of the early nineteenth century, Rio Grandenses in general were "so proud of the glorious name of Brazilians" and so touchy around foreigners that he had to be careful not to provoke fights inadvertently. The traveler suspected that the proximity of Brazil's Spanish-speaking neighbors exacerbated this attitude, and there is evidence to support his idea. Though twentieth-century

Rio Grandenses proudly call themselves "gaúchos"* and other Brazilians think them hispanicized, Portuguese-speaking borderlanders identified themselves culturally and politically with the empire, and they never tired of favorable comparisons between Brazil and Spanish America. In the nineteenth century, they were likely to append the modifier "castelhano" (Castilian) to the word "gaúcho," especially when describing the sort of person whom they thought ought to be in jail.[6] In the 1850s, an imperial administrator expounded this attitude by lamenting, to his superiors in Rio de Janeiro, the plague of bandits and deserters "educated in the school of anarchy that the neighboring Republics constantly provide." When the body of a murdered Rio Grandense appeared carved up in a lonely part of Bagé, local suspicions focused automatically on a party of "castelhanos" wearing Guaraní chiripás and carrying lances. After a foreman for the Silveira family was slain south of the border, a Brazilian official railed about Uruguayan bandits who "often cross into this province to kill people."[7] Tensions between the two countries sometimes ran high during the middle years of the nineteenth century, when horse races at the border became so volatile that the authorities prohibited them. In his report to the provincial chief of police, an officer in Jaguarão referred to marauding Uruguayans as "a horde of cannibals" in the 1860s. Incensed by stories of atrocities against Rio Grandenses in Uruguay, Bagé's local bard called for "War! War of extermination / Against those beasts of the Plata . . ." (and after war began, he sent reports in verse from the various battles in which he took part). The former Farrapo general who championed the cause of Rio Grandense estancia families in Uruguay was deliriously feted (with "A toast as loyal and sacred / As his Brazilian heart") in Bagé after travelling to plead the borderlanders' case in Rio de Janeiro.[8]

Rio Grande do Sul's borderland elite dominated the province through most of the nineteenth century, and it constructed a collective self-image that highlighted its patriotic military traditions. As in Uruguay, these traditions were partly linked to insurgency, though to a lesser degree. The great hero of the secessionist Farrapo rebellion was a borderland caudillo (*caudilho* in Portuguese) named Bento

---

*The Portuguese spelling of *gaúcho,* with an accent mark, will be used with particular reference to Rio Grande do Sul.

Gonçalves, formerly the national guard commander of the Jaguarão border (see map). Eager to end the decade-long Farrapo War, the imperial government had granted the Farrapos an honorable negotiated settlement and afterward accorded special treatment to these unruly cattle barons of its southern marches. Many times in the coming years, ex-Farrapos and their former enemies joined forces under the Brazilian flag to fight in foreign wars, and their camaraderie helped to dissipate remaining rancors. When the emperor toured the Rio Grande in 1865, during the Paraguayan war, he met a festive welcome in Bagé and other borderland towns. Enthused by a discourse of national greatness, borderlanders put noticeably more energy into patriotic rituals during that war. "Who is that majestic star of grandeur and light rising, radiant, on the horizon of South America?" asked Bagé's independence day orator rhetorically as a prelude to announcing Brazil's coming of age as a continental power. By the 1880s, the almanacs published in the borderland featured etchings of Gonçalves and battlefield narratives from Paraguay in a manner reminiscent of similar publications in the U.S. South after the Civil War. "Heroic" and "legendary" were favorite adjectives in ceremonious tributes to this "American Sparta": "This heroic land, Pátria of so many brave warriors, classic land of indomitable liberty, legendary Rio Grande do Sul . . . is invincible." Throughout the century, the referent of the word "pátria" still oscillated between the province of Rio Grande do Sul and the whole of the Brazilian Empire, so both the provincially-oriented Farrapo insurgents and their imperialist adversaries could consider their struggle "patriotic." Although the Farrapos had operated from Uruguayan bases just as the Federalists did later, both waxed indignant when their enemies accused them of joining forces with the castelhanos.[9]

Most important in the relationship between Brazilians and Uruguayans were the repeated invasions of one country by the other. In 1763, Spanish armies overran the southern portion of the Portuguese captaincy of Rio Grande do Sul and dominated it for a decade, and during the Uruguayan war for independence, caudillo Fructuoso Rivera struck another famous blow, "stealing" hundreds of Guaraníes from Brazil. Spanish-speaking outlaws continued to plunder Rio Grandense territory for three generations thereafter. On the whole, however, international conflict at the border usually meant Brazilian imperialism in Uruguay. In the eighteenth century, the Portuguese pushed down the coast toward a "natural" southern limit at the wide, muddy Río de la Plata, twice invading Uruguay to throttle patriot caudillo José Artigas during the Spanish American wars of independence and formally annexing Uruguay in 1820. Uruguayan patriots "threw off the Brazilian yoke" (with help from Buenos Aires), made the country independent (with help from Great Britain), and contributed importantly to forcing the abdication of the first Brazilian emperor in 1831. But Brazil invaded Uruguay again in the 1850s and yet again in the 1860s. At mid-century, the Brazilian regular army and national guard could field a force of more than twenty-five thousand in Rio Grande do Sul, giving them a crushing superiority over their Uruguayan counterparts. Brazilian capital flowed into the Uruguayan republic, a favorite investment site for the leading Brazilian financier of the nineteenth century, the Baron of Mauá, who happened to have been born in the borderland himself. Meanwhile, imperial administrators wrote in supercilious, and eerily familiar, terms about the need to safeguard Brazilian lives and property until Uruguayans could learn to provide the guarantees of law themselves.[10]

Large numbers of Rio Grandenses like the Saravias had migrated across the border and acquired land in the 1830s and 1840s. By mid-century the Brazilian population of northern Uruguay was about twenty-five thousand, and the elite families of the Brazilian side of the borderland had become the chief ranching clans of the Uruguayan side as well. In some parts of the Uruguayan north, Brazilians quite literally owned most of the estancia land. Of 485 ranchers branding cattle in Cerro Largo at one point, 311 were Brazilian. "Across the Jaguarão river, gentlemen," proclaimed a Brazilian deputy during a parliamentary session of 1845, "clothing, language, customs, currency, measurements, everything to the far bank of the Río Negro, everything, gentlemen, even the land itself, everything is Brazilian."[11]

The grandfather of Gaspar Silveira Martins, whose princely riches had helped finance Portuguese annexation of Uruguay early in the century, offers an extreme, but not misleading, example. His patriotic services earned him the title of viscount from a grateful emperor and facilitated the acquisition, at favorable prices, of several vast tracts of Uruguayan territory. The viscount, so it is said, wanted to be able to ride all the way to Montevideo on his own property. Strung together, his eleven estancias almost satisfied his whim. A survey done by the Rio Grandense national guard at mid-century showed thousands upon thousands of square leagues claimed by Brazilians in northern Uruguay. In some years during the Farrapo War, when Rio Grandense borderlanders like the Saravias swarmed into Uruguay, well over half the people getting married in the Uruguayan town of Melo were Brazilians.[12]

So overwhelming was the Brazilian presence in some rural areas that supposedly "Uruguayan" justices of the peace—like the father of Silveira Martins—submitted their reports quite unabashedly in Portuguese. Such officials often had better handwriting and were clearly better equipped for the job than any of their Spanish-speaking neighbors, yet one imagines the unease of the Uruguayan judge who received an officious report concerning the ceremony held in one borderland neighborhood to swear allegiance (in Portuguese) to the "santa constituição" of the newly independent Republic of Uruguay. By the 1860s, Uruguayan officials complained that Spanish "was disappearing almost completely" in the rural north. Not infrequently, Brazilian families simply took land that lay unoccupied because the Uruguayan owner had fled or had never settled there at all. Legitimate title for many such de facto claims was established later in the century by legal action, possibly including token payment to the heirs of the original owners.[13]

Well into the 1860s, frustrated Uruguayan authorities in the borderland wrote to their superiors in Montevideo about Brazilian infringements of their sovereignty. Slavery provides a good example—manifesting the significance of the concept of nation even as it illustrates the fragility of state control. After the Uruguayan republic abolished bound servitude in the 1840s, many Brazilian landowners continued to work their Uruguayan estancias with bondsmen: ex-slaves who, according to a legal fiction, freely entered into contracts of indenture for fifteen, twenty-five, or even forty years. This was a constitutional fig leaf many Uruguayans found humiliating. Still, Uruguayan abolition obliged opulent Brazilian ranchers who owned property in both countries to take most of their human chattel to estancias north of the border. As a result, the abduction of free Uruguayan blacks supposedly owned by someone in Rio Grande do Sul (or simply intended for sale there) became epidemic. During the Paraguayan war, in which Brazil and Uruguay became allies, Brazilian press gangs did not halt their depredations at the border. Like their competition—the Uruguayan press gangs—they seem to have conscripted black and mulatto men most quickly and ruthlessly.[14]

Large, well-organized cattle raids, which Brazilian borderlanders lightheartedly termed "californias" (comparing their profitability to the 1849 gold rush in that territory recently annexed by the United States), constituted a glaring demonstration of the inability of the Uruguayan state to impose its sovereignty. The Brazilian imperial government frowned on the "californias," which were launched by Rio Grandense cattle barons in retribution for losses they suffered at the hands of castelhanos, but it failed to prevent them. The Farrapo leader Bento Gonçalves and his brother Francisco (sporting the sobriquet "Chico Bonito") both led forays in the 1820s and 1830s. At least one fabled leader of californias, the Baron of Jacuí, flaunted an imperial title of nobility, and many others—like Bento Gonçalves himself—were top brass in the Rio Grandense national guard. "Chico Bonito" functioned, at one point, as head of the Jaguarão police force.[15]

The 1880s brought a respite from the internal upheavals that had plagued Uruguay in its first half-century, and a sympathetic Brazilian spokesman came forth to defend the small republic from the slanderous epithet "country of barbarians," so often flung by his own countrymen. Nevertheless, his refutation reveals the stubborn derision of Rio Grandenses who envisioned Uruguay as a land populated by Indians, where abusive police and mindless political wars endangered the lives and property of law-abiding foreign residents. That image, the writer assured his fellow Brazilians, was now out of date. A newspaper in the Uruguayan town of Melo translated the article and reprinted it approvingly. Things had, indeed, changed in the Uruguayan borderland. After the stormy partisan struggles of mid-century, the ordinary insecurities of life on the plains had diminished during the adult lives of Gumercindo and Aparicio. Peace allowed the Uruguayan economy to prosper, and Montevideo, with the best harbor in that part of the continent, had become a bustling import–export conduit, a modernized city of streetcars and impressive buildings, far more attractive than Porto Alegre for either business or pleasure. Although Uruguayans still resented the power of the Brazilian state, they began to feel a certain cultural superiority over their Portuguese-speaking neighbors, whom they deemed the bearers of an indolent tropicality and too many African genes. Brazilian border-landers were belittled for concealing their women from strangers, speaking a language of permanent hyperbole, and engaging in quasi-barbarous customs such as "dancing for the little angel" at the wake of an infant. Uruguayan clerks in bordertowns did occasionally catch an enthusiasm for certain infectious rhythms through their international fraternizing, but otherwise Brazilian culture was little esteemed in the Río de la Plata. By the 1890s, a Portuguese accent had become part of the Uruguayan "hick" stereotype, and the modernizing elite of Montevideo considered the backward ranching practices of border-land Rio Grandenses an obstacle to national progress.[16]

In addition to economic gains, late nineteenth-century Uruguayans reaped the benefits of a highly effective educational reform that began in the 1870s and eventually made the country's general standards of literacy the envy of Latin America. The borderland constituted a major focus of this reform (designed especially to instill a national culture among immigrants) and school teachers near the border earned higher salaries than other rural teachers in Uruguay. Whereas the educational institutions of the Brazilian borderland had been more noteworthy at mid-century, Uruguay took the clear lead by the 1890s. Sheer numbers tell the story. In 1896, there were forty-one public schools for girls and boys in Cerro Largo and—most impres-sively—thirty-five of these schools were in the countryside. The Uruguayan state was making a credible (if not absolutely successful) attempt to put a primary school within walking distance of every child, while in contiguous rural areas across the border there were virtually no schools at all. Rural school masters contrived elaborate patriotic rituals replete with flag-carrying marchers, speeches, and anthems to commemorate Uruguayan national holidays.[17] Because they wanted to preserve their own national culture (and also resisted the idea of educating girls) Brazilian landowners were reluctant to send their children to these schools. Clarion calls to reclaim the Uruguayan borderland for the national language were still heard in the first decade of the twentieth century, but by then the tide had turned. Continued economic prosperity combined with the efforts of rural school teachers to create a preference for Uruguayan nationality in subsequent generations of Brazilian borderlanders south of the border. The importance of public education as a nationalizing instrument should not be underestimated, despite the joke, told as early as 1895, about the child in Rivera who spelled out a word with Spanish letters, p-e-rr-o, then proudly announced its meaning as "*cachorro*" (in Portuguese). According to the civic-minded essay of one Melo schoolgirl in 1894, Greece had its Alexander, Rome its Caesar, and Uruguay its José Pedro Varela (referring to the founder of the country's school reform).[18]

Gumercindo Saravia could claim Brazilian nationality because he was born at a time when Rio Grandenses like his parents took their children to be baptized in Brazil and because his baptism was a matter of institutional record. Along with his brother Basilicio, one year younger than he, Gumercindo got his sprinkling of holy water on 14 September 1853 in the Rio Grandense parish of Arroio Grande, where Propícia and Chico seem to have met in the late 1840s and where both had family. The vicar of Arroio Grande scribbled the requisite formulas on page 119 of the second volume of the baptismal registry, as one can learn from Brazilian and Uruguayan historians who have carefully transcribed this information in their heated dispute over Gumercindo's birthplace and nationality. Nationality is, in fact, a central issue in Manuel Fonseca's carefully researched *Gumersindo Saravia: El general de la libertad* (1957), which argues that Gumercindo must have been born in Uruguay despite his Brazilian baptism. Family traditions collected in Cerro Largo (along with the fact that Gumercindo and Basilicio were baptized at the same time) lend persuasiveness to Fonseca's case. Undaunted, Brazilian historian Sejanes Dornelles refuses to concede an Uruguayan birthplace in his *Gumersindo Saraiva: O guerrilheiro pampeano* (1988).[19]

The variant spellings of the name—Saravia or Saraiva—reflect the authors' opposite orientations concerning Gumercindo's nationality. *Saraiva* is the Portuguese form of this originally Portuguese surname. Gumercindo's parents used the Portuguese form all their lives, but their children all seem to have adopted the Spanish version. In fact, they often wrote *Sarabia,* indicating their Spanish pronunciation, since the letters v and b are interchangeable phonemically in Spanish but not in Portuguese. Gumercindo's Brazilian enemies sometimes said *Sarabia* when calling him an Uruguayan bandit, while his Brazilian supporters insisted on the Portuguese *Saraiva*. On the other side of the border, the pattern was inverted. Aparicio's detractors often spelled his name *Saraiva,* especially at first. The signatures of both brothers serve as an indication of their self-definitions of nationality. Gumercindo wrote *Sarabia* during his thirty years in Cerro Largo and during his combative rise to local power in Santa Vitória do Palmar, but he tended to prefer *Saraiva* more and more as he became involved in Brazilian politics. Aparicio signed *Sarabia* until adopting the more standard Spanish spelling, Saravia, as he gained prominence in Uruguay. I have used the Spanish form uniformly in this book because it is the best-known spelling and also suggests the transcultural qualities of the family.[20]

As for the vicar who baptized Gumercindo and Basilicio in 1853, he wrote *Saraiva* quite automatically. Arroio Grande, after all, was Brazil, and Portuguese was the language of official records there, including church records, of course, since churches—like schools and civil wars—operated strictly in a national context. The vicars of churches in the paired bordertowns Rivera and Santana do Livramento lived and said mass within a few hundred yards of each other, but they took orders from bishops in Montevideo and Porto Alegre, respectively. Until the end of the Brazilian monarchy in 1889, the Catholic church acted almost as a state institution. Tithing was required by law, and vicars performed a variety of functions—beyond keeping the official records of birth, marriage, and death—such as census taking and land registration, that the republican government across the border in Uruguay had assumed after independence. For purposes of record keeping, the Catholic parish was the basic administrative unit in the Brazilian borderland—not so south of the border, where churches were further apart and the connection between church and state more tenuous. For a time in the late 1820s and early 1830s, the vicar of Melo was a republican priest from Brazil, who seems to have taken his holy offices a good deal less seriously than his involvement in Brazilian politics. There are also reports of priest-landowners in parishes north of the border, whereas the clergy of the Uruguayan borderland could be found only in the more populous towns.[21]

Borderland towns were even more nationally oriented than the countryside around them, and logically so, because the presence of the state inhered mostly in urban institutions—schools, churches, courts, notaries, and newspapers. In addition, Uruguayan and Rio Grandense towns looked different architecturally, as could be observed directly at the line separating Santana do Livramento from Rivera, the former plastered and whitewashed, the latter built of the same stone but without plaster or paint. Rio Grandense families who had settled on Uruguayan estancias traveled back to towns north of the border for errands. In Bagé, Jaguarão, or Santana do Livramento they could enjoy the society of other families like themselves (at a religious procession, perhaps, or at carnival festivities held by a local club), learn the most recent political gossip from the imperial court, and visit a doctor, a druggist, or a tailor who spoke Portuguese. In Uruguayan towns like Melo, Rivera, or Treinta y Tres (named for the thirty-three patriots who began the revolt against Brazilian occupation in 1825) they would encounter an entirely different set of people: lawyers, notaries, judges who had studied in Montevideo, Spanish Basque shopkeepers, and newspaper editors who reprinted articles from Buenos Aires or Santiago de Chile more often than from Rio de Janeiro. The Saravia family visited nearby Melo so rarely before the 1890s that, after Gumercindo rose to fame in the Brazilian war, the local newspaper had to explain to its readers that the acclaimed general's family had lived in Cerro Largo for forty years and still lived there.[22]

The communications networks used by urban people were also nationally oriented. Stage coach lines and mail carriers went from Melo to Montevideo much more frequently than to Brazilian towns nearby, and, most of the time, borderland newspapers concentrated strictly on national news. In towns of only a few thousand people (the size of the biggest settlements until the end of the nineteenth century) news of what happened yesterday traveled much faster than local newspapers, and chronicling local events was hardly their specialty. The four-page biweeklies that began to appear in Bagé and Melo after 1860—typically the single-handed production of an editor who wrote himself almost everything not reprinted from another paper—devoted a few columns on pages two and three to snippets of local trivia but put national matters on page one. Quite self-consciously, borderland editors considered themselves exponents of a national culture. Even when born in the locality themselves—not always the case, by any means—they had acquired their journalistic pretensions in Montevideo (if Uruguayan), in Porto Alegre, Rio Grande, or possibly Pelotas (if Rio Grandense), and their discourse invariably took national public life as its frame of reference. Although a Portuguese-language paper appeared in Montevideo during the 1880s, it was no less keenly national in orientation, as indicated by its title *O Brazil* (later, *A Pátria*).[23]

Although they were shy about entering the urban environment in Uruguay, Rio Grandense residents of the country could not avoid dealings with the judicial system, one of the few state institutions that reached into the countryside, and they often complained of friction with unsympathetic Uruguayan authorities. On both sides of the border, justices of the peace and various subordinate officials exercised responsibilities for conciliating quarrels over debts or property boundaries among neighbors, assisting in the investigation of crimes in rural areas, administering the routine procedures of civil law, and issuing permissions of various sorts.[24] The more important judges of Bagé and Melo frequently remitted prisoners and requisite documents back and forth across the border, emphasizing the concept of divided sovereignty and carefully recognizing each other's authority as the surest way to win reciprocal respect for their own. Consequently, Rio Grandense landowners had to retain Uruguayan lawyers to protect their interests south of the border. Entirely separate probate inventories, for example, would have to be executed at the death of people owning property in both Uruguay and Rio Grande do Sul. Puttering through their case records more than a hundred years later, the historian finds the Brazilian judicial system more organized, its justices of the peace more literate, their investigations more thorough, and the accused more often apprehended. The stronger continuity of the colonial bureaucratic traditions in independent Brazil and that country's greater political stability strengthened state institutions in the Rio Grandense borderland. The Brazilian jury system (unlike anything in Uruguay) involved large numbers of landowners in the process of administering official justice. On the whole, such institutions seem more organic to rural society north of the border—those of the Uruguayan side, more like idealized impositions on an indocile social reality.[25]

By far the most ambitious thing that either state attempted to do in rural areas was to police them. When rural Uruguayans spoke of "the authority," they were usually referring to the police comisario of their neighborhoods. Uruguayan comisarios were miniature caudillos, military men with a minimum of formal education, who commanded ten soldiers and reigned supreme from their headquarters in a crumbling rancho on some lonely cuchilla, while Brazilian police *delegados,* their counterparts in Rio Grande do Sul, were urban based, part of a more centralized, and disciplined force. Because they owned a lot of vulnerable property, Rio Grandenses south of the border approved of the police in principle and loudly praised police officials who protected them, but, on both sides of the border, poorer foreigners attracted a disproportionate amount of police attention, little of it favorable. Ideally, the most opulent and powerful families in a neighborhood avoided clashes with the police force by taking it over, as they did, too, with local justices. Rio Grandense families were less able to do so in Uruguay, of course, since the Uruguayan government preferred to have its own nationals in positions of authority, but exceptions (like the occasional "Uruguayan" justices who reported in Portuguese) remained common until the 1870s because of the shortage of rural men literate enough to be justices and thanks to the general predominance of Rio Grandense landowners in the Uruguayan north.[26]

Like the military, the courts, and all other forms of state presence in the borderland, the police fell far short of total efficacy, but rarely were any of these institutions completely ignored. In sum, two national states met at the invisible line that cut so arbitrarily across the rolling pastures of the borderland, and, being the creations of the human imagination, state institutions always had some importance, if only in people's minds. The material, mechanical aspects of governance were roughly comparable on either side of the border, but those of the Brazilian side seemed more effective during most of the nineteenth century. Brazilian institutions were upheld by a comparatively homogeneous ruling class with strong loyalties to the Braganza monarchy that had ruled them for generations. In the Uruguayan borderland, on the other hand, the institutions of a still-unconsolidated republican order encountered crippling barriers: an interminable blood feud between Blancos and Colorados and a quite heterogeneous population, many of whom (among them the largest landowners) were Brazilian. The borderland also played a different role in the two polities. The great landowners of the Rio Grandense side were the bulwark of the provincial aristocracy, closely linked to the central government and its foreign policy, while those of the Uruguayan side often viewed state institutions as hostile intrusions manipulated by their political enemies, undermining the power of those institutions to inspire loyalty and obedience.

This contrast diminished in the 1890s, when the newly created Brazilian republic encountered its own crisis of legitimacy, and the Uruguayan republic, having weathered the worst years of instability, gained a firmer hold on its borderland. An era of burgeoning export earnings brought communications innovations like the telegraph and railroad, while modern rifles and field artillery gave regular armies a decisive advantage, for the first time, over the old-style montonera armed with lances. Independent-minded cattle barons no longer posed much of a threat to state builders in Montevideo or Porto Alegre, or at least so one might suppose, yet borderland Federalists like Gumercindo Saravia and Joca Tavares had not yet absorbed this lesson in March 1893.

6
MARCH 1893

After the capture of Dom Pedrito, the government of Rio Grande do Sul stopped sneering at Gumercindo's Maragatos as Uruguayan bandits and set about trying to annihilate the insurgency. Governor Júlio de Castilhos, by this time, had managed to establish good relations with Republican president Floriano Peixoto, and the Federalist attack on the army garrison at Dom Pedrito gave Castilhos pretext to demand reinforcements from Rio de Janeiro. Unfortunately for the revolution, the insurgents—only about one in eight of whom had a gun—were no match for even half their number of well-trained, fully-armed regular soldiers such as those who would soon arrive in Bagé via the Southern Brazilian Railroad. A network of telegraph lines strung all over the state in the 1870s and 1880s allowed Castilhos to monitor the movements of the insurgents and coordinate the efforts of his own newly refurbished forces. Speed and an intimate familiarity with the terrain would permit the insurgents to outrun and outmaneuver most pursuers, but they were to capture few strongly garrisoned towns during the thirty months of the revolution. The miniature triumph at Dom Pedrito had perhaps induced even veterans like General Tavares to forget their true situation, but arriving outside the town of Santana do Livramento to find its defenders well armed and well entrenched, Tavares had reason to deplore his pitiful firepower.[1]

Since sieges can be won by artillery or starvation, but never by cavalry charge, the insurgents' numerical advantage availed them of nothing. The garrison and townspeople would not soon go hungry since Santana directly adjoined the Uruguayan town of Rivera and, though the Federalists had surrounded Santana on three sides, they had no control over the side that bordered Uruguay and dared not risk a confrontation with that country's authorities. Needless to say, the merchants of Rivera were soon doing a roaring business in basic commodities with the besieged Republicans. Meanwhile, the hotels of Rivera were jammed with Federalist émigrés waiting to join the revolution. According to rumor, even Gaspar Silveira Martins, who had so far preferred to preside over the rebellion oratorically from the lobbies of fashionable Montevidean hotels, traveled incognito to Rivera by train to greet the Liberating Army. Discovering that the insurgents' only artillery was a phony siege gun made of stove pipe and not wishing to appear ridiculous, he beat a hasty retreat to Montevideo. Ten days passed. In the besieging camp, the officers of the Liberating Army issued a manifesto to the nation disavowing imputations of monarchism. In the high-flown rhetoric typical of such pronouncements, they announced that the aim of their revolution was an end to violence and tyranny, that the insurgents' chivalrous conduct at Dom Pedrito showed their moral calibre, and that true Rio Grandenses preferred to sacrifice their lives to the sacred trust of their ancestors rather than face the ignominy of subjugation.[2]

The name of Gumercindo Saravia appears at the bottom of this manifesto, but he played no part in composing it, and on the day it was signed Saravia and the Maragatos were actually miles away skirmishing with army reinforcements. The relief column, an entire division under Gen. João Telles, was already approaching from Bagé, where it had arrived by rail a few days earlier. Gumercindo's lancers could ride circles around Telles's infantry, but little else. The Army of Liberation could not engage such a force without more arms and ammunition, so the thwarted insurgents broke camp and streamed away from Santana do Livramento, leaving the sons of Santana Republicans and the sons of émigré Federalists in Rivera to pelt each other with rocks at the international line. General Tavares might have regretted not destroying the stove-pipe siege gun, which soon became an object of Republican mirth. Ailing and confused, he was learning that his experience as a professional soldier did not equip him to command a guerrilla army.[3] Uncertain of how to proceed, old Joca led his disheartened men around the flank of Telles's menacing column and back toward the revolution's home ground near the headwaters of the Río Negro. Lurking about the outskirts of Bagé and finding it as well defended as ever, he was stymied again. Then, while most of the Liberating Army waited nervously, Gumercindo and the Maragatos demonstrated what they had learned in the Uruguayan school of montoneras. They broke away from Tavares and took up the guerrilla tactics of the guerra gaucha, something not seen in Rio Grande do Sul for half a century. Now Gumercindo began his ascendancy over the other colonels of the Liberating Army to become, within a few months, the hero of the revolution.[4]

The Maragatos generally moved at night through the rocky, treeless hills of the state's southeastern corner, materializing unexpectedly at points along the tracks of the Southern Brazilian Railroad to disrupt communications, if only temporarily. Insistent rifle fire could keep Saravia's lancers at a distance while soldiers calmly rebuilt a section of dismantled track so a train could proceed, but Gumercindo's adroitness and sense of the terrain enabled him to escape and attack at will. Meanwhile, Telles and his division returned to Bagé after reenforcing Santana do Livramento and bottled up the main Federalist force in its hideaway at the headwaters of the Río Negro. A number of skirmishes followed. At the end of March, a group of Maragatos chanced upon an isolated scouting party of Republican cavalry, fair game for the one tactic that did not require firepower—a lance charge—and they gave the revolution another modest bit of inspiration. Galloping at the head of the Maragato charge, leading lancers for the first time in the deadly rush later so closely associated with his name, was Gumercindo's younger brother Aparicio. There were twenty Republican dead and no Federalist losses.[5]

A few days later, Aparicio sat on the ground with his saddle in his lap to write his wife Cándida. This letter in his own handwriting is one of the tiny bundle that have survived to represent all the personal correspondence of one of Uruguay's national heroes. Aparicio apologized for the shakiness of his improvised desk, but under the best of circumstances (and despite assertions to the contrary by Uruguayan biographers who have not seen these letters) Aparicio's was clearly the hand of a rural man unused to writing—his phrasing, that of colloquial speech, his spelling phonetic, his punctuation nil. Jubilantly earnest, he bragged of his win and spoke yearningly of Cándida and his children. Apparently, Cándida had been inquiring when he would come home from Gumercindo's war. Aparicio said he could not leave his brother yet because he would be called a coward, but he promised her that if the revolution headed north out of the borderland he would return to Uruguay.[6]

Tavares and his forces still remained stalled for lack of firearms. Inaction was the worst test for a borderland war party, which would endure many months of mobilization without complaint as long as there was excitement but would melt away after too many weeks of waiting. A rare photograph of the insurgent camp shows members of the Army of Liberation lounging on the grass to have their picture taken. Here are the cannon fodder of the revolution, men with bedraggled ponchos and their hats pulled down over their eyes, about thirty of them, and a pitiful few rifles stacked like tripods in the foreground in a futile attempt to make them seem well armed. Their faces are dark, sunburned no doubt, but also dark with the skin tones of Africa and indigenous America. What did these men, the ordinary soldiers of the revolution, expect from this war? What occupied their minds as the days turned suddenly colder and the southern hemisphere winter began to descend from the Andean slopes far to the west, bringing the first whiffs of icy wind? Winter also meant rain, and there was little shelter in the rebel camp. A number of officers—like the ailing general Tavares—slept at nearby estancia houses, and others had tents. Covered carts with two massive wheels the height of a tall man and drawn by six oxen offered dry spots for some men underneath, but most simply perched on their riding gear to keep it dry and huddled under their ponchos in the downpour. Then they emerged to quarrel or chortle around smoldering fires, to pass the mate gourd, and to toss the taba bone in a favorite pastime not unlike the game of horseshoes.[7]

Colonel Manuel Rodrigues de Macedo and Lt. Col. Adão de Latorre enjoyed the privileges of their fairly exalted rank, but they felt quite at ease with the private soldiers of the revolution, for neither owned a large estancia, and both were mulatto men whose hierarchy bespoke their skill as fighters, not their social status. Macedo, known affectionately to the whole army as "Fulião," always shouted "Long Live His Majesty the Emperor!" before ordering his men to fire, a habit left over from the Paraguayan war. (In addition, an Uruguayan paper reported that some Federalists wore broad hatbands reading: "Long Live the Empire!" Understandably, such quirks attracted spirited notice among the Republicans, necessitating the anti-Monarchist disclaimer issued at Santana do Livramento.) "Fulião" was known for his uncouth language but also for having his men pray before and after the fray. Adão de Latorre had ridden in borderland montoneras for half a century already in 1893, and his association with the Blanco party of Uruguay reached back to that party's mid-nineteenth-century origins. In 1893, he held the rank of lieutenant colonel, the same rank as Gumercindo at the outset of the war. The face of Adão de Latorre was wrinkled but his body still muscular, and his speech was a swirling blend of Spanish and Portuguese, tending more heavily to the latter. This was his first Brazilian revolution, but not his last. Incredibly this tough old warrior took up arms again thirty years later in 1923 and died during the course of that war.[8]

It is only because they held their unusually high ranks that we know the names of non-elite members of the insurgent army like Latorre and Macedo. The huge majority of the five to ten thousand men who fought as Federalists during the thirty-month war figure individually in no records. The greater part were borderlanders—that much, at least, seems sure—and many clearly belonged to the kin and clientele of Federalist colonels, as did Gumercindo's Maragatos. All else about these ragged recruits, however, must be deduced from the material conditions of borderland life in the 1890s. Most mysterious of all, because they are virtually invisible in both the meager documentary evidence and the traditional historiography, are the women who could often be found among the army's supply carts. The majority were dark-skinned like the men they cooked for and took care of. The women's presence seems to have been ubiquitous, yet only a few stray bits of evidence reveal it: an order that the women must not intermingle with the men on the march, a mention of ninety women in one group of nine hundred rebel soldiers. These female camp followers lacked any remnant of respectability, many being prostitutes, a circumstance which could explain why they were so seldom mentioned in public discourse on the rebellions. A rare 1897 description emphasizes their "mannishness": they gathered at a country store, smoked cigars, and rode bareback. Perhaps the conception of war as a consummately masculine activity (the very mark of a "real man," in fact) made these women appear necessarily aberrant, when it did not exclude them altogether from male depictions of the adversities and personal sacrifices of the campaign.[9]

No doubt, many poor people had joined the Liberating Army because times had become so hard in the borderland, and the truly destitute had become so numerous, that many prospective liberators had little to lose in going to war. In the revolution, they could at least hope for a little excitement. The Republicans, who had less stalwart clientele in the borderland, appear to have recruited more indigent and desperate people than did the Federalists, whose war parties drew more on their patronage as landowners. Republican montoneras called "popular forces" or "provisional corps" seem held together by the lure of pillage. Certainly, they rampaged far more destructively than did the Federalist montoneras, taking a high toll on the herds and other property of their high and mighty Federalist enemies. Some former provisional corps even embarked on careers as bandits after the war was over. One encounters many hints of social tension in the behavior of Republican partisans. The leader of the Republicans in a given borderland district was often a poor relation of the local Federalist leader. The most important Republican chief of Herval, a locality between Jaguarão and Bagé, bore the familiar surname Silva Tavares, and when Republican provisional forces looted the estancia belonging to Federalist colonel Vasco Martins, among the pillagers was an illegitimate son of the landowner. There is more than a whiff of social tension in the figure of beardless Carolino de Freitas, who, at the head of a band of provisionals, terrorized the environs of the aristocratic Federalist city of Pelotas with adolescent boastfulness. Clearly, class contradictions had sharpened in the last decades of the nineteenth century, straining the paternalistic, patriarchal bonds that had held this rural society together.[10]

7
HARD TIMES

The violence of the Rio Grandense revolution of 1893 (which left perhaps ten thousand dead) and the popular response to Gumercindo Saravia may both owe something to the social tensions of the late nineteenth-century borderland, where the pressure of rapid population growth on fixed resources gave rural poverty a Malthusian cast. Formed in an environment of frontier abundance and exiguous population a hundred years earlier, this society had adopted a style of economic production that required enormous amounts of pasture land but little labor. Techniques of ranching then evolved little while, with the passage of four prolific generations, the number of borderlanders soared—roughly tripling between Gumercindo's birth and the beginning of the war. As the estancias of the borderland became increasingly subdivided, their profitability declined. To make matters worse, the central governments of Brazil and Uruguay began to challenge local control of the border effectively for the first time, raising tariffs and launching a concerted attack on the borderland's oldest and most lucrative avocation, contraband. It is impossible to know how much the decline in the size of ranches and the relative "closing" of the border lowered borderland standards of living, yet neither can logically have been without deleterious effects. How might these factors be expressed in the war of the Maragatos?[1]

The gruesome violence of this civil war seemed unwarranted and inexplicable to both sides. Perhaps the general decline in the scale of landholding contributed to psychological pressures, and therefore to charismatic response and violence, because its insidious erosion of people's well-being often passed unremarked. After all, there was nothing unusual in the borderlanders' inheritance customs, which followed the general Latin American pattern, and people of the time could not observe the region's changing property map over a period of generations, watching how huge early nineteenth-century estancias were subdivided by successive inheritance proceedings. Indeed, this observation is difficult enough for an archival historian to make, given the imperfect nature of the surviving records—yet the overall contours of the fragmentation are unmistakable: by the 1890s, only a handful of estancias approximated the immense scale quite unremarkable earlier in the century. The explanation is not far to seek. Nineteenth-century borderlanders begat a steady average of about six surviving heirs per family, implying a two-thirds reduction of land for each family member in each generation. Although people cannot have overlooked this fact altogether, it did not become a prominent topic of public discourse.[2]

Another change in the rural environment put still more pressure on social relations. Scattered statistics show that seventeen thousand inhabitants of Cerro Largo in 1860 had become seventy-three thousand two generations later, and the denser population of the Brazilian side followed suit. To make matters worse, by the 1890s the Uruguayan side no longer offered economic enticements to emigrating Rio Grandenses like the parents of Gumercindo and Aparicio. Seemingly, the earlier generation's success in buying up land combined with the imposition of "law and order" in the Uruguayan countryside to raise the price of rural real estate there. For the most part, nineteenth-century borderlanders did not have access to comparative population figures nor did they identify earlier migration as a disappeared "escape valve." They simply yearned for the good old days, when, as one put it, "there was more money than people" and "good faith and pleasant, familiar relations reigned."[3]

This vision of the past has indubitable patriarchal and rose-colored tints, but it is true that, where there had once been food for all, some now went hungry. For a hundred years, the tiny population of the borderland had dwelled among herds of livestock so bountiful that in glut years cattle were slaughtered for their hides alone. Fresh meat had little market value in these circumstances, and landowners readily shared it with their agregados, but by 1884 a Bagé paper chronicled (with obvious astonishment) the starvation of an infant. "It will seem incredible, but it is the unhappy truth," explained the paper's editor. Not so far away in São Gabriel, "a person can now die of hunger!" In 1893, a newspaper in the Uruguayan town of Melo reported a shocking new degree of indigence: a woman sleeping in the street. The Brazilian war was partly responsible, and poverty festered among refugees as the fight there dragged on. Within a few more years, homeless people were no longer novel in Melo. Scores of shanties sprouted in the outskirts of that and other borderland towns, and whole families were seen shuffling through the streets with their possessions in their arms. Many were fleeing the devastation of war, but others had lost their livelihoods because of gradual social and economic transformations affecting both sides of the border.[4]

There was little for the surging population to do in the static pastoral economy. As the scale of estancias gradually declined, landowning families did more of their own labor. Eight of the nine Saravia brothers busied themselves tending the family's livestock, and when borderlanders began to fence their properties in the 1870s and 1880s, their labor requirements diminished further, since perpetually riding herd was no longer essential. Borderland ranchers did not enclose their pastures in order to begin breeding fancy pedigreed stock that, in turn, would require more elaborate care and create more rural employment. Quantity, not quality, defined this rural economy, and the new wire fences were intended less to enable selective breeding of Durhams or Herefords than to stake a more secure claim to thousands of rangy longhorns. Because untended pasture had a carrying capacity (of about two hectares per cow or horse) beyond which it would become damaged by overgrazing, the smaller estancias of the 1890s necessarily supported fewer animals.[5]

Encroaching fences made agregados' livestock less welcome in the dwindling fields of the patrón, and, as wages plummeted, landowners could more easily afford day laborers to supplement their own manpower. Earlier in the century, an advertisement seeking "one or two hired hands" had run fruitlessly for months in a Melo newspaper, but in the 1890s the relationship of supply and demand had reversed. Gone were the days when the landless could easily find a livelihood in the underpopulated borderland and landowners had to pay dearly to attract workers. At the turn of the twentieth century, rural wages in northern Uruguay had fallen to a harrowing three-to-five pesos a month (depending on the skills of the worker) and subsistence privileges for the wage earner's family seldom entered into the bargain anymore. In addition, the agregado's function as loyal retainer of the landowner had lost significance as borderland insurgencies became less frequent and national states policed the borderland more proficiently in the late nineteenth century.[6]

The prosecution of a young agregado named Rufino Silva illustrates the new tensions. In 1893, Rufino was given notice by his patrón that he would have to leave in the spring, because the estancia where Rufino lived had been rented and the new occupant refused to provide the customary ration of meat. Indignant, the agregado took for himself the ration that had not been proffered paternalistically, leaving the hides out in plain sight and expecting that at worst he would have to pay for the butchered animals. Although no mass eviction of agregado families occurred in the wake of fencing, their position immediately became more precarious. On the Brazilian side of the border, the easy availability of cheap wage labor facilitated early emancipation in 1884, four years before national abolition. Many ex-slaves stayed as agregados on borderland estancias, but those who left swelled the ranks of impoverished wage laborers still further. Where pre-1850 enumerations never showed more than a fifth of adult rural males involved in wage labor, a half or two-thirds were wage laborers in the 1890s. The great majority of these people had no regular employment at all and earned their hopelessly tiny pay only when the estancias required extra workers, as at branding or sheep-shearing time.[7]

The unavoidable result was hunger for the rural poor, evidenced particularly by the rash of midnight butcherings in unwatched corners of borderland pastures—obscure events of which we have some record because they constituted the crime of animal theft. Borderlanders had pilfered each other's herds from time immemorial. The ancient activity called "changa" (killing semi-wild cattle for their hides) had always been directed preferentially at someone else's beasts. Early in the century, it was a sort of peccadillo, engaged in by mischievous boys on a lark, and seldom punished with severity. A police officer of the 1820s mentioned "daily stealing by neighbors with little land and few animals, . . . inveterate in the rural districts." One landowner of mid-century (a widow) accused her neighbor, along with his sons and agregados, of keeping cows especially trained to lead stock off of her property and onto his, where it subsequently disappeared. The early *changadores* had sought hides for profit, skinning the carcass and leaving it to rot and frequently eating nothing or perhaps only the tongue, while the animal thieves of the 1880s and 1890s, on the other hand, wanted primarily food. In fact, the evidence against those who were apprehended, in most cases, was meat found in their houses. When the Baron of Upacaraí slaughtered eight cattle to distribute to the families of day laborers and agregados in his neighborhood north of the border, the Bagé newspaper attributed the act to "the impulses of his generous heart," which it may have been, but it was also a form of damage control. By 1886 some Rio Grandense landowners reported discovering the slaughtered carcasses of half a dozen bovine victims on their property in a single week.[8] Across the border in Cerro Largo, the number of prisoners for animal theft also rose steeply in the late 1880s and early 1890s, so that landowners began to speak of their losses in relative levels (up in this neighborhood, down in that one). Customarily, they blamed the inadequate police, but also "the immense poverty that today surrounds the proletarian class." With few exceptions, the accused men were day laborers who lived in the neighborhoods where the "stolen" animals were pasturing, people who had no way to feed themselves and nowhere to go.[9]

The situation of Felisbino Gularte was typical. A poor black man in his mid-thirties, Felisbino lived with his wife and numerous children in a rancho surrounded by a plot of mediocre land planted in corn and beans—a small agricultural *chacra* of a sort that was becoming more common in the borderland's hilly nooks and crannies. Almost certainly he farmed the spot as an agregado, but it did not provide a living, so Felisbino also worked as a day laborer. Gumercindo's brother Chiquito Saravia, the local police comisario in Felisbino's neighborhood, suspected him of animal theft, and a midnight gathering at Felisbino's house in 1893 led the police to catch him with an illicit roast. Saravia arrested Felisbino, who confessed to having killed sheep for over a year, including twenty belonging to the Saravias themselves. Because of Felisbino's poverty, he got only eight months in jail.

Other incidents from Saravia's 1893 police records are similarly suggestive of hard times in the countryside. A young day laborer without fixed domicile was detained for his third (detected) animal theft. Two others were imprisoned for slaughtering a cow, forced to confess under duress, and then released when they turned out to have permission from the cow's owner. Two more day laborers, apparently out searching for some stray horses, had stopped and grabbed a sheep for supper when the owner caught them bending over the carcass, red-handed. During the resulting confrontation, the blood of the owner and one of the thieves soon mingled on the ground with that of the butchered sheep. The surviving prisoner was a nineteen-year-old local boy who had worked a few days for the dead owner at that year's shearing.[10]

Who was to blame for this situation? Early twentieth-century analysts identified the problem as economic "backwardness" and the cure as scientific husbandry: selective breeding, cultivated fodders, and market specialization. Agronomists like Francisco J. Ros argued that the landowners of Cerro Largo ought to modernize their ranching techniques in order to make smaller estancias more productive and provide more employment, and he laid the blame for borderland poverty at the door of the region's unenlightened landowners. By Ros's calculations, improved breeds would quadruple the output of meat and wool, and railroads would make large-scale commercial crops feasible in Cerro Largo, but such transformations required both abundant capital and the disposition to innovate. According to almost everyone, the landowning families of the borderland had neither. The frustrated agronomist lamented that borderland ranchers liked their rustic life too much and that they must learn to desire material refinements and acquire a taste for work ("that redeeming prayer of progress that should be prayed [eight] hours every day") before they could become modern ranchers.[11]

Ros might have used the properties of Gumercindo's father as a case in point. In 1880, already master of eighteen thousand hectares of pasture land, old Francisco lived with his large family in a house with two bedrooms, one bed, a table, sixteen chairs, two trunks, and eight mattresses. In the last years of his life, Francisco Saravia had twelve thousand longhorns, but not a single pedigreed bull. It was not for lack of liquid capital, because at his death in 1893 he had hoarded over fifty thousand pesos. Like most of his less affluent neighbors, old Saravia simply did not believe in innovations. For example, he refused to plant trees to shelter the cattle as agronomists had begun to recommend, nor did he like useless foliage around the house. His brother Cisério, who died the year after Francisco, was of a like mind. According to the inventory of his livestock, none of his three thousand cattle was of the fancy variety, either. Uruguayan historians have concluded that resistance to scientific husbandry and attachment to time-honored practices of livestock management were notable traits of borderland ranching.[12]

Our progressive agronomist would certainly have approved of at least one rich neighbor of the Saravias, Ramón E. Silveira (a relative of Gaspar Silveira Martins) who demonstrated a modernizing mentality and a booster spirit by promoting the diffusion of "improved" breeds in the 1890s. But Silveira is the exception that proves the rule. His purchase of several hundred head of pedigreed livestock and his plans to hold a livestock exposition, both common enough in the south of Uruguay, were unprecedented in the Cerro Largo of 1895, where only fifty-four of almost half a million cattle were purely of expensive blooded stock. Sheep remained far less important than cattle in the borderland, though they had become an economic mainstay in the Uruguayan south, employing more workers and favoring the small producer as well. Sheep raising had still less impact on the Brazilian side of the border during this period. (In Cerro Largo, there were at least enough sheep to make them the preferred—because less obtrusive—target of hungry thieves, whereas in Brazil the "stolen" animals were always cattle.) As for cultivated fodders like the alfalfa that fattened award-winning steers on the showcase estancias of southern Uruguay and Argentina, borderlanders planted none.[13]

Ramón Silveira had acquired his taste for progress in Montevideo. In contrast to most borderland ranchers, he was an absentee landlord who spent his time in the port capital supervising an import–export business and lending money for mortgages. Silveira was also a fattener (who prepared cattle for slaughter on expensive pasture land close to market—the most lucrative sort of ranching), and he was allied by marriage to families who owned slaughterhouses, the most important industrial enterprises of the period in Uruguay and Rio Grande do Sul. Having escaped from the arithmetic logic of the long-horns and learned to make money increase geometrically, Silveira had become just the kind of businessman that most borderland ranchers emphatically were not.[14]

There is no evidence that Rufino or Felisbino or other hungry borderlanders of the 1890s shared Silveira's booster vision. Nor is there any evidence that they saw the problem as "structural," originating in the appropriation of property rights by the Iberian families who had shouldered aside the earlier inhabitants of the borderland at the beginning of the nineteenth century. Their resentments were much more likely to be personal, directed at the patrón who denied his customary obligations. These resentments could be explosive in the context of paternalistic bonds that, although strained, continued to be crucial in people's lives, stirring strong emotions in landowners and agregados alike. Such considerations help us read the case of two rural men who were quietly drinking mate on the doorstep of the house where both lived, when one very suddenly stabbed the other to death. The shocked widow of the victim explained to the police that her husband had just told the murderer, his agregado, that he would have to leave.[15]

If paternalism sometimes mitigated the suffering of the borderland poor, it also added psychological complications. For instance, Chiquito Saravia, who arrested Felisbino Gularte, had a reputation for generosity in Felisbino's neighborhood and was called a *pai dos pobres*—"father of the poor"—in the Brazilian idiom. Oral tradition tells of his insistence on roasting a fat steer and providing proper drink for the people thronging Saravia estancias at round-up and branding, a practice that the day laborers of the neighborhood heartily endorsed, and crowds of poor mourners attended his funeral after his death in an ill-advised lance charge in 1897. Felisbino, whose family preyed on Saravia flocks, must have felt the injustice of his hunger in the presence of great wealth, but which would he have preferred: the Saravias' traditional paternalism or the progressive gospel of Ros and Silveira?[16] For the most part, day laborers, agregados, and their families seem to have identified with the values of the conservative landowners on whom they depended, directly or indirectly, for a livelihood. Perhaps the borderlanders who suffered dispossession without a satisfying rationalization or a clear target for their resentment became more capable of charismatic response—and also of unbridled violence—during the civil wars of the 1890s.

One finds reason for apprehension among the landowners as well as the landless. Although they did not face hunger as did the rural poor, most landowning families nevertheless experienced decline— and, no doubt, distress—because they had little hope of setting up their children with commodious estancias. The average property inherited around Bagé on the eve of the civil war of 1893 would support only a very small herd of cattle, the kind a well-off agregado might have had at mid-century. Even the impressive domain amassed by the Saravia family, one of the largest in Cerro Largo by the 1890s, was barely enough to provide *estanciero* status for the twelve legitimate heirs—not to mention the six children that old Francisco had after Propícia's death with another woman whom he did not marry precisely so as not to over-divide the patrimony. The estancias inherited by the siblings of Gumercindo and Aparicio Saravia at the end of the nineteenth century were about the size of one that Manuel Amaro da Silveira, a rich Rio Grandense landowner, had bequeathed to his son by a slave woman two generations earlier. And Amaro da Silveira left much larger parcels to each of his fifteen legitimate heirs![17]

The squeeze was tighter still among the landowning families who could not equal the unusual accumulation of property accomplished by Gumercindo's parents. Very few, in fact, could do what the Saravias had done—not even all the Saravias could do it. The eleven children of Gumercindo's cousin Francisco Saravia (rather an important man in the 1850s) became poor relations by the 1890s. Something similar had happened to the children of his uncle Manuel Saravia. When Manuel died in the 1890s, three of his children could not be located and at least one son was thought to have migrated— along with thousands of other Rio Grandenses—to the Mato Grosso cattle frontier in the far west of Brazil, because the nearer Uruguayan frontier no longer beckoned as it had in earlier generations, and these relatives of Gumercindo and Aparicio stood to inherit only tiny sums of money and no Rio Grandense estancia land at all.[18]

In the 1870s and 1880s, the sons of Rio Grandense ranching families began to leave the estancias more often to study a liberal profession or seek another sort of urban livelihood, and landowners' daughters felt increasingly compelled to seek favorable matches with notaries, apothecaries, and successful merchants in town. Such outlets were too small to keep landed families from steadily subdividing the land, however. In 1890 Cerro Largo had twenty professionals but several hundred landowning households whose sons might aspire to become such. By far the preferred career for young men of property was law, and there were only two practicing lawyers in Melo—only eighty-five in the entire country—and competition had become intense. There were ten times as many store owners as professionals in Cerro Largo, but the sons of landowners only exceptionally engaged in trade, partly out of preference and partly because local commerce and small manufacture were activities dominated by European immigrants with closely-knit business networks. Most of the Basque and Italian storekeepers and artisans in borderland towns had immigrated as bachelors, and well-to-do rural storekeepers were proverbially eligible to marry landowners' daughters. A similar situation prevailed north of the border. In sum, the grown children of landowning families, particularly young men, often had to choose between reduced status on shrinking estancias and the challenges of a competitive and unfamiliar urban environment. It is hard not to read these anxieties into the front-page suicide of Abílio Amaro da Silveira, a descendent of one of the fifteen Amaro da Silveira heirs recently mentioned. In the 1890s, this young representative of one of the borderland's richest founding families seems to have experienced downward social mobility in Porto Alegre where, at the time of his suicide, he roomed in a boarding house and worked as a sales clerk.[19]

In addition to the shrinking estancias and the teeming ranks of rural poor, new and more effective anti-contraband measures exacerbated hard times in the 1890s. Smuggling had been a way of life for borderlanders since the seventeenth century, when parties of gauchos and soldiers of fortune had smuggled Bahian tobacco and Peruvian silver across the ill-defined no-man's-land lying between Brazil and the Río de la Plata. The rampant illicit commerce became a primary concern of Spain's late colonial reformers, who warned that borderland ranchers "play cards with two decks," but their attempts to control contraband failed notoriously, in part because the Portuguese considered silver for tobacco a good trade and—from the vantage point of their port citadel at Colônia do Sacramento—did what they could to encourage it. After the border had been clearly defined, international movements of cattle became a regular matter of contention between cattle barons and the agents of central authority. Because of their proximity, the slaughterhouses of Pelotas constituted the natural destination for landowners on both sides of the Saravias' borderland.[20] As much as half to three-quarters of the cattle raised in the Uruguayan north crossed the border to slaughter—most of them illegally. In addition, Rio Grandense landowners often sent cattle for fattening to the superior grazing lands south of the border before driving them back north to market in Pelotas. Attempts by the central government of Brazil to collect taxes on these herds had contributed to the rebelliousness of the Farrapos in the 1830s and 1840s, and after the Farroupilha the imperial authorities helped prevent further trouble by guaranteeing Rio Grandense cattle barons a permeable border. An 1851 treaty prohibited the Uruguayans from levying any tax of their own on cattle being taken to slaughter in Brazil, and thanks to the national influence of Gaspar Silveira Martins, Rio Grande do Sul eventually enjoyed a special exemption to the import duties paid throughout the rest of Brazil.[21]

Prominent borderland families scarcely bothered to hide activities that both Uruguayan and Brazilian officials found themselves unable to prevent. As the police chief of Cerro Largo wrote in 1866, attempts to tighten tariff collection threatened disastrous consequences for the officials charged with enforcing them. Infrequent legal actions against contraband, such as those involving two northbound herds in the 1840s, give us some indication of movements that generally passed unchallenged and unrecorded. The cases involve the powerful Tavares and Amaro da Silveira families, as well as elements of complicity on the part of the authorities. Such complicity was the normal means of attempting to avoid direct conflict—here, unsuccessfully. Tavares had received faulty assurances that his drovers would find the ford unguarded, and Manuel Amaro da Silveira had gotten the nod from one Uruguayan official but encountered a different one when his herd reached the Jaguarão River. Undaunted by the defiant attitude of the guard, Amaro da Silveira announced his intention to export his eight hundred longhorns with or without authorization. Such cockiness depended not on imperial approbation but on the power of the cattle barons themselves, and uncircumspect Brazilian customs officials risked as much as Uruguayan ones. When a relative of the Amaro da Silveira clan, Col. Astrogildo Pereira da Costa, arrived at the Jaguarão River with four hundred cattle for fattening in Cerro Largo and a lieutenant of the Brazilian border guard tried to stop him from crossing, Colonel da Costa drew his saber, signaling one of his henchmen (he had taken the precaution of setting out with twenty) to shoot the offending lieutenant, and the herd proceeded on its way. A trail gang in the employ of the Baron of Mauá was involved in a similar shoot-out as late as 1886.[22]

The free movement of cattle across the border mattered most to landowners, of course, but other elements of contraband mattered to anyone who used buttons, handkerchiefs, thread, thimbles, pomade, cotton fabric, rice, coffee, sugar, mate, tobacco, or cane liquor—the sort of products that crossed the border on the backs of peddlers' mules or in the lumbering carts that creaked through the streets of borderland towns in the middle of the night to unload at the rear door of some local business.[23] The brunt of this trade was underwritten by local merchants who hazarded their capital in combination with carters who risked their freedom to carry out the actual contraband, but few borderlanders passed the border with their saddlebags empty in the course of their normal activities. When official correspondence did not avoid the topic altogether, it usually pointed out the virtual impossibility of policing the border effectively and politely explained that, well, almost *all* manufactured goods passed untaxed. As a general rule, borderlanders favored contraband even when they did not practice it themselves, and most local authorities sooner or later became active participants. Very simply, contraband improved the borderlanders' standard of living, and as long as the cattle barons retained their political influence in Rio Grande do Sul and Uruguay, the agents of the state power were unwilling or unable to interfere decisively.[24]

By the 1890s, however, times had changed. The control of Rio Grande do Sul and the support of the central government were slipping away from the military and landowning elite of the borderland, even as state-builders to the north and south bid to affirm their own authority at the border. In Brazil, the new republic eliminated the special tariff privileges formerly enjoyed by Rio Grande do Sul and began a concerted campaign against borderland contraband. In Uruguay, the export tariff was raised and officials sent out from Montevideo took over the responsibility of patrolling the border from locals who inevitably "served both God and the devil."[25] Anti-contraband measures collided with a practice so massive and inveterate that it remains a central fact of borderland life a century later. Nevertheless, rising tariffs and more vigorous customs enforcement must have eroded borderland living standards in the 1880s and 1890s. Some effect can be gauged in protests signed by landowners surnamed Amaro da Silveira, Tavares, and Saravia among many others, and arrests for contraband proliferated. The police chief of Rivera proudly claimed to have filled his jails with prisoners as a result of his anti-contraband campaign in 1895, most of them small fry nabbed with a pound of tobacco or a few dozen tins of guava jelly.[26]

Three other elements completed the disheartening economic prospects of the borderland on the eve of the Saravias' revolutions. In 1890, a financial crisis in London had powerful, if temporary, effects and was widely blamed for a poor Montevidean cattle market for several years. Meanwhile, the surging Brazilian inflation of the early 1890s caused a contraction in the buying power of slaughterhouses north of the border as well. Brazil's paper currency, the milréis, became so weak vis-à-vis Uruguay's gold peso that a few pesos of Uruguayan tax on cattle moving north to slaughter presented a serious problem for Brazilian buyers. Finally, the market for borderland longhorns had long been flaccid, and by the 1890s, it seemed clearly doomed. The flesh of longhorn cattle made good jerked beef—a common slave ration (cheap and high in protein) that had also become a basic ingredient of the traditional Brazilian *feijoada* (a bean dish)— but European consumers found it nauseating. Furthermore, by the 1890s, African slavery had finally disappeared, having been abolished even in the last holdouts: Cuba (1886) and Brazil itself (1888). To expand their markets, borderland ranchers would have to introduce the expensive new breeds suitable to European tastes, just as the modernizing ranchers of Argentina and southern Uruguay were doing, but the new breeds made poor jerked beef and would require modern packing plants (not built until 1904 in Uruguay, 1917 in Rio Grande do Sul). In the meantime, the exports of jerked beef remained flat and the price barely kept pace with inflation.[27]

As for the Saravias, with estancias on both sides of the border and all their wealth in longhorns and rocky pasture ill-suited to cultivated fodder, they were just the sort of landowners for whom access to markets in both Pelotas and Montevideo constituted a critical advantage. Gumercindo's estancia in Santa Vitória do Palmar lay quite near the border and offered an excellent platform for surreptitious cattle drives to Montevideo, should he have chosen to send any there. We know that Gumercindo and Aparicio had worked together as drovers during the late 1870s and early 1880s, sometimes conducting as many as five thousand animals to market when the full moon made nocturnal vigilance more practical. Although there is no record of their travels, it would be highly unusual if they had not occasionally visited Pelotas and avoided the tax by gathering the herd on an estancia within a few hours' ride of the border and setting out after nightfall to cross it before morning with no customs officials the wiser. We have good evidence that their cousin Terencio attempted this trick with about four hundred animals one night in 1888, when a few strayed and, the next day, fell into the hands of a border patrol. Everyone knew Terencio in the neighborhood where the stray cows appeared because he had an estancia nearby, right on the northern bank of the Jaguarão River, in fact, and the Saravia brand on the impounded cattle became state's evidence against him in Uruguay. To avoid prosecution, Terencio stayed in Brazil (where Republican partisans murdered him in 1892).[28]

We cannot know, beyond the foregoing sort of informed speculation, what impact the increase in rural poverty, the shrinking estancias, the assault on contraband, or sundry other economic pressures had on people's behavior in the Rio Grandense civil war. Contemporaries rarely mentioned economic developments in their own constructions of political events, but the occasional exception is telling. For example, a telegram sent to the Brazilian finance minister before the war, in 1892, warned him of the risks of his new tariff policies by referring to the military potency of coronéis like Gumercindo Saravia, who had temporarily ousted Republican governor Júlio de Castilhos:

> Huge number Brazilians own almost all Uruguayan border-land. Sent many regiments recent revolution. Neither just nor prudent to injure interests.[29]

8

APRIL-OCTOBER 1893

During the month of April 1893, Gumercindo Saravia's Maragatos remained encamped near General Tavares at the headwaters of the Río Negro. Meanwhile, far to the west, another column of Federalists finally received a shipment of firearms arranged by Silveira Martins. After the abortive siege of Santana do Livramento, this second insurgent column had left Tavares and marched west into the corner of Rio Grande do Sul where the Argentine, Brazilian, and Uruguayan borders meet. There the long-awaited shipment finally arrived from Montevideo: 680 Remington rifles and 250 bullets for each. The boat Carmelita, that brought the weapons and ammunition, had been preceded by a sophisticated regular army officer, Colonel Luís Alves Leite de Oliveira Salgado, who had resigned his commission to join the revolution at the top level, as general. Salgado's hesitation to take over before the guns arrived left some borderland Federalists uneasy with their new general, but when the rifles were finally distributed and Salgado assumed command with an elegant harangue, they cheered loudly. Perhaps now the revolution would achieve its first real success.[1]

This western corner of the Brazilian–Uruguayan borderland shared many characteristics with the eastern corner where the Saravia family lived, but economic differences made it less friendly to the Federalists. To begin with, while the Saravias' eastern borderland suffered hard times, the western economy showed vitality. Isolated by transportation difficulties from Porto Alegre and the principal seaboard settlement areas of Rio Grande do Sul, the western borderland along the Uruguay River had developed strong commercial ties with Buenos Aires and, most especially, with Montevideo and its bustling deep-water port. Steamboat lines linked the Rio Grandense river ports of Uruguaiana and Itaqui to Montevideo after mid-century, and railroad construction tightened the link in the 1880s. These connections led to the creation of a major slaughterhouse center on the Brazilian side of the border, exporting jerked beef by rail south through the port of Montevideo, a new and highly advantageous situation for the area's landowners. Because it was more recently settled and less populous, the west did not seem to be experiencing as much subdivision as the Saravias' borderland. Nor had General Tavares and Silveira Martins ever possessed as much influence here as on their home ground in the east. Therefore, the Federalist appeal to the past—emphasizing old habits, loyalties, and leadership—did not play so well in the west. As a result of these factors, it would appear, the Republican party had prevailed among the western region's landowners, who mobilized traditional rural patronage networks to support the government rather than to oppose it. Local Republicans clearly controlled the Missions district of strong Guaraní and mestizo population around São Borja, where Coronel Nascimento Vargas (father of Getúlio) was helping to organize a column of twenty-five hundred Republican irregulars. In conjunction with a strong regular army force, the Republican irregulars moved to trap Salgado's newly armed Federalists in the narrow cul-de-sac of the state's southwestern corner, where the Carmelita had unloaded her precious cargo.[2]

Aware of the danger, Salgado's insurgents quickly moved back east toward Tavares, who agreed to rendezvous with them and did so just in time to make a common front against a Republican force of seven thousand near a stream called Inhanduí, site of an insurgent victory in the Farrapo War. At dawn on the day of the battle, the Federalists peered across a stretch of low, rutted ground toward the top of the next low hill, where well-armed regular infantry and eight artillery pieces—in addition to three proto machine guns—formed a formidable uniformed line, flanked by Republican provisional corps on horseback, flags flapping in the late fall breeze. Gumercindo looked quickly at the government army and at the field, then galloped to the tent where Tavares and Salgado (whom he had never met) were planning their tactics. Gumercindo cut pleasantries short to tell Tavares of the weak point where he intended to put the Maragatos because it would be the most difficult part of the battlefield to defend. Then he hurried off, not paying much attention to Salgado, who was suitably impressed, since, moments before, he had been expounding to Tavares the vulnerability of that same portion of the battlefield. The insurgent army at full strength now numbered six thousand Federalists, but most of them were the lightest of light cavalry, lancers without guns. Only one in three men of Salgado's column had received rifles from the Carmelita, and his column was by far the better armed of the two. So once the battle of Inhanduí had begun, half of the insurgents remained in the rear, holding the horses and listening to the bullets drone over their heads, unable to do anything while other Federalists died.[3]

This was another battle that could not be won by charging lancers, but still they charged over and over for six hours, the very first assault being led by an impatient Aparicio Saravia, who was getting a reputation for leading the Maragatos in their favorite maneuver. Eventually, government troops came to dread "the charge of the Castilian" (meaning Aparicio) in any encounter with the Maragatos. At Inhanduí, though, no amount of galloping around could prevail over Republican firepower. The Federalists' successive attacks withered in the hail of bullets and artillery shells, so that only a few lancers from any given charge actually reached the Republican line, bristling with bayonets. On such occasions, the handful who managed to breach the line could do little more than lunge in the direction of a rival commander, or if possible, seize a flag and try to escape with it alive.[4]

When night fell, Tavares and Salgado decided to retreat under cover of darkness. "Revolution strangled," hooted the victors in their telegram to Porto Alegre the following day, as the Federalist army with its jolting carts full of wounded slogged back toward Santana do Livramento in a steady, cold rain, riding thousands of their horses to death in a frantic week-long retreat. As the rains continued, streams rose into rushing torrents and spread out of their banks, creating sheets of water that reflected the leaden clouds, and the going got even harder. When the chastened insurgents approached the headwaters of the Río Negro, a Republican force under their old adversary General Telles came out from Bagé to cut off their retreat, and a third

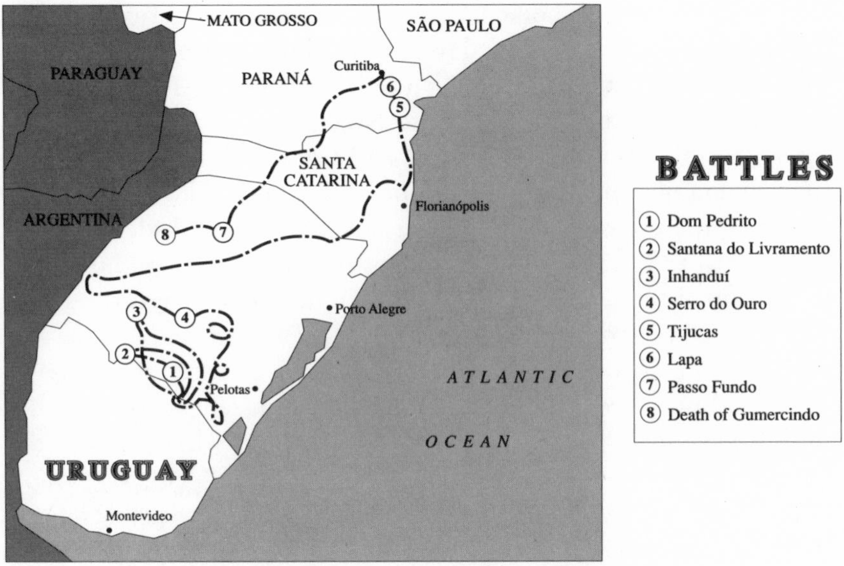

Map 3   Campaigns of Gumercindo Saravia

Republican force closed in from the north. At a swollen stream called the Upamarotí, Republican cavalry fell on the Federalists from behind when they were already halfway across, but Aparicio led the Maragatos though a string of high-speed rear-guard maneuvers, keeping the government forces back long enough for the rest of the insurgents to get through the flood and leaving Telles to claim only a lackluster victory: the capture of a number of supply carts and reserve mounts.[5]

After crossing the Upamarotí, the insurgent army camped only few miles from the border and, that night, began to unravel as several hundred deserted into Uruguay. The next morning, as the men waited nervously, the commissioned officers of the revolution held a council under a solitary ombú tree. Salgado, the only one with formal military training, spoke of the futility of continuing the struggle given the inequality of weapons. Those who rose in opposition to Salgado's arguments pleaded that martial honor be sustained at all cost, and argued that, even without hope of victory, true Rio Grandenses must not give up. Gumercindo arrived late at the council, and all eyes were on him after the Maragatos' performance at Upamarotí. "His word is decisive," writes an admiring biographer (in a stagey present tense):

"It touches the virile fiber of the assembly. They acclaim him. They follow him. He is the caudillo of the revolution!" Whether or not his rise was really foreshadowed this way in a moment of charismatic response during the council of the ombú, Gumercindo defiantly became the hero of the revolution when the rest of the Liberating Army abandoned the field in the winter of 1893.[6]

Soon after the council of the ombú, while Gumercindo somehow took the Maragatos through the encircling enemy forces without being detected and rode north into Brazil searching for badly-needed horses, Tavares and Salgado surrendered to Uruguayan officials at the border along with most of their men. Although supposedly in custody, they enjoyed complete liberty of movement and, a few days later, met at the house of a Brazilian landowner just south of the border to declare themselves not beaten yet. During the rainy winter months of June and July, the Maragatos were the only Federalist revolutionaries on Rio Grandense soil, and the flooded streams helped shield their movements through the hilly southeastern grasslands Gumercindo knew so well. The Maragatos would appear on the outskirts of a lightly garrisoned town, do some mischief, then disappear—moving at night and lying low in the thick woods along some watercourse while the sun shone—to surface again far away a few days later. The Republicans received a disquieting intimation of what lay in store when Saravia's men crept into the outskirts of Bagé in the small hours of the morning and made off with most of the garrison's two thousand mounts. A few weeks later, Saravia's column paraded into a town almost halfway to Porto Alegre, routing a tiny garrison and receiving a hero's welcome from the townspeople. He was gone before Telles could react. Saravia tied his Republican pursuers in knots as he turned and twisted through the area east of Bagé, then back through the headwaters of the Río Negro, trouncing the Republican cavalry just as often as he could separate it from the infantry whose murderous firepower he could not match. Hotly pursued by government forces at a place called Serrilhada, Aparicio led the Maragatos in a feigned retreat followed by a sudden reversal and a compact counterattack against the pursuing cavalry (who had left their supporting infantry behind)—a classic gambit of the guerra gaucha, a smashing small-scale triumph, and another fillip for the growing fame of Gumercindo's younger brother.[7]

Meanwhile old Joca Tavares was encountering the limits of his age and health. Even after the winter, which was particularly severe that year, Tavares was not well enough to campaign. General Salgado, on the other hand, was eager to vindicate his honor after the somewhat embarrassing conclusion of his earlier invasion. As winter turned to spring, Salgado's force filtered back into Brazil through the headwaters of the Río Negro and joined with Gumercindo, whom Tavares had by now raised to the rank of general, too. The relationship between the two had started badly on the morning of Inhanduí, when Gumercindo gave Salgado's effusive greetings short shrift, and it proved stormy ever after. Since most of the insurgents wore their normal ponchos and had no uniforms, Salgado had them put on red hat bands (*divisas*) to signal their Federalist affiliation. Red was the color adopted generally by Federalist insurgents, but Gumercindo, Aparicio, and all the self-respecting Blancos among the Maragatos— which included most of the Uruguayan contingent—refused to wear them. To the Maragatos, the color red represented their sworn enemies, the Colorados, and they took the matter seriously, indeed. Aparicio wrote to Cándida that the "revolution had almost been lost" because of it, and Gumercindo's insistence on white divisas led to further friction with Salgado.[8]

Accompanying Salgado was another outlander, one who got along much better with Gumercindo and who became something of a mediator between the two generals. This was Angelo Dourado, a "Bahiano" (Rio Grandenses labeled other Brazilians "Bahianos" rather indiscriminately, but Dourado really was from Bahia), a physician and a resident of Bagé since the early 1880s. Dourado had enthusiastically joined the first Republican city council of Bagé before becoming disillusioned with the authoritarian exclusivism of Júlio de Castilhos. He had fled to Uruguay when the Republicans seized Bagé in 1892 and emerged as the chief voice of the insurgents' partisan imagination with his philippics printed in Portuguese by Melo newspapers for an émigré readership. Dourado soon left Salgado to become the camp physician of the Maragatos, and his diary of the campaign has survived as the single most important narrative of the revolution of 1893. In late August, within a few weeks of joining the Maragatos, Dourado described the most important pitched battle since Inhanduí, this time a victory for the revolution.[9]

The battle at Serro do Ouro involved several thousand combatants, and several hundred died there. Again, the better-armed Republican regulars took an advantageous position on the field, but they were many fewer than at Inhanduí, and this time they had no artillery. In front of them ran a stream with densely wooded banks, a barrier which would greatly slow any assault, but during the night some of the Maragatos cut a path through this thicket, and by dawn they had passed through it, ready to attack from the quarter that the defenders least expected. According to the plan, Salgado's column was to divert the attention of the defenders to assure the element of surprise, but when the morning mists rose and the Republican forces discovered the Maragatos in their exposed position, Salgado was nowhere to be seen. During agonizing minutes, Aparicio—whom Gumercindo had entrusted to lead the flanking attack—rode back and forth in front of the restless line of lancers, awaiting Salgado's diversion as bullets thudded into the earth around horses and riders. Finally, he doubled his reins in one fist, wheeled his horse, and spurred toward the Republican line with his cousin Cesáreo Saravia, "Fulião" Macedo, Vasco Martins, and others close behind. Letting out a roar of relief, the Maragatos charged up the rocky hill.[10]

The advance was slow and rough, and the Republican infantry intensified its fire, opening gaps in the charging line. Long minutes passed. Then the leaping horses and their howling riders slammed into the massed Republican infantry, trampling and impaling their enemies, who scattered, terrified, in all directions. Salgado's men arrived only in time to participate in the pursuit. As the Republicans fled on foot, they became easy targets for the galloping lancers and much of the firing stopped. Particular carnage was done at a narrow place between two hills, where Republican supply carts jammed together and obstructed the escape. From a high overlooking hill, Dourado watched the distant rout in horrified jubilation as the lances dipped and rose, their white pennants fluttering red with blood. Dourado's account of the battle features tragic vignettes and poetic interludes, but while the melancholy doctor was contemplating cadavers and musing on the horrors of civil war, most of the Maragatos gave themselves over to carousing around the camp fires in gleeful celebration of the first major victory of the revolution. Aparicio, too, wrote to his wife about the "marvelous" impact of a charge that had bolstered his personal prestige in the montonera. Such a charge, announced Gumercindo in his official report of the battle, "must have made our ancestors shiver with pleasure in their graves."[11]

Shortly after Serro do Ouro, in mid-September 1893, the Maragatos received the gratifying news that a major naval revolt in Rio de Janeiro had shaken the republic. Just as had occurred briefly in 1891, a number of conservative admirals had turned their ships and crews against the government—a move with dramatic implications in a country where almost every major city was a seaport. This time their action led to no quick presidential resignation, however, and after a prolonged and inconclusive artillery duel with the shore batteries around the harbor at Rio, the mutinous ships steamed away from the capital city. A few days later, the naval rebels occupied Desterro (today Florianópolis), the island capital of the state of Santa Catarina, just to the north of Rio Grande do Sul, where they instituted a provisional government. Suddenly, the revolution appeared closer to victory than most borderland Federalists could have dared dream, and Saravia and Salgado marched north toward Santa Catarina to join forces with the provisional government. Their trek north took them off the open plains, gradually into more forested and higher mountains. As the slopes grew steeper and the paths narrower—sometimes barely wide enough for horses to pass—the Maragatos developed an enthusiasm for pushing boulders loose to watch them go crashing down the mountain sides. Like the rest of his men, Gumercindo had never left the plains in his life, and, as he watched the Maragatos file deeper into country so unsuitable for their horses and tactics, he became increasingly taciturn and, Dourado thought, uneasy. Surely Saravia feared that his skills as a captain of borderland lancers would lose their magic so far from home.[12]

9
STRONGMEN

G umercindo Saravia became the hero of Brazil's 1893 insurgency because of his experience as a leader of montoneras,
experience that the other Federalist colonels did not have.
Saravia's rapidly growing prestige suggested to Angelo Dourado the
possibility of independent political initiatives, such as marching on
Porto Alegre, but Gumercindo had no such plans. Actually, he seemed
more worried about the sequels of victory than about the consequences of defeat: "The minute we get there," he told Dourado,
referring to a hypothetically captured Porto Alegre, "a *government*
will appear, and then everyone will scramble for offices and forget
about the enemy." Speechifying and founding provisional governments were definitely not for Gumercindo. Despite the grand sepa-
ratist schemes that are sometimes attributed to him, his political
interests seemed focused on Santa Vitória do Palmar, and his role in
the revolution remained strictly military.[1]

In this he exemplified a general characteristic of political leadership
in nineteenth-century Brazil and Uruguay: the dichotomous distinc-
tion between leaders whose specialty was rhetoric—the bacharéis
(called *doctores* in Spanish)—and leaders like Gumercindo, whose
specialty was violence. Indeed, Brazilians of the period tended to
understand the terms *coronel* versus *bacharel* (and Uruguayans, the
terms *caudillo* versus *doctor*) as binary opposites, the former military
and the latter civilian by definition, complementary lead players in
political life. Caudillos and coronéis had the ability to mobilize and

direct armed men, a basic element of political power. Ordinarily they were landowners, enabling them to gather fighters among the rural men who lived on and around their property. Rural men made the best occasional soldiers because they were more likely to use cutting tools (the common improvised weapons) with dexterity. For these reasons, nineteenth-century *caudillismo* and *coronelismo* are political phenomena unquestionably rooted in rural life, a central aspect of the "ruralization of power" that took place in Latin America in the wake of independence.[2] Gumercindo's career provides an excellent example of these rural roots, less in his brief exploits as Federalist hero than in his twenty years as a local strongman—first in Cerro Largo, later in Santa Vitória do Palmar.

As an Uruguayan caudillo or a Rio Grandense coronel, Gumercindo protected his friends and terrorized his enemies with his commanding presence, his strong arm, and his ability to organize collective violence. Violence was an endemic condition of rural life in the nineteenth-century borderland. From its creation and by its nature, the borderland had always been contested ground—a zone where various forces competed—and the medium of this competition was deadly force at close quarters. In fact, because of their consummate horsemanship and dexterity with blades of various kinds, borderland males became social specialists in the use of force, employed by the Portuguese and Spanish crowns—then by the governments of Brazil and Uruguay—in wartime, but also operating "free lance" in banditry, contraband, and revolution. Most families of strongmen, the Saravias included, had at least one member who became an outlaw: Gumercindo's uncle Cándido was shot down as a bandit during the 1870s. An early nineteenth-century traveler described parties of contrabandists "always armed and always on the march, fighting the soldiers, militias, and customs officials of both nations indiscriminately." The early nineteenth-century caudillos Bento Gonçalves of Rio Grande do Sul and José Artigas of Uruguay both began their careers as freebooting borderland contrabandists whose ascendancy was subsequently identified by imperial authorities as a superlative qualification for government service in the region. Both eventually rebelled against their respective colonial empires and then attempted to secede from the resulting independent countries. Male borderlanders as a group gained considerable military experience during the decades of war that ensued. The ruralization of power made it impossible for either state to monopolize the use of violence in borderland society, and there existed, instead, a sort of competitive market in which national armies and police vied with outlaws and cattle barons on fairly equal terms. Men like Gumercindo Saravia, who excelled at organizing collective violence, took on a commanding position—"prestige" they called it—in the minds of other rural males, who particularly admired both physical courage and dexterity in feats of horsemanship and bloodletting.[3]

What city-bred man could leap upon the back of a half-broken mustang—of the sort commonly pressed into service for a montonera's reserve mounts—and ride it without a saddle? Herding cattle, the most ubiquitous of all borderland activities, generated skills that made borderland males natural light cavalry, as horses and riders used their bodies, day in and day out, to block or turn darting longhorns, directing their mounts through quick, complex feints and dodges using only subtle pressures of their legs. Riding herd from the time they were very young, rural borderlanders became adept at maneuver on horseback, and, for this reason, could use a lance effectively in combat without spending half their time practicing, as the knights of medieval Europe had to do. This ability sharply separated them from city-bred males, who virtually never learned to wield a lance at all. Vigilance and defense (of livestock and people) were the most basic aspects of a man's labor on borderland estancias, where the protection of law was so tenuous that, when a party of strangers approached an isolated estancia, the men of the house reached for their weapons automatically. In addition, the lives of mounted herdsmen usually involved more mobility (and therefore more willingness to travel a long way from home on campaign) than normally characterized agricultural communities in nineteenth-century Latin America, making borderlanders (along with Argentine gauchos, Venezuelan llaneros, and Mexican vaqueros) especially useful as soldiers. Herding cattle on long trail drives gave borderlanders other qualities essential for the mounted guerrilla's war of speed and surprise: wide knowledge of the topography, of the rivers and their fords, and of the location of good pasturage. It was said of a number of renowned caudillos that they could tell their whereabouts on a moonless night by feeling or tasting the grass.[4]

Then too, all borderland men dealt, quite literally, in "blood and guts" as a simple fact of life, beginning with their relationship to livestock. The fact of their strongly carnivorous diet put male borderlanders in the habit of butchery, so that, by inveterate custom, they became inured to the spectacle of blood and their sensibilities hardened to suffering. Or so twentieth-century museum goers can guess, at any rate, while contemplating huge cattle brands that charred a large area of flesh for easy visibility, and spurs—especially the rosettes of long steel barbs called *nazarenas*—that must have made horses' flanks quite bloody. If a calf refused to be weaned when its mother was destined for fattening (one reads, in accounts of their husbandry) the men simply amputated the cow's udders. Inevitably, one also recalls the scene described by an English traveler who, after admonishing two boys whom he saw cut the throat of a dog one day in northern Uruguay, received hasty reassurance that it was their dog. Every few days, and more often as the family accumulated mouths to feed, estancia boys would go to watch one of the men slaughter an old or weakened animal by cutting its throat, often hoisting it up by its feet to empty the blood most efficiently from the slowly dying animal. Because they had so often cut the throats of animals, borderlanders also had the knack of killing each other by *degola*—in Spanish, *degüello*—the single, massive slice from ear to ear that constituted the routine manner of execution, when such was called for, in the ammunition-scarce guerra gaucha. What Montevidean clerk or stevedore, what Porto Alegre mason or shopkeeper, could spill blood with the equanimity and control of a man who had done it routinely hundreds of times?[5]

The best symbol of a rural male's intimacy with physical violence was his facón, the long blade without which he did not feel fully dressed and which he used at all hours of the day for a thousand things around the estancia, including meals. Most borderland males sought to be pugnacious machos, able to compete physically with other men, most especially in the knife fights that took the place of the North American cowboys' showdowns with six-shooters. A borderlander fought with his poncho wrapped around his left forearm as a shield, and most often tried to wound rather than kill, because a visible scar on a defeated opponent's face served to commemorate his victory in a manner less likely to bring prosecution. Knife fighting was an activity that borderland boys practiced with an index finger dipped in soot to mark a hypothetical gash on the opponent, or sometimes with real blades in a game that might go out of control—as happened once, apparently, when the Saravia brothers were fencing playfully with their cousins. Eventually, young Gumercindo became confident enough to take on a tough black gaucho who proved more than a match for the overweening boy. According to the story, only his father's intervention saved Gumercindo after his *facón* of brittle steel shattered. Supposedly, too, the encounter cemented a friendship between Saravia and his black opponent, who, many years later, became a Maragato. In another story, a seventeen-year-old Aparicio answers the open challenge issued by a pugnacious drifter, who takes one look at the boy, gets on his horse, and leaves. During the 1880s and 1890s, Aparicio used pieces of barrel stave to train his own sons in the techniques of knife fighting.[6]

An examination of judicial records suggests that borderland knife fights arose most often over disputed claims to masculine hierarchy. Most frequently they began in country stores, where men from different estancias had gathered to drink, talk, and establish their pecking order. Over and over, the crabbed script of a local comisario or justice of the peace tells the curiously straightforward story of men who fought for what seem to us trivial reasons. Sometimes the men were known enemies, but, often enough, they were total strangers whose relationship to one another had yet to be established. Typically, one insulted the other, gave him a shove, or dared him to back up a brag, and then both pulled their knives, and the contest began. Afterward, in response to police questioning, the witnesses established who had made the first move (since the issuer of the challenge bore the onus of the law) and went on to describe the fight that all had watched without interfering. At least occasionally, the fighters were friends, and then onlookers felt they had reason to intervene. According to a story told of Angel Muniz, caudillo of Cerro Largo in the 1860s and 1870s, the disputed outcome of a horse race led him to cross blades with a friend. The men sought out a quiet spot to avoid well-meaning meddlers and prepared for the contest. "Take off your spurs, Angelito," said the caudillo's affectionate challenger, "I'm afraid you'll trip," but friends located the two men and separated them before blood was spilled.[7]

Borderlanders of all races, including enslaved men, shared in the belligerency of the region's nineteenth-century culture. Judicial records indicate that some slaves carried weapons and guarded outlying areas of large estancias. Fights such as the one recounted of an earlier generation, between Gumercindo's uncle Cisério and the slave Justino, were not uncommon. Consider the 1839 incident that occurred when two slaves, riding from estancia to estancia to look for strays, roped a horse claimed by a third slave, Gabriel, whose response was what we might expect from any other self-respecting borderland macho. Pistol in one hand and facón in the other, Gabriel charged the other two, shouting "either you give me that horse or kill me, or I am going to kill one of you!" Black men were strongly overrepresented in the ranks of almost all borderland armies—regular and irregular—in the nineteenth century, both because of impressment practices and because, as economic dependents of the landowners, they sometimes had little choice but to join the patrón in insurgencies. In addition, escaped slaves from Brazil often found protection in Uruguayan armed forces, both those of the government and those of the perpetually rebellious Blancos. An 1850 list of escapees provides examples: Benedicto (twenty years old, from Africa, a skilled horse tamer) had run away to join the Blanco militia in Tacuarembó; Antero (twenty-seven, light-skinned, experienced at ranch work) had served in Brazilian forces before escaping to join the Blanco militia in Cerro Largo, and so on. Borderlanders respected strength and valor in men of all colors, as the successful military careers of "Fulião" Macedo and Adão de Latorre illustrate. One white Uruguayan of the elite class wrote with almost mystic reverence (in a memoir that, nevertheless, also reveals the racist attitudes of the day) of a black soldier who showed the whole army how a "real man" faced death.[8]

Nineteenth-century borderlanders considered knifeplay and horseplay male prerogatives, defining aspects of gender. Women, of course, were not supposed to use violence, nor go to war, yet much of the men's violence related to women as prizes to be conquered or defended from other men. Men played the dual roles of gallant or patriarch—the gallant challenging the sexual exclusivity of others' wives and daughters; the patriarch attempting to insure the exclusivity of his own. Many a borderland marriage began with the abduction of the bride.[9] Bride stealing, or *rapto,* might also be called elopement, since women actively cooperated most of the time, and therefore, more than violence against women, borderland rapto represents competition between the suitor and the woman's father, the defender of her virginity. Gumercindo's mother, Propícia, had thus been stolen away from her father's house in the 1840s, and a similar midnight gallop helped Aparicio overcome the objections of Cándida's parents to their union in the late 1870s—the rapto being immediately sanctioned, in both cases, by the family of the *raptor*. Aparicio took Cándida straight to an estancia, El Cordobés, provided by his parents.

Knife fights frequently originated in male competition over women. Because men outnumbered women (as was normally the case on nineteenth-century cattle frontiers) and because men frequently went away (two or three days to attend a horse race, several weeks to take a herd to market, months or years to join a revolution) women were often left to fend for themselves. If they turned to another man for help and solace, or simply to insure their survival (as was often the case for poor women) the husband felt honor-bound to fight the newcomer upon his return. Recourse to the law would only publicize the husband's failure to play the role expected of him. When such an incident occurred with Gumercindo's cousin Juana María, her husband did go to the police, but quickly repented and let the case drop.[10]

The Saravias maintained stern patriarchal traditions. They addressed their father with conspicuous formality and routinely asked his blessing, in the Brazilian fashion, when meeting him. One friend of the family tells how Gumercindo, already a grown man, leapt to his feet and threw his cigarette away at his father's approach because to smoke in his presence would have been disrespectful. Another story tells of a difficult childbirth suffered by Gumercindo's mother. When the midwife warned her husband that perhaps only mother or child could be saved, old Francisco answered dourly: "save the child—the mother is doing her duty." Although Aparicio received parental support when he convinced Cándida to elope with him, his uncle took an entirely different stance when Aparicio's cousin Cecilia eloped, promptly disowning her. Subsequently abandoned by her husband, she lived with four children in a shack on a neighbor's land until she gained control of her inheritance after her father's death.[11]

The roles of patriarch and gallant seem aptly exemplified in Gumercindo and Aparicio Saravia, respectively. Very few anecdotes speak of Gumercindo's relationship with women, and all suggest patriarchal severity. Upon setting out for Brazil with his montonera in 1893, for example, Gumercindo directed only an impassive farewell to Amélia, sending his brother-in-law back to comfort her afterward. Aparicio, on the other hand, was reportedly a "ladies' man" who liked dancing and playing the guitar. His courtship of Cándida bloomed originally at fandangos at her parents' house, then culminated, as we have seen, in rapto. The deteriorating economy of the Saravias' borderland in the late nineteenth century may have deprived many young men of the wherewithal to play a patriarchal role convincingly. No property was required, however, to demonstrate one's manhood through the violence of the insouciant challenger to authority. Could this last circumstance be a factor, too, in the 1890s revolutions?[12]

Gumercindo's emergence as a local strongman began quite early. In 1870, while he was still a teenager, Gumercindo had joined a Blanco revolution, and he had returned, in his early twenties, to represent his party as a police comisario in the Saravias' rural neighborhood. In this, he followed in the footsteps of other members of the family who had begun to exercise police power in Cerro Largo as early as 1853, when the area's police chief put eight men under the command of Gumercindo's cousin Francisco. Or was this his *father* Francisco? No one knows any longer. At any rate, in 1855 the name Francisco Saravia appears on a list of rural justice officials, and in 1859, as a national guard officer, and, regardless of which Francisco held these offices, the Saravia family as a whole gained influence as a result. Another document, this one an official communication from the central government in Montevideo, grants Francisco Saravia (again, which Francisco?) remission of property taxes for his "services to the cause" of the Uruguayan caudillo Venancio Flores in the 1860s.[13]

Gumercindo did not last long as comisario in the early 1870s because his political appointment was cancelled as quickly as it had appeared, but he remained a local strongman ever after—alternately the police chief and, when out of office, the police chief's rival. In 1875, Gumercindo antagonized the Uruguayan government by going (along with Aparicio and Chiquito) to another revolution. By now, his proven fighting ability and his prestige in the neighborhood (demonstrated by the number of horsemen he took to the revolution) merited him the rank of lieutenant in the Blanco militia. When the Uruguayan government began to encourage the formation of private police forces (as a way of farming out the expensive and difficult task of imposing law and order on the borderland) the Saravias formed a force of their own. Within a few years the political chief of Cerro Largo was looking for reasons to dissolve the Saravias' private gendarmery owing to tensions with the official police in their neighborhood, and he found an excuse to do so when they killed a drifter accused of preying on cattle. By the early 1880s, Gumercindo and the comisario of his neighborhood, a Colorado, had become quite explicitly competitors for local dominance, and the slightest rumor of armed actions by "Gumercindo's people" sent the authorities galloping out to his estancia in a lather.[14]

The 1883 incident that forced Gumercindo to leave Uruguay to escape prosecution apparently had its origins in this rivalry. Legal depositions provide the details of what happened on the high road of the Cuchilla Grande on a wintery evening of that year. Boxed in by wire fences on both sides of the road, a herd of fifteen hundred longhorns had lumbered along for much of the day without fodder and, at nightfall, its situation became critical. Not finding a gate, the drover cut the fence wire and moved his desperate animals into the pastures of La Pandorga, an estancia whose linguistically hybrid name betrayed the presence of a "Luso-Uruguayan" family, in this case, the Saravias. Gumercindo and three other men brandishing lances confronted the intruders, a fight ensued, blood flowed, and the local comisario soon took the opportunity to harass his rival Gumercindo with legal charges. The comisario must have done so with relish, because—himself a drover—he had once been similarly expelled from Saravia property. The drover who invaded La Pandorga in 1883 was yet another personal enemy, apparently, and Gumercindo provoked him on purpose in a letter written two days after the incident, a letter the drover later submitted as state's evidence. "I should warn you," wrote Saravia, "that when I challenge someone who thinks he's a big man (even though he's not) I never do it with ridiculous pretensions and much less by bothering the authorities. You [the drover and his brother] are men and if you've gotten the worst this time you should take it like men of honor. I'm plenty healthy and maybe you'll have your chance to get even." Saravia closed by wishing the drover's brother a speedy recovery from his bullet wound. So, by the inexorable logic of borderland enmity and rivalry—the necessary inverse of friendship and alliance—the drover-turned-comisario pursued the comisario-turned-drover and, with the weight of the Uruguayan government behind him, forced Gumercindo to move his family across the border into Brazil and settle on an estancia in Santa Vitória do Palmar.[15]

Gumercindo had not been in Santa Vitória long when (in a clearly repeating pattern) he became the sworn enemy of one of his neighbors, Jacinto Senturião, a local police official. Gumercindo's estancia house at Curral de Arroios stood not far from the sandy shores of large Lake Mirim, and from the lookout atop its main house, one could see the sails of cargo boats and the shallow-draft steamer on its weekly run to Jaguarão. Anyone who visited Curral de Arroios noticed immediately that the rectangular compound, formed of walls almost ten feet high and pierced by occasional loopholes, was built to withstand a siege. Isolated Santa Vitória—surrounded by Lake Mirim on one side, Uruguay on another, the Atlantic ocean on a third, and vast marshes on the fourth—had always been a lawless place, and like other parts of the borderland, it was experiencing a rash of animal theft in the 1880s. Gumercindo announced that anyone caught filching one of his animals would be shot on the spot, and he soon acquired a reputation for effectively repressing thieves, the worst of whom, he declared, was Senturião himself. The feuding neighbors skirmished at every opportunity, including a protracted gun battle in which the house of Senturião's mother was burned to the ground. One witness thought Saravia had forty or fifty armed men living at Curral de Arroios, and half a dozen were said to patrol the estancia day and night. Predictably, the police began an investigation of Gumercindo's activities despite his protests that official intervention in a private dispute amounted to partisan persecution. There may be something to the charge of partisanism, since by this time (the mid-1880s) Saravia had become a client of Liberal leader Gaspar Silveira Martins and the police investigations were being carried out by a Conservative administration. Even the special investigator sent by that administration admitted in his report that Senturião had been stealing Saravia's cattle.[16]

Obviously, the legal accusations made against Gumercindo owe a great deal to his political enemies' determination to discredit him, yet even the most skeptical reading of them must give us pause. Let us discount as sensational, for example, the report that Gumercindo had the head of one enemy mounted on a pike in Curral de Arroios, but the killing itself (by degola) seems credible enough in view of the evidence. Also, why doubt the testimony of the seventeen witnesses, including several women who had been domestic servants in the Saravia house, who testified that Gumercindo sent men to abduct, torture, and kill a spy employed by the Senturião family and that this had been common knowledge at Curral de Arroios? The reports that Gumercindo sent "*capangas*" (Portuguese for "thugs") to liquidate a number of enemies in Santa Vitória come from numerous witnesses, including one who claimed to have taken part in such missions and who also reported that Gumercindo offered a two-hundred-peso reward to whoever killed Jacinto Senturião. Material evidence for these crimes was almost always lacking, but after the Republicans forced Gumercindo out of Santa Vitória in 1890, they did exhume a body at Curral de Arroios. Was this Preto Simão an ex-slave who had died from natural causes at the age of almost a hundred, as Saravia's partisans asserted? Or can we believe the (no less partisan) autopsy that described the remains of a much younger man, his penis and one hand missing, his skull crushed? As with all the other charges, witnesses testified against Gumercindo only in his absence, and juries acquitted him unanimously when he returned to Santa Vitória in 1891. Whatever our doubts, it is clear that, true to the standard modus operandi of a local strongman, Gumercindo dealt with the rustlers of Santa Vitória, not by rounding them up and bringing them to justice, but by running them down and killing them.[17]

The general prosperity enjoyed by the Saravia family amid the hard times of the late nineteenth-century borderland owed something, no doubt, to these same talents. Of course, one should not diminish the importance of the various small businesses that provided liquid capital for their early land purchases: the provision of fresh horses for a stage coach line and the rural store run by Basilicio. Still, wealth of any kind had to be protected on the lawless frontier. Because they were numerous and tight-knit, enjoyed an enviable reputation for family solidarity, and frequently controlled the local police, the Saravias could hold their own in the violent environment of northern Uruguay at moments when less hardy families withdrew to Montevideo, Pelotas, or Jaguarão. Even the Saravias sometimes retreated across the Brazilian border in the early years, while their oldest boys were still young (on one such occasion, buying their first property in Santa Vitória do Palmar), but they never stayed very long. For them, the perils and opportunities of borderland life went hand in hand. This was, after all, what had first attracted the family to Uruguay in the previous generation. The early land speculators of the Uruguayan side of the borderland had bought and sold their huge tracts so cheaply at the dawn of the nineteenth century precisely because these properties were so hazardous to occupy.[18]

The original Saravia estancias in Cerro Largo formed a small part of one such tract, an extension of about 1,450 square miles of pasture purchased from the crown in October 1810 for a mere 1,500 pesos, then subdivided and resold within a month. The new owners left Cerro Largo during the turmoil of independence, selling to a Rio Grandense family in 1822. Long years of political warfare in the middle years of the nineteenth century convinced not a few landowners to sell their properties and abandon Cerro Largo. So it was that Gumercindo's parents bought their first piece of land from a family that had retired to Jaguarão to escape an Uruguayan civil war. Gumercindo's uncle Cisério made four purchases in that same year (1866), all from people who had fled to Rio Grande do Sul. The price of one of these purchases (less than one peso per acre—considerably more than the one peso per square mile of 1810, but still a bargain) shows why the normally city-shy Saravias were willing to travel to distant urban centers to close these deals. Another burst of acquisitions followed the Blanco revolution of 1870–72, when Gumercindo was named comisario in the neighborhood. A month after Uruguay's contending parties made peace, Gumercindo's father, Francisco, set out for Pelotas, and then made a similar trip to Montevideo a few months later—both times to buy land from former neighbors who had given up on the idea of living there. Just after the Uruguayan revolution of 1875, his father made further acquisitions, traveling first to Melo and then again to Montevideo. Once established in Santa Vitória, Gumercindo continued to build his landholdings by acquiring land inexpensively amid the insecurities of the late 1880s and early 1890s, the safety of his investments guaranteed by his own intimidating presence.[19]

Gumercindo's rise as a caudillo was firmly rooted in his two decades as a local strongman, much admired—as well as feared—by his rural neighbors. As for landholding, so often invoked to explain the power of local strongmen like Gumercindo, it did contribute to his strength, of course, by providing a ready means of recruiting and maintaining followers, but, while all landowners shared this means, only a small portion of them became caudillos. If several dozen local strongmen can be identified in the nineteenth-century history of Cerro Largo, for example, many thousands of Cerro Largo landowners never held that sort of "prestige" in the eyes of their neighbors, nor did political prestige correlate directly with the size of landholding. Across the entire Uruguayan north, the largest estancias were owned by Rio Grandense families who rarely played an important part in Uruguayan politics—the Saravias being quite exceptional in this regard. More than wealth, prestige like Gumercindo's reflected male admiration for the strongman's skills, an admiration virtually universal among borderlanders who practiced those same skills and considered them the essence of masculinity. Gumercindo's prestige began with his personal strength and daring, then spread over his neighborhood because of his skill at organizing small groups of armed men to exercise (or defy) police power, and finally soared in 1893 when he emerged as the only Federalist commander who won most of his battles against the Brazilian army. As the revolution erupted north into the states of Santa Catarina and Paraná in early 1894, Republican fears and Federalist hopes alike centered on the gaucho caudillo whom the famous Rio journalist José do Patrocínio dubbed "Napoleon of the Pampas."[20]

10

JANUARY-AUGUST 1894

umercindo Saravia's capture of two well-defended cities in the state of Paraná marked the high tide of the revolution, but at a high cost in blood. As Saravia's lancers bore the brunt of the fighting, General Salgado and the insurgents' other regular army and naval officers frittered away the military momentum of the revolution comfortably lodged in Desterro (the "liberated" capital of Santa Catarina) attending soirees hosted by the city's most distinguished society, proclaiming their willingness to make the supreme sacrifice, and arguing about who would hold what post in the provisional government. Meanwhile, farther north at the town of Tijucas in Paraná, the Maragatos rode unknowingly into a well-fortified emplacement of modern Krupp cannon that suddenly opened fire, blowing horses and riders apart. Angelo Dourado, who had stayed on as the Maragatos camp physician when Gumercindo and Salgado parted company, spent that day kneeling in the bloody mud of his makeshift field hospital to saw through splintered bones and tie off arteries, bullets buzzing close above his head.[1]

For once, however, the insurgents had more ammunition than their enemies. Aparicio paraded around on horseback carrying an umbrella instead of his lance, complaining loudly about the "mosquitos" and otherwise trying to goad the defenders to use up their bullets. The tactics worked. After a week, the garrison of Tijucas ran out of ammunition and surrendered. This was the first time in the war that the Federalists had taken a strongly garrisoned town, and this victory was to be followed by a greater one at Lapa, where Saravia's column headed immediately. Here the Republican commander preferred death to surrender. For almost a month the Maragatos besieged a well-organized defensive perimeter that contracted slowly with the passing days. As days became weeks, the government artillery pounded the outskirts of the town into a rubble-filled no-man's-land that made attacks ever harder. During the battle, the Maragatos displayed their own peculiar attitude toward death. Dourado watched in amazement as some of them danced to accordion music so close to the lines that one of the dancers was occasionally toppled by the impact of a stray bullet. The surviving defenders of Lapa finally surrendered at the death of their iron-willed commander.[2]

After the battle, Saravia and Dourado went with a trainload of wounded men to Curitiba, the capital of Paraná, and Dourado had a trumpeter play lively marches to cheer the wounded as they rolled through the tall-timbered countryside so different from the borderland. In Curitiba, they found the train station thronged with people who had come out for a glimpse of the famous Gumercindo. Dourado describes how, as the battered Maragatos tried to make their way through the lobby, an impromptu orator climbed onto a table and waxed lyrical on the subject of courage and heroism until Gumercindo had him interrupted so that the wounded could be taken to the hospital. Dourado wrote angrily to his wife about how the rags of the Maragatos (many of whom went barefoot) contrasted with the fine uniforms of the regular officers who represented the provisional revolutionary government. Hearing that Salgado planned to take the port of Rio Grande by sea, Gumercindo scoffed at the idea and talked nostalgically of returning to take the town himself. On 24 February, Gumercindo wrote to his wife Amélia that he hoped soon "to tread borderland soil" with his army.[3]

A statement issued in Saravia's name on 7 April projected the Liberating Army's move north toward the state of São Paulo. The elaborate rhetorical periods of the document, with its effusions about a "Holy Republic," are clearly the work of a ghost writer or secretary, not of the rude borderlander who sometimes asked Dourado to do his talking for him on public occasions. Still, for a moment anything seemed possible, and a heated atmosphere of revolutionary enthusiasm produced a gale of rumors and pronouncements in Santa Catarina and Paraná. Within days, "confirmed" newspaper accounts narrated a string of revolutionary triumphs, including the capture of not only the port of Rio Grande but also the cities of Pelotas and Porto Alegre, announcing that Governor Júlio de Castilhos had been taken prisoner by insurgent forces. In rapid succession the astonished populace of Paraná learned of a smashing rebel victory at sea, an uprising in the state of Minas Gerais in central Brazil, and feverish preparations for a transition government in Rio de Janiero. Unfortunately for the blissful insurgents, Salgado's assault on Rio Grande had in fact fizzled when the disembarked force was given misleading intelligence about the strength of the garrison there. Refusing to attack, Salgado instead reembarked and sailed to Buenos Aires, where his men surrendered themselves, their ship, and their weapons to the Argentine authorities. The other reports were pure imagination— "goiabas," in the Brazilian expression of the time. In fact, by the end of April 1894, the principal warship of the naval rebellion had been torpedoed and sunk, and the Maragatos could expect little further support from the provisional government. Brazil's most powerful state, São Paulo—strongly Republican and boasting its own quite formidable armed forces—waited directly ahead, and Saravia's column, numbering now no more than a thousand, began its long retreat back to Rio Grande do Sul.[4]

The Maragatos marched west, away from the coast, on an arduous journey through the backlands of Paraná and Santa Catarina, reaching Rio Grande do Sul in June. The Rio Grandense Republicans sent their seasoned Division of the North to meet them, and, at a place called Passo Fundo, in the northern part of the state, Saravia's column fought its last major battle. When Aparicio was hit by a bullet in the hip, Gumercindo, who had rarely used a weapon during the war, picked up a lance for the last time, and led a charge to rescue his wounded brother. The insurgents inflicted terrible casualties on the Division of the North, but the lancers' repeated charges failed to break the massed infantry squares. Many hundreds died in the battle, where Aparicio achieved definitive fame as a military athlete by impaling two Republican soldiers in a single lance thrust. But when darkness fell, Gumercindo's bedraggled Maragatos retreated as relentlessly as after the defeat at Inhandui. They were finally nearing the open plains of the borderland when, on 10 August, the pursuing Republican force caught up with them again.[5]

Gumercindo was out surveying the field between the armies when Republican snipers shot him off his horse. The wounded general's aides carried him to camp, where he pleaded for cold water, continued to issue orders ("tell Aparicio to watch his flank"), and begged those around him to keep his personal riding gear from falling into Republican hands. Aparicio took one look at him, turned away in anguish, and left without speaking. Gumercindo covered his face with his hands. "They've killed me," he said several times, but he was still alive when they loaded him into a cart after dark, and as the stricken Maragatos marched through the night, Dourado, fearful of panic in the ranks, rode beside the cart issuing optimistic prognoses. When the hopeful insurgents camped in the morning, however, he let the army know that Gumercindo was dead. The remaining insurgent officers chose Aparicio to lead them west toward the Uruguay River and across it, as quickly as possible, into the Argentine province of Corrientes.[6]

Once in Argentina, the Maragatos moved slowly south toward home, and they began to hear more details of the disasters that had befallen the revolution in the borderland during their march north to Santa Catarina and Paraná. At the end of 1893, General Tavares had thrown everything into an assault on Bagé. The attack of two thousand Federalists on the army garrison of Bagé began with sweet revenge for the followers of Tavares when, in an initial victory, they caught an outnumbered party of Republican irregulars on the Federalists' home ground in the headwaters of the Río Negro. The commander of these Republican provisional forces, Manuel Pedroso, was the man who had allowed the looting of Bagé after Tavares fled to Uruguay on the eve of the war and, when the Pedroso surrendered, the imperatives of vengeance brought a blood bath. Who gave the orders for dozens of prisoners, including Pedroso, to be executed by degola? Certainly it was not Adão de Latorre, who carried out the orders, to the eternal infamy of his name. On the other hand, a report that Adão's wife and daughters had been brutally raped by Pedroso's men also casts some light on the role of the executioner, and the Federalist taste for retribution was hardly unique. At this point in the war, a number of government directives reminded local Republicans "to neither spare nor give quarter" to the rebels. Throwing everything into an assault on Bagé, Tavares failed to overcome the stubborn resistance of the Republican garrison of eight to nine hundred men commanded by Carlos Telles, relative of Joca's old nemesis, Gen. João Telles. (The hard-fought defense of Bagé won for Carlos Telles a first installment of military fame throughout Brazil, fame augmented years later by his participation in the even harder fought destruction of the millenarian community at Canudos in the state of Bahia.) After two weeks of intense house-to-house fighting, Tavares had to give up and slink back to the border. His army—now mostly on foot, its ammunition consumed utterly by the attack on Bagé—split into three columns and finally dissolved into Uruguay, definitively bested.[7]

Returning to such dim prospects after their own demoralizing experience in the north, many of the Maragatos now deserted the revolution. With Gumercindo dead, one might expect Aparicio to have done likewise, but instead he stayed on and began to prepare a new invasion of Brazil. When Cándida and his children traveled to see him in an insurgent camp in northwestern Uruguay (recalls his son, Nepomuceno) they found Aparicio changed, speaking to them now only in Portuguese and without his familiar mischief and booming laugh. Why did Aparicio Saravia stay with the Federalists, when he could not even be one? After all, he had joined the insurgency as an Uruguayan personally loyal to Gumercindo, with no particular grievance against the Republicans aside from their harassment of Gumercindo and the murder of his cousin Terencio. His personal declaration to his wife in a letter dated 20 November shows how he explained his staying to her. "I didn't want to stay mixed up in the revolution," he wrote in the colloquial syntax and unconventional orthography so different from the language that secretaries would later produce in his name, "but since they say that the tyrants dug up Gumercindo and tore him apart I have to fight to avenge what they did to his body."[8]

11
THE WILL TO BELIEVE

When the Republicans marched their army past Gumercindo's body, forbad his burial, and finally collected his head as a scientific specimen—the modern equivalent of displaying it on a pike—they provided us with a clue about the imaginative dimensions of caudillismo. It was not enough for Gumercindo to be dead; his death had to be as public as possible. Gumercindo's mere disappearance, the absence of his skilled leadership on the battlefield or on the long marches between battles, would hurt the Federalists, but the *idea* of his death would demoralize them utterly. In a private letter, Silveira Martins disconsolately described the collapse of Gumercindo's column—morally, though not militarily, defeated. The Republican police chief of Santa Vitória do Palmar crowed (telegraphically) upon learning the news: "Revolution considered over in view of Gumercindo's death." But for months afterward, the Federalists refused to believe the discouraging claims of their hero's demise. As the days passed, rumors of Gumercindo's death lost ground, it seemed, to other rumors saying that he was only wounded (in the foot—and the bullet had been removed and he was recovering in Argentina), then to other rumors saying that he had recently issued new orders (someone had seen a copy—no, someone had seen the originals), and finally to still other rumors saying that Gumercindo's family had just received a letter in his handwriting and that the wily caudillo only pretended to be dead in order to confuse the Republicans. Unhappily for the Federalists, the rumors of Gumercindo's survival were greatly exaggerated, but these fertile "goiabas" powerfully suggest their will to believe in him, a will that the Republicans sought to destroy along with his body. Exactly what did Gumercindo represent in the minds of his followers, and why were those things so important?[1]

Evidence about the ideas of Gumercindo's followers is scanty. Among the Maragatos, only the camp physician, Angelo Dourado, kept a detailed diary (none other, at least, survives), and it cannot be considered representative of the illiterate, rural men who made up the majority of Gumercindo's column. About them, we have only broad indications. In scattered narrative passages, we hear the voices of anonymous soldiers exulting about their general—"a God of revolutions!"—and read about their "fanatical adoration" or about their avid response to his "hypnotizing" gaze. Dying soldiers supposedly struggled to their feet to shout a final tribute as he rode across the battlefield. Of course, these things were written by literate people who owned property and whose personal perspective inevitably differed from that of poor, illiterate people. Still, such are the only surviving sources of information, and we must therefore read them closely, sometimes "against the grain" (seeking to glimpse what the writer said without intending to) with particular attention to the distinctions created or erased by their class perspective.[2]

Local newspapers are another helpful source because they give clues about the "intersubjectivity" of the borderlanders, that is, how attitudes toward Gumercindo jibed with other political, social, and economic concerns. In local papers, we encounter fragments of the written discourse of everyday life. Embedded in these chunky, uneven columns without pictures or banner headlines, are letters from ordinary "correspondents" in the countryside, brief personal announcements, jokes, advertisements, descriptions of theatrical events, riddles, and word games (Can readers identify the stylish, but unnamed, local belle in the following description?), as well as plenty of editorializing. The Federalist newspapers of Rio Grande do Sul were shut down during the war, but the editor of Melo's *El deber cívico* was quite sympathetic to the revolution and published a lot of war-related materials (including Angelo Dourado's column in Portuguese) and a Federalist newspaper in the Uruguayan bordertown of Rivera also continued "to fight virilely in defense of its sacred rights" throughout the conflict. Even more than conduits for information on the fighting, newspapers were themselves combatants in a propaganda war.[3]

A miasma of horror hangs over the rhetoric issuing from both the Federalist and Republican camps at the time. Perhaps this is unsurprising given the rising social tensions and proliferation of political vendettas in the borderland of the 1890s and given, too, the literary vogue of naturalistic horror in police reporting and fiction. The newspapers of Rio Grande do Sul routinely featured lurid crimes, many of them from outside the state, in the years before the revolution. In December 1892 (when the rash of degolas was spreading across the borderland along with rumors of impending invasion) Porto Alegre's comparatively staid *Jornal do comércio* printed a meter-long front-page story under the heading "Human Ferocity" about a woman murdered and chopped to pieces in Paris.[4] A month later, Bagé's Republican newspaper was carrying "horrid" new explicit details of the torture, murder, and mutilation of a leading Republican, Evaristo Amaral, and a few days after that, borderlanders read the invasion proclamation of Joca Tavares, which opened with a passage about government-condoned assassins "dancing on the cadavers of their victims." In one of his newspaper columns of about this time, Angelo Dourado imagined Republicans rounding up Federalist women in a corral for each soldier to lasso his own. Republican journalistic discourse was every bit as shrill. Take, for example, the following apostrophe to the deceased Gumercindo: "Heavy as the Andes be the earth that generously cloaks your damned cadaver, and heavy over your stinking burrow weigh the concentrated grief of the mothers you sacrificed, the virgins you violated . . ." and so on. Another view of the discourse of horror may be found in a pamphlet, *The Truth about the Revolution,* that went through three printings in 1894. The author, Germano Hasslocher, was a Federalist who left the revolution declaring that the insurgents had become drunk with their own rhetoric. The final straw for Hasslocher had been the description of the degolas of Manuel Pedroso and other prisoners, recounted to an enthusiastic audience of Federalist émigrés by an eyewitness who brandished Pedroso's withered ears as a visual aid. When the other men sneered at Hasslocher's squeamishness, he fled into the dark and wandered for hours "to absorb the horror."[5]

For the Republicans, Gumercindo himself exemplified the horror. He was "the Tiger of Curral de Arroios," a "famous bandit" bizarrely raised to a position of authority, a local despot who had his enemies whipped in the streets of Santa Vitória and forced an accordion player to provide musical accompaniment for his own torture, a gratuitously evil Spanish-speaking caudillo who, when offered a sumptuous meal by a family mistaking him for a Republican, repaid them afterward by having all their throats cut. The term "cannibals" sometimes replaced "Federalists" even in official police telegrams. In a word, Saravia appeared to the more progressive of Rio Grande do Sul's political parties as an appalling atavism, a barbarian enemy of progress and civilization highly reminiscent of Sarmiento's portrait of Facundo Quiroga.[6]

At the opposite extreme, Federalist propagandists presented Gumercindo as a redeeming paladin, a knight without stain, a paragon of civic and patriarchal virtues, selfless and uncompromising. This Saravia never permitted looting and never aggrandized his own interests. Where his enemies painted a picture of bestial impulsiveness, his admirers emphasized self-control and restraint in the face of provocation. Angelo Dourado depicts Gumercindo as a man capable of lending his own poncho to a trembling prisoner, but capable also of righteous reprisal when one of his own retainers was caught menacing the defenseless women and children of an absent landowner. Though tearful when giving the order, Gumercindo had the offending soldier shot (along with an accomplice) and then marched the Maragatos past the executed men's bodies as an object lesson in military discipline.[7]

Unsurprisingly, one senses a nostalgic outlook among the borderlanders who championed the cause of former monarchical bastions like Joca Tavares and Gaspar Silveira Martins. In their representations, the past signified calm and order, the peaceful seasons of the good old imperial days, with current violence a nightmarish intrusion on the scene. In Dourado's melodramatic rendering:

> the carter, the drover, the gaucho rested together in the
> greatest harmony, and argued merely about which pastures
> were finer, which cattle sleeker and more beautiful. . . .
> Then strange figures arrived. The joy and laughter were

transformed into silence and fear. Suddenly cries were heard, laments, prayers, then a dull groan from the violated bed, a satanic guffaw, women fleeing, children unable to comprehend the horror even afterward, and somewhere a shout: Long live Legality! Long live Júlio de Castilhos.[8]

The Republicans had, indeed, disrupted the past order that many Federalists regarded wistfully. Most of the Republican activists who seized the reins of power in the early 1890s were young men. Júlio de Castilhos himself was only twenty-nine years old when he became leader of the Rio Grandense Republicans, only thirty-one when he became governor with sweeping powers. The striking generational contrast between the young Republican leadership and Federalist graybeards like Silveira Martins and Joca Tavares was jarring to people steeped in the prerogatives of patriarchy, who must have viewed Castilhos's rise as a violation of the proper social hierarchy. There are rich implications in the fact that Castilhos himself became styled "the Patriarch" among Republicans, though he died in his early forties.[9]

Images of social inversion and violation of the family combine with a notable anxiety about the future in Dourado's campaign diary published after the war as *Volunteers for Martyrdom*. Violations of the family constituted a standard element of Republican atrocity stories and functioned, for Dourado, as a social metaphor as well. Accelerating immigration seemed to menace a "Brazilian family" that, as a whole, possessed noble idealism but not the competitiveness needed for the emerging social order. Dourado admired many qualities of the German immigrants whose colonies he visited during the war, but he also feared that Order and Progress, the positivist slogan of the republic, would "annihilate our offspring so that this foreign people can cover the surface of Brazil." For Dourado, the violence of the 1890s reflected the loss of past virtues and the inroad of modern materialism and individualism—Brazil for sale to the highest bidder, its leaders harkening only to the voice of ego—resulting in a generalized dread and disorientation: "My poor Patria! They have torn asunder the bonds that held you in equilibrium, and on that fearful grade, in the grip of vertigo, where will you come to rest?" To borderland ranchers witnessing the crumbling of their familiar world (the decline of their rural economy, the threatening transformations of their society and the eclipse of their political importance) Dourado's call for redeeming struggle may have been quite compelling. Disillusioned Germano Hasslocher lamented that, most cruelly of all, poor rural people with no real stake in the political issues of the war also became swept into a self-perpetuating vortex of rage and revenge. The popular reaction to Gumercindo Saravia must be understood, then, in the context of a climate of fear that compounded the dismay of those who saw him as the new Attila and redoubled the fervor of those who yearned for a hero.[10]

Caudillos were inevitably the heroic protagonists of narratives like Angelo Dourado's. "He is the savior," wrote Dourado to his wife in 1893, after recounting how Gumercindo had rescued the revolution "single-handedly" during the winter months when the Maragatos fought alone in Rio Grande do Sul. This rhetorical reduction of an army to the person of its general, hardly peculiar to Dourado, constituted an extremely ingrained habit of thought and expression, and the view of leaders as epic protagonists seems as common in borderland popular culture as in the writings of elite males. Borderlanders tended to view leaders as heroes and villains locked in a titanic contest. To paraphrase a Porto Alegre newspaper of the 1930s, there was no corner of Rio Grande do Sul—no estancia with hired hands sharing a mate, no polite gathering in town—where heroes' deeds of valor were not told and retold. The newspaper referred to the Federalist and Republican "chiefs" of 1893 (Gumercindo preeminent among them) but the same could have been said in the 1890s about an oral tradition that reached back to the Farrapo War of 1835–1845 and earlier. The hundreds of anonymous quatrains that circulated during and after the Farrapo War incessantly rehearsed the reputations of various leaders, lingering on their triumphs or humiliations (for example: "With forces three times larger / On a field both flat and even / The loyalist Silva Tavares / Was definitively beaten") and engaging in wordplay with their names. Half a century later, similar quatrains covered Gumercindo with the Farrapo mantle: "The heroes of thirty-five / From the tomb arising / Proudly do repeat / Gumercindo is arriving."[11]

After the winter of 1893, Saravia clearly emerged as the favorite subject of borderland storytellers and versifiers, the hope of the revolution, and borderland Federalists assured each other that he would soon return from the north. As his reputation grew, various Federalist leaders claimed the credit for having discovered him. In one of these ex-post-facto prefigurings of the hero's rise (a rather standard element of such legends), Silveira Martins relates how he dramatically told a mystified Federalist assembly in 1892 that "the leader we seek is already among us." In another, Salgado recounts how, after his first momentary meeting with Saravia on the morning of the battle of Inhanduí, he informed Tavares: "That gaucho is a military genius!" The stories of Gumercindo's 1890 imprisonment and escape, circulating with multiple permutations in Santa Vitória do Palmar, also fit a common pattern of borderland hero legends—most notably that of Bento Gonçalves who had been elected president of the Farrapo republic even though he languished in a faraway prison, then escaped and made his way secretly across half of Brazil to assume the presidency. Amélia takes on an aura befitting the wife of a hero in these tales, at one point flying bedsheets like flags in an attempt to warn her husband of plans to arrest him, then carrying a gun to defend herself while Gumercindo was in jail, and finally making a wax impression of the lock on the cell door to aid his "historic" escape. When a first key was made to open the door it broke off in the lock, said the storytellers of Santa Vitória do Palmar, but Amélia extracted the fragment with her teeth to avert disaster. (Other residents preserved a "historic bottle" of drugged wine used to dispose of Saravia's guards.) Stories of women in a caudillo's family often indicate "masculine" qualities, as if to imply a superabundance of testosterone in the bloodline. Gumercindo's mother was said to have helped work the stock, the reader may recall, and another story has her single-handedly facing down a Colorado war party that approached the house in Chico's absence.[12]

In late 1891, Gumercindo returned to face trial at the head of a hundred armed men. "The scene when the great General went before the jury is vivid in my imagination," explained an old-timer of Santa Vitória in 1938, describing Gumercindo's full beard, dark hat, poncho and colored neckerchief, and the way he strode into the courtroom to face down his enemies and walk out absolved. "This was in 1892," specified the adoring informant, glorying in the spectacle of the hero's solitary stand, and supplying a date to place the account in an historical context. On the other hand, he declined to mention that any jury so rash as to convict Gumercindo when his men controlled Santa Vitória would have run an unreasonably high risk of physical injury.[13]

A hundred years later, people in Santa Vitória do Palmar continued to tell contradictory stories about Gumercindo. In one, he catches a poor countryman in the act of slaughtering one of his cows. "My wife and children are hungry," protests the man. "You need not steal," answers Gumercindo. "When your family is hungry, go to my estancia and I will give you meat." Then, according to this version of the story, he allows the man to finish butchering the cow, saying "Go ahead, but never do this again or I will punish you severely." Another version of the story ends a bit differently: Gumercindo simply cuts off the man's head and leaves it on top of the slaughtered animal as a warning to others. Other stories refer to a secluded spot on Gumercindo's estancia where he liquidated (by inches) any cattle thieves he apprehended. To this day, say the storytellers, no horse will graze the luxuriant grass that grows on that spot.[14]

Borderlanders collected, refashioned, or even invented outright the memorable words of their political protagonists—for example, a racial slur flung in the face of Adão de Latorre by Manuel Pedroso, the leader of Republican montoneras, when he was executed at Río Negro, or the exclamation of famous Republican leader José Gomes Pinheiro Machado upon contemplating the exhumed cadaver of Gumercindo: "And to think that this upstart made the Republic tremble." Gumercindo's own words were few. One of his rare sallies responded to a question about why he—a Brazilian insurgent general—spoke Spanish instead of Portuguese. "I'd rather not mistreat *our* language," he answered with a wry wink toward his Brazilian interlocutor and a nod toward Aparicio and Cesáreo, "but *theirs*!" Overall, however, the elder Saravia gave the weavers of his legend less yarn than did many more flamboyant caudillos.[15]

Undeterred, borderland Federalists constructed an image of the hero they wanted. One orator, for example, saw in Saravia not only "the bravery of Garibaldi" but also "the virtue of Lincoln." Here, in the sort of effusion that generally confounds U.S. historians (who vastly underestimate the degree to which most caudillos were admired as well as feared) the distance between the rhetoric and its referent indicates a strong "will to believe." True, Gumercindo had a reputation for a certain austere rectitude closely associated with property rights. "He'd sooner pardon a killer than a thief," said his advocates in Santa Vitória, and his column does seem to have been comparatively restrained in its requisitions of cattle and horses as it marched across the borderland. Whatever the true virtues of the caudillo, however, a powerful will to believe was clearly at work when cultured men like Dourado (who interrupted his diary, at one point, with a religious allegory of over five thousand words) projected their own values onto the strongman: highlighting his tears because they prized sensitivity, calling him "a Homeric figure" because the classical allusion transformed him from a mundane local enforcer into the kind of sublime and elevated hero they desired. More rustic borderlanders wanted a hero as well, and the values they projected reveal their own, quite different brand of admiration. Consider the following "goiabas" that circulated in the borderland for weeks after Gumercindo's last battle in faraway Passo Fundo. The reader will recall that the Maragatos charged fruitlessly against the disciplined infantry squares on that day and reeled away sorely hurt, but, during the weeks after the battle, successive Federalist versions created a more satisfying narrative of the battle, detailing Gumercindo's laughably easy victory in ever more elaborate scenarios, until, two months after Passo Fundo, the pro-Saravia goiabas had his lancers surrounding their enemies and dragging them out of the squares, one by one, with lassos, so that only a few government soldiers survived to tell the tale.[16]

Here was an image to make Gumercindo's rural admirers shake their heads and chuckle in appreciation. Was the general not known, at times, to make a show of his own skill with the lasso when the Maragatos slaughtered cattle? Was he not, after all, a "gaúcho"? The word *gaúcho*, constituting an insult in earlier years (when it referred exclusively to drifters and social marginals of mixed race), had lately taken on more positive associations in Rio Grande do Sul. This semantic evolution was parallel to that of the same word in Spanish, and was very probably influenced by the popular gauchesque traditions that had developed during the early nineteenth century in the Río de la Plata. By the 1890s, verses about *El gaucho Martín Fierro* by the Argentine poet José Hernández were recited with a Portuguese accent in the Brazilian borderland, and Rio Grandense authors had also begun to produce and popularize literary gaúchos of their own.[17]

"Gaucho" or "gaúcho" was coming to signify a proud cultural identity applicable to anything native to the Argentine, Uruguayan, or Rio Grandense countryside, an identity defined particularly by clothing, speech, and the habits and skills of rural life. After becoming the leading general of the revolution, Gumercindo wore a dark blue uniform for the sake of military decorum, but a life-size oil portrait painted and exhibited during the war represented him in full gaucho attire, with careful attention given to the details of his saddle, bridle, and other gear, down to the tiny golden stars inlaid on his silver spurs.[18] Rio Grandense newspapers of the late 1880s sometimes had "gaúcho" correspondents who wrote in borderland dialect, who cracked jokes about how city boys ("so-called Rio Grandenses") rode like sissies, and who always found some reason to mention their own "gaúcho" dress. One of these "gaúcho" columnists imagined in detail how dashing Gaspar Silveira Martins would look in *bombachas* (the baggy, peg-bottomed trousers then fast replacing the Guaraní chiripá and still worn by rural men today), spurs, poncho, and neckerchief—the characteristic accoutrements of a gauchesque "monarch of the plains."[19]

Another identifying trait of the gaúcho persona (well exemplified in the "Letters from Silvério" published by the Federalist paper of Rivera) was a mistrust of "Bahianos" from other parts of Brazil. Symptomatically, when the crusty Silvério used the word *pátria,* he always meant Rio Grande do Sul rather than Brazil as a whole. During the war, insurgent rhetoric tried to appropriate this cult of nativist pride, and logically so, given the Federalists' general attachment to the notion of tradition and the location of their stronghold in the rural borderland where these images resonated so powerfully.[20]

The earlier Farrapo insurgency of the borderland constituted a crucial element of the Rio Grandense nativist identity. When, at the high tide of his advance into Paraná, Gumercindo sent a (ghost-written) telegram to Brazilian president Floriano Peixoto announcing his victories, he called himself the "descendent of a Farrapo." In his family history there is no evidence for this claim (possibly improvised at the

instigation of a secretary), but many Federalist leaders did have Farrapo forebears. When Col. Ladislau Amaro da Silveira harangued his
troops about "sustaining the glorious traditions of the Spartans of
'35," he might have been thinking of his own Farrapo father, who
died in that war. Whether or not Saravia was actually a lineal de-
scendant of the Farrapos, his supporters viewed him as the spiritual
heir of the earlier Rio Grandense rebels. Liberal followers of Silveira
Martins had kept "the legend of '35" in the masthead of their Porto
Alegre newspaper throughout the late empire, and Rivera's *Canabarro* (the Federalist paper that printed "Letters from Silvério") took
its name from David Canabarro, a local Farrapo general. A later
Federalist paper also published in Rivera, the *Maragato,* provides a
full orchestration of this imaginative genealogy in its homage to the
heroes of the 1893–95 revolution, published as a pamphlet a few
years afterward. The Farrapos appear four times in the pamphlet's
brief prologue, followed by the revolution's famous martyrs
(Gumercindo and Admiral Luís Felipe de Saldanha da Gama, the
latter killed in the fruitless final invasion of 1895). The stirring por-
trayal of Joca Tavares reveals the absorbing power of the Farrapo
myth. "The gaúchos gather, arm themselves, rebel, and proclaim him
their military leader. Behold him at their head, in spite of his eighty
years, nimble as a young wrangler . . ." Federalist propagandists made
old Joca a Farrapo by association, carefully neglecting to explain that,
almost uniquely among the insurgents of 1893, Joca had actually
fought in the Farrapo War himself—but on the side of the anti-
Farrapo loyalists![21]

Whatever his appeal as a symbol of gaúcho nativism or past glories,
Gumercindo's prominence had clearly rested most of all on his efficacy as a war leader—one not given to reckless and flamboyant
acts of battlefield daring like his brother Aparicio, but one who knew
how to pick his battles and win them—and so his death left more
disillusionment than inspiration in its wake. Had there been two
Gumercindos, suggested a Federalist orator on the occasion of the
commemorative mass held in Melo by the Saravia family six months
after Gumercindo's death, the war would already be won, and many
Republicans expressed a similar estimation of the defunct hero. In his
official justification for carrying away Saravia's head, the responsible

Republican officer explained that profound scientific study of the cranium would lead to the discovery ("as mathematically must occur") of the constitutive principles of military genius. Despite the elegy offered by Melo's pro-Federalist newspaper, *El deber cívico,* explaining that the tombs of fallen heroes would become parapets for the fighters who took their places, the Federalist insurgency gradually ran out of steam in the year following the death of Gumercindo.[22]

Aparicio now permanently donned dark clothes in mourning (an important custom to borderlanders, who sometimes even covered their silver bridle ornaments with black cloth), and he did his best to repay the "atrocious insult" done to his brother's body. "Aparicio's on the way / Gumercindo didn't die," offered a hopeful Federalist bard in the pages of the *Canabarro* during the ill-fated final invasion led by Aparicio and Admiral Luís Felipe de Saldanha da Gama. Unfortunately for the insurgency, Gumercindo's replacements could not rival his efficacy in the field—though Saldanha da Gama, thanks to his own poignant martyrdom, did come close to eclipsing Gumercindo's aura in the Federalist imagination for a time. As for Aparicio, he had always declared his Uruguayan nationality, and, especially as the beleaguered insurgency moved toward a negotiated peace with representatives from Rio de Janeiro, Uruguayans in the Federalist ranks became an increasingly embarrassing political liability. Thus, while "the unforgettable name of the immortal Gumercindo" remained a Federalist talisman, Aparicio, whose montonera was one of the very last to lay down its arms, became utterly invisible in the Federalist press during the last months of the war.[23]

Aparicio's fame had begun in Brazil, but it resounded far more in Uruguay. While Gumercindo's wife Amélia returned to Santa Vitória after the war, and her children seem to have identified themselves as Brazilians, Aparicio returned to Uruguay, careening unexpectedly toward national influence there, and ultimately, toward his own death in an Uruguayan insurrection. "I'm Oriental I'm not Brazilian" (*llo soy oriental nosoy brasilero*) he wrote to Cándida in his own hand (and spelling) sometime in 1895, using the adjective—Oriental—that Uruguayans prefer to describe their own nationality. In the careers of the two Saravia brothers, the contrast between Uruguay and Brazil seems as important as the personal contrast between the two men. As we will see, the Uruguayan state was much less formidable an adversary for a borderland montonera when compared with the Brazilian state, and Aparicio's image as a hero drew resonance from an entirely different national context.[24]

12
OCTOBER 1895

When Aparicio Saravia returned from the Brazilian war in October 1895, a reporter from a major Montevidean daily rode out with the police escort that the Uruguayan authorities had designated to meet him at the border. Aparicio was returning to his estancia in Cerro Largo with the last two dozen Maragatos. The reporter found "the brother of the famous Gumercindo" a bit shorter than expected, sunburned from so many hours on horseback, and wary, but when the party halted at noon by a shady stream and brought down a cow for the midday meal, Aparicio's habitual suspicion of men like the city-bred reporter apparently subsided. As the two sat together watching the meat roast and drinking a brew out of Saravia's personal mate gourd, the reporter mentioned rumors, rife in Montevideo, that Saravia planned to lead a Blanco revolution against the Colorado government. Aparicio replied that an Uruguayan who loved his country should forget revolutions. Still, when the party rode on after eating, he reined his horse at one point and sighed, gesturing toward a smoothly contoured stretch of ground: "Here's a nice spot for a skirmish. . . . It's fun once you get used to it."[1]

Aparicio's acquired taste for lance charges seemed out of step with the Uruguay of 1895, a country no longer wracked with chronic civil war as it had been during so much of the nineteenth century. On the other hand, Uruguay was not yet characterized by the civil democratic traditions for which it became famous in the twentieth century. Au-

thoritarian modernizers comparable, in some ways, to the Rio Grandense followers of Júlio de Castilhos had seized control of Uruguay
in the mid-1870s and ruled for over a decade through military dictatorship, banning the partisan politics and brutally but efficaciously
imposing order on the countryside. The construction of railroads
and telegraph lines, the purchase of modern weapons for the army,
and the multiplication of rural police (including private police forces
such as the one formed by the Saravias) allowed authoritarian rulers
to gain a secure hold on the whole country and pass it, eventually, to
civilian Colorado governments. The civilian Colorados continued
to determine the outcome of elections through force, however. In
1893, one local official proudly announced to the central government
an electoral victory for local Colorados, an achievement all the more
praiseworthy, it seems, because they were "outnumbered four to
one."[2]

Landowners could now accelerate the importation of expensive
pedigreed livestock in the confidence that their investments would not
shortly be devoured by a passing montonera. Although affecting
southwestern Uruguay especially, the transformation of ranching
was extensive enough to generate increasingly profitable exports and
a matching optimism among the Uruguayan ruling classes. Their capital, Montevideo, quickly lost its somewhat traditional ambience of
an administrative and commercial city to become, by the turn of the
century, a cosmopolitan center of belle epoque society, with fashionable shops, cafés, parks, theaters, and beach front. Already in the
1880s, about half the city's inhabitants were recently arrived immigrants, Italians especially, like the reporter who interviewed Aparicio
Saravia in October 1895. Urban construction boomed as electric
streetcar lines radiated out to new immigrant neighborhoods. This
was a place in which unlettered rural men like Aparicio were considered (and felt themselves) to be complete rubes.[3]

In fact, Aparicio cut a somewhat rustic figure even in the town of
Melo, the administrative and commercial center of Cerro Largo,
where the Saravias rarely went. Although boasting no more than five
thousand inhabitants in 1895, Melo was distinctly an outpost of
urban society. True, many streets still became virtually impassable in
the long, heavy rains of borderland winters, the houses (painted in
pastel colors at the time, though no longer) remained compactly one-

storied, tile-roofed, and vernacular in style, and without a railroad, Melo lagged behind even Bagé regarding certain technological talismans of progress. The town's old theater threatened to collapse at any moment, and a measles epidemic like the one of 1889 could still carry away six hundred souls at one fell swoop. Leaving aside the lighted store windows that had made their debut in 1895, Melo did not mirror the physical transformation of Montevideo. But the old church of mud daub construction (its bell tower so low that mischievous boys could ring the bell with well-flung rocks) had at last been replaced with a more substantial structure. Melo now had four hundred agricultural chacras in its immediate environs, and a profusion of minor businesses, crafts, and trades—particularly busy in recent years thanks to the influx of Federalist émigrés. More importantly, Melo possessed well-developed institutional representations of national urban culture, from its legal system, public schools, and periodical press (which had produced twenty-eight different newspapers in the last three decades), to its "Venetian Festival" celebrated in boats on the small Tacuarí River, its recreational society organizing sports, picnics, and hunting events, its Club Wagner, and its social club boasting one of the best libraries outside of Montevideo. *El deber cívico*, published by the director of that library, was the most polished, responsible, and long-lasting small-town newspaper in Uruguay.[4]

Aparicio's rural neighborhood had shared little in the economic transformations of southern Uruguay or the cultural changes evident in Melo. His estancia El Cordobés (taking its name from the stream that flowed along one side of it) lay in isolated, rocky, and broken country with the lowest tax assessments in the republic. Encompassing two thousand hectares of pasture—a substantial spread, but modest by the standards of his parents' generation—the estancia had a main house of plastered, white-washed masonry and tile that stood in a hollow rather than on a hill because, according to Aparicio, enemies approaching in the dark could be detected by their silhouettes against the night sky. Aparicio had not had time to dabble in scientific husbandry, and rather than spend money on agronomical innovations, he and Cándida had invested their savings in a traditional manner, acquiring more unimproved pasture land across the Río Negro in the borderland districts of Tacuarembó and Rivera, seeking to accumulate a landed patrimony sufficient to give each of their six children a respectable estancia. The furnishings of their house, listed in the inventory done some years later, show they had not yet abandoned the sober simplicities of their parents' generation. Besides the relative luxury of an iron bedstead for themselves and another for each of their six children, El Cordobés resembled most borderland estancia houses in that it contained only rudimentary furniture. A table and chairs of exceedingly plain materials and workmanship (the chairs being appraised at eighty cents apiece), one equally plain dresser, a wardrobe, three washstands, a couple of mirrors, and an abundance of pillows completed the furnishings of the house. As had been true in his father's house, too, all furnishings together did not reach half the value of Aparicio's silver and gold inlaid harness and bridle. In the kitchen at El Cordobés, the skulls of cows and horses (the habitual, rude benches of the plains frontier) were arranged around an open hearth with no chimney. Aparicio and Cándida set a table without refinements, and they and their brood dressed like any other estancia family, making many of their own clothes. In the early years their children generally went barefoot, and one of them recalled his father often wearing the Guaraní chiripá instead of pants.[5]

Surely, though, this was before Aparicio became a general, a rank that he had officially received during the last phase of the Brazilian war. To be a general held large significance in this militarized society and attracted no little esteem among the borderlanders who gathered at November's important horse races in various neighborhoods of Cerro Largo. But if Aparicio's new prestige quite transformed his status in the eyes of his neighbors, he still had never been at the center of local power and conflict like Gumercindo, and he was not there now. His brother Chiquito, the comisario—fairer and taller than the other brothers and known for his open hand and boyish smile—came closer than Aparicio to being the neighborhood "caudillejo." As became evident in the early days of the coming insurgency, Chiquito could gather a larger group of personal followers among his neighbors than could Aparicio, who was a general without an army. The two brothers were about the same age, both high spirited and well liked among their neighbors, and they owned contiguous estancias. They seem to have been personally close, as well (Chiquito having helped look after Aparicio's family during the thirty-month Brazilian war), and Aparicio would be visibly shaken by Chiquito's death early in the coming rebellion.[6]

From Chiquito, and from other Blancos in the vicinity of El Cordobés, Aparicio heard the details of political developments in his absence, particularly of the widening rift between two factions of the Blanco party, a rift that undermined the party's existing leadership and provided an opening for the emergence of a new caudillo. Within a year of Aparicio's return from Brazil, the course of national political events, his influential neighbors, and personal motives that we can only suppose combined to put him once again at the head a montonera, directly challenging the authority of the current Blanco caudillo, Justino Muniz. By chance, Justino Muniz and Aparicio Saravia, the only two Blanco generals in Uruguay (saving valetudinarian exceptions), lived not far from each other and thus, according to the logic of borderland life, seemed destined to be rivals, much as Gumercindo had always clashed with the police authorities during his years as a local strongman. One imagines the spirit in which the people of Cerro Largo viewed that season's local horse races, in which the Muniz and Saravia families both fielded lead contenders. Odds are that most local Blancos favored Muniz, who exercised so much influence in that corner of the country that the military government of the 1870s and 1880s had been obliged to endorse his rule in Cerro Largo while insisting on Colorados elsewhere.[7]

Until now, the Saravias seem to have been careful not to cross Justino Muniz, though they may have voted against Municista candidates in 1887, during the first election to be held after a long decade of military dictatorship. Muniz determined the winner of that and the ensuing two elections in Cerro Largo, partly because of his popularity, but also because he left little to chance, using soldiers and police to intimidate and, occasionally, to intervene overtly in vote counts. Justino himself customarily went to his neighborhood polling place with a score of henchmen. One part of Cerro Largo where the Municistas appear to have polled fewer votes than their adversaries in 1887 was the Saravias' neighborhood. Nevertheless, in the government tally, the names of both Aparicio and Chiquito—along with most of their neighbors—appear as supporters of the officially victorious Municistas, but the government tally had plainly been "cooked" after the ballots arrived in Melo, simmering quietly for several days in the house of a Municista. There were so many witnesses to the manipulation of the vote count after the ballots arrived in Melo that opponents of Muniz made legal accusations of fraud, opening a formal inquiry, and El deber cívico published an alternative, allegedly unadulterated, list of votes in which only one Saravia, Aparicio's brother Mariano, appeared in the Municista column. An army detachment finally settled the matter by breaking open the strongbox where the ballots lay and issuing their own definitive count: a clear, if unsurprising, victory for the Municistas.[8]

Interestingly, no one from the Saravias' neighborhood was eager to continue the legal investigation—at least, not enough to come forward to provide corroborating testimony—and the matter was forgotten. In 1890, a few Saravias added their names to a list of 1,450 Muniz opponents in Cerro Largo, but Aparicio and Chiquito apparently demurred. Chiquito preferred not to antagonize Muniz, since he was about to assume the comisario's position in the Saravias' neighborhood and would have to work within the Muniz sphere of influence. Thus, the Saravias' accommodation with Municista rule in Cerro Largo allowed them to continue to control their comisariato through the mid-1890s, passing it eventually from Chiquito to Benito Viramontes, a brother-in-law. As long as they could exercise official power directly in their own neighborhood, the Saravias were willing to get along with Muniz, just as Muniz, for his part, was willing to supply votes to the national government (overtly Colorado after 1887) in return for its endorsement of Municista home rule in Cerro Largo.[9]

Justino Muniz would not easily be replaced by the new general in the neighborhood. Eighteen years older than Aparicio Saravia, large, battle-scarred, and bewhiskered, Muniz held strong claim to leadership in the Blanco party of Cerro Largo, having taken over as the party's caudillo from his uncle Angel Muniz, who had taken over, in turn, from his own uncle, Dionisio Coronel. The Muniz–Coronel family had local roots reaching back to the 1790s, when a Coronel had been among the original settlers of this Spanish outpost on the edge of Portuguese territory. This Coronel (who had come from Paraguay like many early settlers of Cerro Largo) had married a woman surnamed Muniz, and the couple had received a grant of land for an estancia and a town lot in Melo, where they built a house and founded something of a local dynasty well before the Saravias ever set foot in Uruguay. By the 1840s, their son Dionisio Coronel, a veteran of the war for independence against Brazil, exercised supreme powers in Cerro Largo—powers that included (if one cares to believe all credible reports) the power to confiscate property from enemies and reallocate it to friends, the power to lift and impose taxes at will and without remitting them to the national treasury, and most importantly, the power to wipe stubborn adversaries off the face of the earth altogether. And while one Coronel enforced the law (so to speak) another member of the family, Nico Coronel, illustrated the tendency of borderland strongmen to go freelance. Though he never occupied important political office, Nico's feats included the assassination of Gen. Justo José Urquiza, one of the most powerful men in Argentina, and, in murkier circumstances, the liquidation of an entire troublesome family during a midnight raid. Enemies of the Coronel clan (the inevitable source of negative reports) no doubt prolixly embroidered these transgressions, yet such stories are hardly unbelievable. Political "prestige" could not be maintained in the nineteenth-century borderland without violence or the threat of it.[10]

Justino Muniz, a rural strongman who could not read or write but wielded a lance famous for its heft and length, exemplified the caudillo of the mid-nineteenth century. He had succeeded his uncle Angel Muniz as the leading Blanco in Cerro Largo through family connections, of course, but Justino's family connections were not entirely auspicious and hardly offer a complete explanation of his rise. He had, in fact, been an illegitimate child (deserted by both father and mother before a year old) and he used the surname of his matriarchal grandmother, Catalina Muniz. Catalina provided family antecedents as good as any borderland caudillo could wish, however. One day in the 1830s, when an intruder tried to rape her daughters in her own house, Catalina sent him stumbling out the door with a knife protruding from his chest. Overall, Justino's celebrated boyhood duel against a much older neighborhood tough called "Longhaired Felisberto" and his battlefield exploits of the 1860s and 1870s best reveal the nature of his prestige. Justino's reputation had been dimmed a bit, in recent years, by his collaboration with Colorado governments in Montevideo. He had received his general's rank, for instance, as a political plum from the hand of a Colorado president, and such cozy relations with the ruling Colorados rankled deeply in Cerro Largo, a historical stronghold of the country's perpetual opposition party, where—or so the Blancos liked to brag—"the blood of men and cattle alike ran white." Yet who had more claim to Blanco leadership there than Justino Muniz? Muniz seemed to fear little from Aparicio Saravia, but that would change rapidly when the brother of the famous Gumercindo became a popular hero in 1896.[11]

13

THE MYTH OF THE PATRIADA

A s a hero, Aparicio would be different from Gumercindo: less feared but more beloved, less efficacious a commander but more attractive a symbol. The great mystery of Aparicio's career is his sudden rise to national leadership of the Blanco party in the period of less than a year. What enabled him, the unlettered son of Brazilian immigrants, to eclipse other prospective leaders well known to Blancos throughout Uruguay? Even more than has the career of Gumercindo, the career of Aparicio Saravia will challenge us to understand the will to believe in a hero. My argument is that, more than Gumercindo, Aparicio came to embody, in his followers' imagination, an attractive picture of their own shared identity, drawing on a well-established set of beliefs and images which I call the "myth of the patriada." The career of Aparicio Saravia suggests that during the hero's life this myth conferred on him what is sometimes called "charisma." Because myths live less in archives than in newspapers, political oratory, fiction, or drama, our exploration of the topic will lead us to that sort of source material. It will also lead us temporarily away from the figure of Saravia himself, because the patriada myth was born long before his rise as a leader, and its prior existence is crucial to this argument.

A few definitions will provide clear starting points for what follows. The Uruguayanism *patriada,* to begin with, refers to a revolt of montoneras. The first patriadas were the wars of independence, and Blancos then called their repeated nineteenth-century insurgencies patriadas as well. As for the word *myth,* it can mean many things, but here it refers to any image or story that holds transcendental significance at a particular moment, for particular people. For turn-of-the-century Blancos, to take the example at hand, the patriada myth offered something quite transcendental: moral regeneration. Blancos had once been heroic and virile, so the story went, but they had degenerated and become effeminate during their protracted, humiliating submission to evil Colorado tyrants. Only by imitating their warlike forefathers could the Blancos vindicate their masculinity and reclaim their lost political glories.[1]

So summarized a version provides little sense of how this story resonated for those who took inspiration in it. To get the requisite overtones, we must seek the tellings of those who felt the mythic qualities of the story. Some of the most skillful renditions of the patriada myth appear in the fiction of Javier de Viana, one of the major authors of the current Uruguayan literary canon. Viana spent much of his life as a partisan journalist and narrator, and is best known today for his collections of short stories, many of which first appeared in Blanco periodicals. The documentary value of Viana's early writings is enhanced, for our purposes, by Viana's direct experience in the borderland of the 1890s, where he edited a partisan newspaper of the kind that sprang up ephemerally before elections and dealt primarily in highly inflammatory personal invective. (Still in his twenties, Viana at one point publicly offered to fight the "miserable cowards" who surrounded the Colorado political chief and proclaimed himself "a thousand times *más hombre* than any of them.")[2] In the weeks before Aparicio Saravia's first Uruguayan rebellion, Viana wrote a most explicit (if slightly ironic) version of the myth of the patriada:

> On distant hills, the trumpet had sounded the call, and
> someone had glimpsed grim riders slipping through the hol-
> lows, mounted on war horses and carrying makeshift
> lances. Among the low trees, amid the long hills, one could
> hear a low murmur like a rising stream, the seething sound
> of rural rebellion. Farther away, daily work had ceased on
> the rich estates, and all was gloom and stillness, and be-
> yond, in the great and powerful capital city, young men of

refinement and education milled about—unquiet, determined, and brave—waiting to hurl themselves into the fight
at the first cry, their vigorous and selfless chests throbbing
with eagerness, expecting to see their elders unfurl the banner and raise it aloft. The long struggle had not yet ended.
New blood would mingle with so much blood already
spilled, and the clamor of combat would echo again
through the countryside like the voice of the archangel.[3]

This story, to which we will return later, exemplifies three key
elements of the patriada myth: manly chests, a generational passing of
the torch, and intimations of redemption through blood sacrifice. A
fourth element may be gleaned from the etymology of the word *patriada* itself. The root is *patria* (as in patriotic) followed by the suffix
-ada denoting action, and the phrase *hacer la patria* (what one did in
a patriada) helps clarify the sense. A patriada "made the patria."
Because Blancos felt themselves excluded from the political community by decades of Colorado tyranny, they believed that the true,
inclusive Uruguayan nation had not yet been formed. Several generations of Blancos had maintained a sense of collective identity
founded, in part, on this sense of themselves as an oppressed group.
In two generations, the Blancos had governed the country for only a
few short years, and they tended to remember the patriadas as the
defining events of their history.[4]

Memories of the patriadas were signaled by the colors white and
red, which gave no indication of party platform but instead invoked
a history of conflict between the Blancos and their Colorado enemies.
White and red "divisa" hatbands had first been used to designate
Uruguayan political polarities in a 1836 rebellion, when the followers
of Gen. Manuel Oribe identified their side with white ribbons and the
followers of Gen. Fructuoso Rivera adopted red ones. Ever afterward,
these colors in a divisa or neckerchief provided instant party identification in peacetime as well as wartime. The colors gave Uruguayan
borderlanders like Aparicio (whose strong feelings about white and
red became famous but do not seem to have been atypical) a way
constantly to reaffirm partisan identity. For example, the oil-cloth
coverings on estancia dining tables typically showed the family's political color. Aparicio, it seems, had been among the most adamantly

opposed among the Maragatos to adopting Federalist red as an insignia during the Brazilian war, and he evinced a marked preference for white among his cats, dogs, and chickens, not to mention his saddle horses. He had the interior walls of his ranch house painted with the white and sky-blue stripes of the Uruguayan flag (Muniz gave his house a similar paint job) and, on campaign at least, Aparicio would tolerate no red garments in his presence. This color coding was enthusiastically reciprocated by those on the opposite side, like José Saravia—along with Basilicio, one of the two Colorados among the Saravia brothers. José Saravia used only red paint on his estancia, had children at a nearby school wear red ribbons, and was said once to have returned a red bedspread to the store upon detecting a seam sewn with white thread.[5]

At this point, the gendered qualities of the patriada myth deserve specific comment. Like most physical violence in the borderland, patriadas were specifically masculine activities. As with other "patriotic" wars, however, the patriadas were envisioned partly as a collective defense of daughters, wives, and mothers. Women did serve the colors, but only in ways designated by their gender. For instance, Blanco women tended the white robes of the Immaculate Virgin, the Blancos' patron saint in the church at Melo while Colorado women favored the Nazarene Christ, dressed in crimson. Wives and companions sometimes sanctioned their men's participation in civil war by providing divisas they had embroidered personally. Women also sewed battle flags and presented them to their men in public ceremonies. During a patriada women were expected to tend the wounded and stoically endure the loss of sons or husbands.[6]

An Uruguayan stage play from 1897, Antonio N. Pereira's *Fratricidal Struggle and Conciliation: A Historico-Dramatic Sketch*, dramatizes the prescriptive gender roles of the patriada. In the play, several families are divided against themselves. The two daughters of doña Leonor, a stalwart matronly character, love two brothers who belong to opposite sides in the revolution, and both daughters protest the senseless conflict. Doña Leonor reproves them, declaring repeatedly that their father would have done just as the two brothers, and we learn that the girls' father perished in an earlier patriada. "As a wife and mother, I must grieve," announces doña Leonor, admitting the difficulty of her prescription. "I may be a woman / But as an

Oriental / I am proud to say / He did his duty." The play dignifies the character of doña Leonor and her message that men must go to war and women must let them go. As one of the brothers announces:

> *Each must maintain*
> *His beliefs and his party.*
> *We must give ourselves*
> *In defense of a cause.*
> *And I don't blame the man*
> *Who has different ideas.*
> *Shame only on those*
> *Who don't shoulder the burden*
> *Or hold to their creed*
> *(Whatever it is)*
> *Steadfastly with courage.*
> *For each is obliged, after all,*
> *To defend his party.*[7]

Thus, Admiral Saldanha da Gama's letter to Amélia Saravia after the death of Gumercindo in 1894 merely repeated a commonplace of the time in exhorting her to face her bereavement with the austere pride of a Roman matron. Did women aspire to live up to these socially prescribed requirements of womanhood? "Today I learned that they cut off my dear boy's leg," wrote Cándida Saravia to Aparicio when she heard her eldest son had been wounded in 1897: "I was very sad, but at least it happened defending his country and his father, because if it had been an illness it would bother me much more." Three more of her sons were wounded in 1904. Whatever the variations in women's behavior, we must suppose that the cultural standards always had some influence.[8]

Another example of the patriada myth will illustrate how its propagators could play persuasively on gendered identities. Uruguay's first major novelist, Eduardo Acevedo Díaz, was among the most assiduous exponents of the myth of the patriada. A radical partisan journalist since the 1870s, Acevedo Díaz had spent much time in Buenos Aires exile, where he published a cycle of historical novels about the first patriadas. In 1895, he returned to Montevideo, took over the Blanco partisan daily, *El nacional,* and launched an oratorical crusade that seems to have contributed significantly to preparing the party for the revolt of Aparicio Saravia. Like his historical novels, Acevedo's partisan journalism and public speaking referred often to the masculine exemplars of the heroic past. Now was the time for the "virile element" of the party to take inspiration in its epochs of greatest glory and regenerate itself by reenacting them. Scattered throughout Acevedo's inflamed editorials and, even more pervasively, in his hyperventilated oratorical campaign of 1895 and 1896 are explicit appeals to the redeeming power of the patriada: "Pull down the defiled altars of the Patria and raise others, though blood be spilled, for there is blood even on the images of Christ!" he fulminated during one of his speaking tours outside Montevideo. (One recalls the rhetoric of Angelo Dourado, who went so far as to envision his comrades in arms as illustrations in a *Book of Brazilian Martyrs*.) Modulating his presentation for a rural audience, Acevedo Díaz told his listeners that the Colorados saw them—these descendants of the "fiercest and most valiant caudillos"—as passive, inert, and by implication, feminized. When he addressed women, Acevedo Díaz took inspiration in the ideal of the Spartan mother packing her sons off to battle.[9]

The sometimes satirical stories of Javier de Viana contrast markedly with the ever solemn novels and oratory of Acevedo Díaz, though both authors draw on the patriada myth. Viana's disillusionment seemingly stemmed from his own experience in the disastrous Quebracho revolution of 1886, when, at the age of eighteen, he had stolen away from his mother to join the insurgents, begging her to understand his "sad and sacred duty to follow in [his] father's footsteps." The revolt was quickly crushed, and the resulting deaths of many of Viana's idealistic young companions apparently drained much of his enthusiasm for civil war. In a fictionalized description of the defeat, written not long afterward, Viana describes the bitter disillusionment of an urban youth watching the carnage. This "doctorcito" is an avid reader who, "in hours of burning hallucinations," had imagined the caudillos and their patriadas to be "the arm of God on earth, avenging and sacred." Viana's young protagonist reflects on the disappointing real-life qualities of his romantic heroes on horseback. The story further deflates the myth of the patriada by giving us the thoughts of the caudillo at the young man's elbow: a critique of suave but duplicitous "doctorcitos" with friendly smiles who manipulate rural people into patriadas using "the magic prestige of the symbol of partisanism" and then vanish, leaving them to pay the worst consequences of inevitable defeat. Interestingly, several of Viana's early stories paint ironical portraits of young Blanco agitators who seem modeled, at least partly, on his own experience as a political operative.[10]

Even the earlier Viana quotation about the trumpet, the grim riders, the selfless chests, and the voice of the archangel (cited to exemplify the spirit of the patriada myth) appears in a satirical context. The story's protagonist is an aged veteran—a humble agregado on an estancia in Cerro Largo—who tirelessly recounts his experiences in the wars of independence. Taken to Montevideo by the landowner to give the city's elite youth a dose of patriotic authenticity, the old warrior walks into a political club where he is scheduled to speak but where he finds nothing but effeminate dandies. His grieving heart bursts on the spot, and the thrilling patriada described in the cited passage never materializes. Thus, Viana's story condemns manipulative uses of the patriada myth—the rhetorical centerpiece of Acevedo's revival campaign, which organized clubs just like the one in the story—but it also plays on some of the same ideas, including the loss of patriotic virtue and virility. The juxtaposition of Viana's satire and Acevedo's furious, "frontal" partisanism helps us see how the uses of the myth were occasionally contested among the Blancos themselves. The texts of Acevedo Díaz and Viana also indicate that, by the early 1890s, the patriada myth had become an important constitutive element of the Blanco party's collective identity. The link between myth and identity is vital, because it helps account for Aparicio Saravia's sudden influence over a party that had scarcely heard of him before 1896, a party whose leadership was inclined at first to view Saravia as a Brazilian import.

The Blanco identity was structured, in some respects, like a national identity, and a discussion of this point will help explain why Eduardo Acevedo Díaz could appeal for masculine self-sacrifice on the battlefield in a manner exactly analogous to the appeals of wartime patriotism in international conflict. By the 1890s, some Blancos conceived of the party almost as a proto-national group (like the Children of Israel, wandering in the desert) defined in peoples' minds by images of heroic forebears and a shared past. It is no exaggeration to say that the basic polarities of Uruguay's two-party system were constituted more through narratives of war than through administrative programs, and nothing did more to crystalize the binary opposition between Blancos and Colorados than the decade-long Guerra Grande at mid-century. During the great siege of Montevideo (that led some to call the city a "New Troy") the Colorado government could not have survived without French and British assistance and, for most of that time, it effectively ruled only the streets of the capital, while outside the city walls the besieging Blancos ruled the rest of the country with their own president, ministers, and legislative institutions. Thus, for ten formative years Blancos and Colorados pursued parallel national visions, both attached to the same territory, and though the Blancos' separate institutions disappeared after the siege, the Blanco sense of a parallel nationalist project did not.[11]

During the two decades of continued partisan fighting after the Guerra Grande, each party added to its pantheon of heroes and martyrs and actively cultivated the memory of its conflicts with the other side. The Colorados erected a sculpture-studded crypt for their martyrs near the main gate of the Montevideo cemetery. The Blancos made do with more portable monuments like the long narrative poem *Los tres gauchos orientales* (1872) that enumerates battlefield deeds of partisan valor and devotion. Indeed, the importance of partisan writing in a number of genres reminds one of the role played by the print media in "imagining" national communities into existence all over the world during the last two centuries, and the Blancos' narratives of their shared past plainly reverberated in oral tradition, as well as in print. Manuel Coronel (a cousin of Justino Muniz who opposed him politically) wrote in the Melo newspaper about his childhood during the 1840s when he had gone to stay on the estancia of his grandmother, Manuela Muniz, while seven of her ten sons were away fighting for the Blancos. Coronel described long storytelling sessions in which folk tales about characters like "Juan Soldado" and "Pedro Malasartes" alternated with stories of battles between Blancos and Colorados. Coronel remembered learning reverence for the Blanco caudillo Manuel Oribe, "The Defender of the Laws," and practicing imprecations against the "savage" Colorado caudillo, Fructuoso Rivera, and his European accomplices. Twice, armed bands of Colorados had sacked his grandmother's estancia, forcing the family to emigrate temporarily to Brazil. Coronel also wrote stirring editorials protesting the electoral fraud that the Montevideo government euphemized in the early 1890s as its "directing influence." The Rio Grandense descendents of the Farrapos had honored their ancestors by revolting in 1893, lamented the Blanco editorialist. How long would the heirs of Artigas, Lavalleja, Oribe, and Rivera (Uruguay's great caudillos of the early and mid-nineteenth century) remain servile dupes of a tyrannical government? Echoes of Federalist rhetoric are not coincidental here, since Coronel expressed strong sympathy for their cause and himself wrote the elegy for Gumercindo (mentioned earlier) in which the tombs of the fallen become parapets for the next generation of heroes. To apply the metaphor to Uruguay, one merely changed the names on the tombstones.[12]

The twin imperatives of loyalty and revenge accumulated in almost half a century of patriadas had made being Blanco (or Colorado) a blood commitment. For nineteenth-century Uruguayans, especially rural borderlanders who equated politics with revolution, one's party was something to die for. Self-sacrifice in war demanded a transcendence of individual and family interests, a demand associated most often with nationalism, and the constant appeals for self-sacrifice in the patriada myth show that, at the turn of the century, Uruguayan partisan identities could compete with the official national identity for people's primary loyalty. The play *Fratricidal Struggle and Conciliation* explicitly illustrates the analogy between these two definitions of primary identity. Toward the end of the drama, after the character doña Leonor has established that self-sacrifice certifies the moral caliber of those who make it, her male counterpart, Colonel Valiente (the father of the warring brothers and the most authoritative figure in the play), comes on stage to build partisan reconciliation on that consensual point. Colonel Valiente relates the heroic deeds of doña Leonor's husband, who helped lead a famous lance charge against German mercenaries in the service of the Brazilian emperor during the Uruguayan war for independence. "Those were real battles! That was real courage! That was real patriotism!" Valiente takes this spiritual progenitor as a model, confirming the virtue of blood sacrifice but commemorating the wars of independence instead of partisan civil wars and thus redirecting the shared ideals of masculine duty and honor toward a more inclusive group identity. Valiente indicates that, in their willingness to risk all, his sons have shown themselves worthy of the name Orientales. Finally, one of them enters carrying his bleeding brother and announces that a peace has been signed. As a result of the bloodletting, the opposing sides have recognized their shared primary identity, and the brothers are able to embrace, while doña Leonor covers them with the national flag in a final tableau.[13]

The drama presents tidy schematic formulations of matters better conceived as hopelessly entangled in the messiness of life. Among the complexities not yet addressed at all is the presence of competing myths, such as the myth of progress—the panacea offered by capitalism, industrialism, rationalism, and science. The myth of progress coexisted competitively with the myth of the patriadas, both in discourse and in practice. Although Uruguayan playwright Florencio Sánchez made his reputation as founder of a national theater that highlighted rural, nativist themes, he could just as convincingly deploy the familiar rhetoric of material progress. Sánchez acknowledged his early zeal for the image of Aparicio astride a charger in his famous white poncho, and he was heard to shout the general's name "incessantly" during one battle in 1897, but later, in a different mood, he lamented seeing young intellectuals "searching the yellowed tomes, determined to uncover wisdom in the epic wars of our miserable American experience, instead of studying the beautiful scientific problems that stir contemporary minds."[14]

The discourse of science and progress jostled—in the contested terrain of people's political imagination—with images of collective identity and visions of redeeming heroism, and their response to Aparicio Saravia depended on how his image related to their other beliefs. People of progressive, urban orientation, excited by the social and economic transformations of the day, were unlikely to respond strongly to Aparicio Saravia. Nor can we posit a uniform charismatic response even among tradition-minded rural Blancos. The myth of the patriada cast no automatic spell over all members of the party. Some of Acevedo's listeners surely scoffed at his over-blown philippics, as Viana's satire plainly invited them to do. In addition, fervent believers could become disillusioned, as happened to Sánchez. Acevedo Díaz, who expressed elation that "virile" Blancos had finally offered "to water the beloved soil with their blood" when Saravia announced his initial uprising, did not long remain a Saravista, as we shall see. Javier de Viana's view of Aparicio took the opposite turn. Refusing to join the revolution of 1897, Viana donned a white divisa during the larger war that followed in 1904 and wrote some of the most misty-eyed contemporaneous descriptions of the caudillo.[15]

Among the borderlanders who composed the majority of Saravia's army, the hard times of the 1890s may have added special attractiveness to the patriada myth. Although not suffering personally, the Saravias lived in a generally depressed part of Uruguay, where the technology of production had hardly evolved and where even large landowning families—who measured well-being in square leagues of pasture—were beginning to feel overcrowded. It now took outstanding economic success (of a kind exemplified by the Saravias, with their rapid territorial expansion of the 1870s and 1880s) to allow a landowner of the 1890s to leave viable estancias to each of his children, as had been the normal goal for previous generations, and in a finite landscape, one family's territorial gain was necessarily another family's territorial loss. The psychological impact of hard times must remain a speculative matter, but it comports fully with the notion that social stresses often encourage charismatic response.[16]

As a final consideration before resuming the narrative, we should observe how a factional division within the party made Saravia's rise easier by providing an opening for new leadership. In many ways, the division represented differences between urban and rural Blancos. Ever after the Guerra Grande, the Blancos had remained dominant in the countryside that they had occupied throughout the war, and the Colorados had retained their hold on Montevideo. Of course, Blanco elites also considered Montevideo their capital city, and there were many Colorados in the countryside, so Uruguay's partisan dichotomy and its rural–urban dichotomy did not perfectly coincide. Every so often, Montevidean elites of both parties found common ground in their urban, progressive orientation and attempted a blurring of color-coded political divisions in order to work together, but country people were notoriously skeptical of bipartisan chicanery, believing that parties might pact, but never blur. They preferred confrontation (which yielded local control in areas where the party was particularly strong, like Cerro Largo) to cooperation (which yielded access to public employment in Montevideo). Control of the local comisariato meant more to most rural Blancos than did access to positions in the national congress and ministries. Young elite Blancos of urban orientation, on the other hand, often aspired to a political career and naturally valued representation (and employment) in the national government over the achievement of home rule for local strongmen. When elections began again in the late 1880s after a decade of military dictatorship, this polarization expressed itself in the party's leadership, dividing a majority faction rooted in the countryside (headed by caudillos like Justino Muniz) from an urban-oriented minority.[17]

In 1896–97, Aparicio Saravia would reunite the Blanco party, at least for a while. He was able to do so at the beginning because, like his brother Gumercindo, he had a reputation as an effective fighter, an experienced general who made a practical war leader for frustrated Blancos with revolution on their minds. Once in the field, however, Saravia's role as a practical war leader seemed less important than his function as a symbolic rallying point bringing together rural caudillos and urban doctores in a full-scale reenactment of the myth of the patriada.

14
MARCH-DECEMBER 1896

Aparicio Saravia's small Uruguayan uprising had its nucleus in a political club nourished by the heady rhetoric of the patriada myth. By mid-1896, twenty-five such clubs had been organized across Uruguay in solidarity with Eduardo Acevedo Díaz's campaign to revive Blanco "intransigence." Most were formed in Montevideo or in Uruguay's handful of major towns, including Melo—where three hundred members gathered on a March afternoon in the town's grassy park to hear the telegraphic exhortations of Doctor Acevedo Díaz. Before dispersing, this "Club Dionisio Coronel" (named in honor of the Cerro Largo's most famous Blanco caudillo) marched to the house of Agustín Muñoz, a veteran of the wars of independence, to wish him a happy one-hundredth birthday, and the club's directors (surnamed Coronel and Muñoz, respectively) summoned its members to weekly "gymnastic military exercises" that predictably infuriated the Municistas. The political chief of Cerro Largo later banned the military gymnastics and Acevedo Díaz incited the virile club men to ignore the ban.[1]

Rural Acevedista clubs—especially the "Club Gumercindo Saravia," formed by about fifteen-hundred Blanco true believers in late August—were even more threatening to the government. On the morning of the first meeting held by the "Club Gumercindo," groups of fifty to a hundred horsemen—their best white neckerchiefs carefully knotted, their mounts well-groomed and in dress harness—converged at the meeting site, each led by some landowner of local prestige, a graybearded Blanco captain, sergeant major, or colonel whose rank had been won in the party's glory days. When a thousand-or-so riders had arrived, a band (hired in Melo) struck up the national anthem, and the men listened hat in hand while the fifty-two women in attendance sang. The men then presented themselves for review by General Saravia, who had returned less than a year earlier from the Brazilian war. Aparicio ordered them to mount and led them in a parade while the women applauded and hired hands dismembered and roasted sixty cattle on spits over open fires—quite a carnivorous feast even by the standards of rural Uruguay, where mutton was becoming a common substitute for beef in the leaner 1890s.[2]

Although the powerful draw of the "Club Gumercindo" clearly owed much to the prestige of Aparicio, Chiquito Saravia seems to have done more to convene and organize the meeting. As comisario, Chiquito had established numerous friendships with influential Blancos in surrounding neighborhoods, and though the comisariato had now passed to his brother-in-law Benito Viramontes, Chiquito's networks of personal alliances remained operative. None of the Saravias, however, was the kind of public speaker who could confer political legitimacy on such a gathering, and that role fell to others. Despite its bucolic setting and attendance, the foundational meeting of the "Club Gumercindo Saravia" included no fewer than nine speeches. Sergio Muñoz, son of an important Blanco family whose estancia lay not far away and who seems to have been an important animating force in the club's formation, spoke first. Two other distinguished doctores from Melo also held forth, followed by Bernardina Muñoz (in praise of selfless Blanco soldiers past) and another woman (also related to the organizers) who discussed the partisan duties of mothers, wives, and virgins. The women then presented the club with an Uruguayan flag. Chiquito spread his poncho on the ground to collect contributions, and someone led vivas for Doctor Acevedo and General Saravia. Before leaving the next morning—after an evening illuminated, for the club's leadership, by a "historico-literary soiree" during which Aparicio and Cándida heard a patriotic recitation by their son—each of the ranking officers put himself and his men formally under the general's command.[3]

In the second half of 1896, rumors of revolution multiplied, and the Colorado government had to worry about news of maneuverings by other Blanco dissidents who had set up a "war committee" in Buenos Aires. A marked change in political mood had occurred throughout the country, and the Municista collaborationists of Cerro Largo felt increasingly isolated within the Blanco party. One Municista representative in the national legislature received catcalls from fellow Blancos on the floor of the legislature. Another Municista representative (Francisco J. Ros, the progressive agronomist who recommended the eight-hour prayer of progress) sent the Melo political chief worried letters from Montevideo describing "a dangerous heightening of political passions presaging untranquil days." Justino Muniz, he said, should sleep with one eye open. Of course, Muniz knew to expect trouble from the "Club Gumercindo" in the event of war, and he did take the precaution of removing Benito Viramontes from the comisariato in the Saravias' neighborhood, replacing him with a cousin of his own, but no one expected Aparicio Saravia to end up the leader of an entire Blanco revolution.[4]

Nor, apparently, did Aparicio expect to find himself back at war only a year after returning from Brazil. True, he did have some reason to want to prove himself, not having notably avenged the desecration of Gumercindo's body. The Brazilian war had ended in frustration for him, and the Federalists had begun to ignore him totally now, so that, when news of Aparicio's Uruguayan uprising finally broke, Gaspar Silveira Martins was at pains to say that Aparicio's importance in Brazil had been exaggerated. Silveira Martins attributed the uprising in Uruguay to the influence of flatterers who had surrounded Aparicio since his return to El Cordobés. Aparicio certainly had been the object of new attentions since returning from the Brazilian war. The men Silveira Martins called "flatterers" were probably members of the Muñoz family, Blanco partisans whose historical associations with the party rivaled those of the Muniz–Coronel clan, with deep roots in Aparicio's part of rural Uruguay but with strong connections to Montevideo, too.[5]

Converts to Acevedo's gospel of partisan intransigence, several educated members of the Muñoz family saw in Aparicio just the war leader that the Blanco revival movement needed. Sergio Muñoz became first one of the principal organizers of the "Club Gumercindo" and then Aparicio's secretary (secretary being the customary post of the "doctor" who inevitably accompanied a caudillo to draft his correspondence and public statements). Basilio Muñoz, Sergio's cousin, became one of Aparicio's most trusted commanders, later serving as political chief of Cerro Largo after the Saravista victory. Accounts written by Sergio and Basilio Muñoz constitute the only first-hand accounts of how Aparicio got himself into another revolution so soon after the Brazilian war. Totally unacquainted with the national party scene that the Muñoz family knew so well, and not possessing a local following like Chiquito, Aparicio took no active role in recruiting for the rebellion. His role, instead, was to be military figurehead. One finds Sergio Muñoz visiting Aparicio and Chiquito frequently during these months, sending them examples of the publicity given to the inauguration of the "Club Gumercindo" in the Montevidean press, and encouraging them continually with news of further promises of support from around the country. The club president, Ceferino Costa (who came from a "cultured" family among the Saravias' neighbors), joined the Muñozes in shuttling back and forth to Montevideo.[6]

The Blanco party's official directorate (itself not ill-accommodated to the status quo) still resisted the idea of revolution, however, and Aparicio finally volunteered to go to Montevideo with Basilio Muñoz for a personal meeting with the national leadership. The party directorate remained unmoved by the Muñoz–Saravia initiative and explained that there was no money for revolutions. In a gesture of selflessness that later became famous among his followers, Aparicio then offered to mortgage his property for money to buy arms, but the directorate remained adamant. Meanwhile, Eduardo Acevedo Díaz threatened to abandon his political pulpit if the November elections passed without some kind of popular reaction against the Colorados' manipulation of electoral results. According to the Muñoz accounts, the leaders of the "Club Gumercindo" believed that, without Acevedo Díaz, the "revolutionary spirit" of late 1896 would soon fade. When, in early November, Acevedo Díaz promised to "break his pen" and leave the country unless there were an uprising before the end of the month, Sergio Muñoz traveled a last time to Montevideo to assure the famed orator and journalist that a series of synchronous uprisings had been scheduled to coincide with election day.[7]

Aparicio's part of this "armed demonstration" against electoral fraud was to begin at an estancia he had recently acquired not far from the border, close to his old haunts in the headwaters of the Río

Negro, where the first meeting of yet another Blanco club had been announced for 25 November, with promises of a small band and a monumental barbecue. Chiquito set several men to work making lances, and horsemen began to gather on his estancia and on El Cordobés. A few were veterans of the Brazilian war, and more old comrades in arms from across the border were expected to be at the meeting on the twenty-fifth, but almost all let Aparicio down. (The sole exception was old Adão de Latorre, who never had to be invited twice to a revolution.) When Aparicio arrived with about eighty lancers at his property near the border, he found in attendance only the three Italian musicians contracted for the inauguration of the club. Aparicio explained to his crestfallen followers that, despite the look of things, the rebellion was even then being proclaimed all over the country, so they could not turn back now. Sergio Muñoz wanted to issue the formal proclamation that he had written (about honoring the party's "glorious antecedents" and sacrificing "generous blood"), but Aparicio was not much in the mood. "A viva for the Patria, a viva for the party, a viva for the revolution, and that's enough," he recommended. "The rest doesn't matter." Muñoz declaimed his composition anyway, and the band of Italians did their best to produce the requisite martial airs on clarinet, trumpet, and flute. Somewhat mollified, Aparicio offered them thirty pesos apiece to accompany the revolution.[8]

Then, for two weeks, Aparicio Saravia led what amounted, for the most part, to a traveling reunion of the "Club Gumercindo"—a column of horsemen that numbered close to a thousand at its zenith—overrunning a comisariato or two and trying to rendezvous with other rebel groups that had supposedly "pronounced" at the same time. In fact, however, no other Acevedista forces had joined Aparicio and the club's three colonels—Chiquito Saravia, Cornelio Oviedo, and Eusebio Carrazco—in the planned synchronous uprisings, and, like the Maragatos in early 1893, this was an army in which only about one in ten had a gun. At the tiny hamlet of Sarandí del Yí, the revolutionaries captured a cache of thirty firearms and received divisas and a flag from the local Blanco women, but they also got the bad news that the larger movement had not materialized as promised. The men around Aparicio became nervous at the rising tenor of his excitement when, coming in sight of enemies wearing red divisas, their leader began to shout things like: "I'm Aparicio Saravia! Come kill me, you savage!" Aparicio behaved even more recklessly as his frustration increased. Confronted by a sizable government force, he brandished his lance and summoned whoever wanted to follow him in a charge. His sons, Gumercindo's son, and some other young men were ready to do so, but more experienced officers surrounded him and restrained him. After Aparicio calmed down, he led his armed demonstration back north into the woods of the Río Negro, where it began to break up. An army patrol was waiting to finish off his last sixty followers at the Brazilian border, but Aparicio's old friend Adão de Latorre appeared with enough lancers to save the day, allowing the last of the failed insurgents to cross the border into Brazil.[9]

Aparicio had good reason to be frustrated. One of the movement's very first objectives—entrusted to Chiquito, who sounded his call to rebellion in the Saravias' own neighborhood—had been to invite Gen. Justino Muniz to join the revolution, but the attempt miscarried terribly, leading to a shoot-out and fire at a rural store belonging to the general's son-in-law. A sixteen-year-old son of Muniz died in the blaze, and with him, all hope of avoiding a showdown with the caudillo of Cerro Largo. Aparicio's fast-moving column had avoided a clash with Municista forces, but his house and Chiquito's had been ransacked, along with the house of Benito Viramontes. Their cousin Cesáreo Saravia had openly joined the Municistas and, rewarded with the comisariato of the Saravias' neighborhood, began to hunt those members of the disbanded revolutionary column who still hid in the woods along the Río Negro. News of throat cuttings there now confirmed the reputation for ruthlessness that Cesáreo had gained in the Brazilian war. (In later years, Cesáreo had to surround his house with a dozen particularly large and fierce dogs as a precaution against revenge seekers.) Cándida and her younger children had long since traveled to a small piece of property in Bagé that she and Aparicio had bought precisely for such occasions, and he retreated there now to consider his next move.[10]

Aparicio hardly meditated in solitude, however. Soon he had visitors from as far away as Montevideo and Buenos Aires, attracted by his sudden national visibility as the caudillo of the opposition. Eduardo Acevedo Díaz was spotted in the Brazilian bordertown of Jaguarão, presumably on his way to meet with Saravia, and, in a letter, the celebrated orator directed fulsome praise to the caudillo and regards to his intrepid brother, Chiquito. Another inveterate revolutionist, Abdón Arósteguy, who represented the Blanco war committee of Buenos Aires, wrote to Aparicio and then joined him in Bagé, where he began to gather a group of young doctoral types who wanted to be part of the next revolution. Chiquito Saravia, Basilio Muñoz, and Benito Viramontes traveled to Buenos Aires to secure help from the Blanco war committee in acquiring weapons. For the first time in a generation, urban dissidents saw the opportunity to join forces with a credible rural caudillo. Somehow, despite its multifaceted failures, the uprising of 1896 had moved the Blanco party decisively toward a larger insurgency the following year. Within weeks, the imminence of a civil war was taken for granted in Montevideo, and that city's stock exchange plummeted. In Melo, *El deber cívico* had condemned all political recourse to arms and blamed the revolutionaries for the unfortunate incident involving the son of Justino Muniz but found itself muzzled for almost three weeks by the Muncistas anyway. The paper stopped publishing altogether in mid-February 1897, apparently considering that counsels of moderation now fell on deaf ears.[11]

On the other hand, the paper's last issue contained a hint of something that Uruguayan borderlanders seemed quite eager to hear. A small traveling circus was in town, one of many that featured a daredevil acrobat or two and promised to end its program with a performance of "Juan Moreira," the swashbuckling melodrama of a courageous Argentine countryman forced, by cruel destiny and by his own pugnacious sense of honor, to lead a life of crime. (Perhaps the story had particular resonance in Cerro Largo, where people celebrated the memory of a local desperado named Tomás Moreira, another good man gone wrong.) Although an outlaw, the gaucho character Juan Moreira exercised a clear attraction among Argentine and Uruguayan audiences who saw—or wanted to see—themselves in the nativist attitudes he represented. Something analogous, I believe, happened with Aparicio Saravia during and after the Uruguayan revolution of 1897.[12]

15

A COUNTRYMAN IN REBELLION

To Uruguayans of the 1890s, Aparicio Saravia represented a rural culture and identity. In calling him a "gaucho," those who adored him agreed perfectly with those who despised him, and Aparicio appears to have enjoyed and played to that image. "He makes himself more gaucho than he really is," asserted one of his early biographers, a Colorado who knew him and his family and wrote of them sympathetically in a Montevideo newspaper. Gumercindo's hero legend had similar overtones, as we have seen, but "gaucho" nativism had a larger resonance in the case of Aparicio. Since well before his birth, since before his family came to Uruguay, in fact, the gauchesque tradition—exemplified particularly in popular verse—had constituted an important element in an emerging discourse of Uruguayan (as well as Argentine) national identity. The defining aspect of this nativist discourse was its celebration of rural culture, always more closely associated with the Blancos (because of their predominantly rural base of support) than with the Colorados. During the century since his death, the figure of Aparicio Saravia has offered enduring inspiration to Blancos for whom the memory of the patriadas or the symbols of "gaucho" nativism hold transcendent meaning. Can certain yearnings for self-loss and belonging also help explain the charismatic response to Aparicio Saravia during his life?[1]

Aparicio's was not a mesmerizing gaze, and he did not exude any unusual personal magnetism. One does not find stories of passersby becoming suddenly spellbound by a chance encounter with him. Nor does charismatic response seem to have been important in the making of his 1896 insurrection. When, at one point during that uprising, Aparicio became overwrought and was prevented by his officers from leading a reckless charge, his influence over them seemed limited enough. Likewise, *Chronicle of the Insurrection: Its Origin, Beginning, March, and Defeat,* an 1896 pamphlet, points out that Aparicio's prestige was, at the time, significantly "reinforced by that of his late brother, more powerful and better deserved than his own." The serialized pamphlets called *The Echo of War: Scenes of the Present Campaign with Illustrations of its Principal Leaders; Biographies, Episodes, Anecdotes, Sacrifices, Examples of Heroism, Etc.,* which appeared during the 1897 insurgency, picture Aparicio as one in a gallery of leaders, not the overwhelmingly central figure that he becomes in later, retrospective descriptions of the war. Apparently, Aparicio gained his original followers primarily because he was the only experienced general available, and he became a transcendental hero only gradually, during the course of the war and then after it as a result of the victory. Pamphlets like *The Echo of War* and *Chronicle of the Insurrection* (which might express reservations about Aparicio's leadership but also featured his bearded face on the cover) documented that process and served as its vehicles.[2]

The expansion of public education and the development of the print media in turn-of-the-century Uruguay gave Saravia's image a new sort of projection among those who never saw him personally. About five thousand men, altogether, rode with General Aparicio (as they tended to call him) over the course of the six-month war, but many more people read about the "countryman in rebellion" in newspapers and pamphlets. While only Angelo Dourado, among the Maragatos of 1893, published a detailed account of the campaign and its hero, the Blanco insurgent army of 1897 had, quite literally, a battalion of chroniclers. Among those on hand to record their impressions were a number of more-or-less canonical figures of Uruguayan literature (Florencio Sánchez, Carlos Roxlo, and Eduardo Acevedo Díaz) as well as Saravia's twentieth-century successor at the head of the Blanco party, Luis Alberto de Herrera, and Abdón Arósteguy—historian, revolutionist, journalist, and dramatist. Several of them had a chance to write the proclamations, manifestos, and correspondence issued by General Saravia over the course of the war. Literary topics formed a regular part of these men's campfire discussions, and some even tried to publish peripatetic newspapers for the army. Herrera managed to print a few issues of a sheet he called *La revolución oriental,* and Florencio Sánchez wrote out *El combate* by hand in a manner that mimicked normal newspaper layout. These newspapers have been lost, but the published narratives that survive offer the best window we have—despite its inevitable tint—on the experience of Saravia's insurgent army.[3]

Therefore these chief chroniclers of the campaign and disseminators of Aparicio's image must occupy our attention disproportionately. Many of them were young men in their twenties, sons of elite Blanco families who joined the revolution in a spirit not unlike Theodore Roosevelt's in going to "rough it" among the cowboys, or, even more analogously, organizing the Rough Riders to fight in Cuba. The revolution's chroniclers were acutely conscious of being *puebleros* (in the Uruguayan expression), urban men viewed as pathetic tenderfeet by the countrymen who composed the vast majority of the insurgent volunteers. The young men from Montevideo congregated in a "Patria Battalion" that did not number more than a few dozen but seems to have swarmed around the general, operating as a staff of aides and secretaries. They yearned to prove themselves physically in the strenuous life of the campaign. Luis Ponce de León (poet, orator, founder of the fire-eating Blanco newspaper *El nacional*) recalled encountering his friend Luis Alberto de Herrera during the campaign and finding the Montevidean "dandy" transformed—made stronger and more robust—by his new life. These young men were also searching the rural interior of their country for a sense of authentic national identity—much like Brazilian journalist Euclides da Cunha, who reported on the millenarian uprising of Canudos in northeastern Brazil during that same year. Interactions with Aparicio Saravia ranked among their chief delights. Ponce took obvious pleasure in announcing, at the beginning of his published war diary, that "by a special favor of General Saravia, my cousin Rodolfo . . . and I were the only puebleros who lived with him on his property" in Bagé during preparations for the 1897 invasion. In a letter to Aparicio, Ponce's contemporary, the poet Carlos Roxlo, wrote longingly: "I want to believe that you haven't forgotten the *maturrango* who loves you dearly." *Maturrango* means clumsy horseman, a concept that borderlanders elided into "urban outsider."[4]

A close personal connection to Saravia would become a political asset for young Blancos interested in political careers at the turn of the century, when longtime Colorado control of the national state, immigrant domination of commercial and industrial activities, and a proliferation of advanced degrees among native-born males combined to frustrate the ambitions of many. "It is hard, very hard, to get even a poor position," wrote a friend to Javier de Viana, speaking, for the most part, of public employment of the kind that young men of native elite families had traditionally considered the next step after a law-school education. Thus, *The Advantages and Disadvantages of the Growing Number of Persons Acquiring Degrees to Exercise Liberal Professions in Our Country* ranked among the "palpitating" public issues of the time according to a pamphlet published by Luis Alberto de Herrera a few years later. Herrera was arguing against the "common consensus" that overproduction of professional degrees explained the chronic underemployment of elite males, but whatever the cause, advantageous employment for young elite males was clearly scarce.[5]

Puebleros and borderlanders came from different worlds, and during the campaign they tended to associate with their own kind. Ponce mentions intimate conversations that could easily begin, in the camaraderie of the march, among "friends from the same town or of identical social condition." Like some of the others, he was accompanied on the campaign by a (black) personal "assistant." Herrera, who became the most popular of the Montevideans among the army at large, nevertheless lets slip an occasional sign of revulsion for rural people. Witness the occasion in which he and an (urban) friend took shelter for the night in the miserable house of a poor man who, much to Herrera's disgust, turned out to have tuberculosis. Finding that Herrera's friend was a physician, the man offered them every comfort that he could, in hopes of receiving a cure. "It was really funny to see the emaciated Brazilian, still young despite his yellow complexion, bestowing a thousand attentions on his future savior," recalled Herrera. The next morning, the physician offered his patient a discourse salted with fancy words and prescribed an herb tea with assurances that it would cure the tuberculosis in two weeks. The two visitors then rode away laughing about their misadventure.[6]

Young men like those of the Patria Battalion thus came from a social context so distant from that of their rural comrades in arms that one wonders how they made common cause. The Saravista army—including young doctors of laws with a need to advance their political careers, borderland ranchers and agregados with personal commitments to maintain, and indigent countrymen with nothing to lose—did not rally around a set of overt goals relating to their disparate material interests. Whatever their individual interests were, members of the army seldom talked about them publicly. This was more a matter of taste than of secrecy, for they regarded the injection of personal interests as inappropriate to the matter at hand. On the contrary, selflessness and transcendence of all personal interests, material and otherwise, were the values they celebrated. Ponce wrote home that he relished being "among the true-hearted country folk, without ambition, capable of a thousand sacrifices for the cause," and he found Aparicio's son Nepomuceno to resemble the type of "legendary countryman" he had read about. As has already been suggested, the will of certain Uruguayans to believe in Aparicio Saravia had much in common with the same yearning for self-loss that gives modern nationalism much of its emotional force. Several different definitions of collective identity seemed to intersect and sometimes to compete for primacy in their minds: family, party, and nation (the three at issue in the play, *Fratricidal Struggle and Reconciliation*), along with a fourth—the army itself.[7]

Even after the victory of 1897, when he had become the second most influential man in Uruguay after the Colorado president, Aparicio stayed away from Montevideo, and, except for the people of Melo, urban Uruguayans knew him only through the press. In contrast, the members of his small army saw him every day. Evidence about how they viewed him is sketchy but unanimous on one point. The private soldiers of the army gave him "their love and confidence." His equestrian skills and knowledge of the cattle country constituted a key element of this rapport, an affinity that had linked many prior caudillos to their armies as well. Unlike Gumercindo, Aparicio frequently joined the fighting himself, leading lance charges on more than one occasion. On the march, he could always be seen at the head of the column, and at night he wandered from campfire to campfire talking and drinking mate with the men. Aparicio was reported never to eat unless his men had food, and then to content

himself with unsalted meat, thrown directly on the coals. A reporter
from a Montevidean daily found Saravia's intimacy with his soldiers
undignified and sneered at his improvised tent with a lance for a
ridgepole, where (Aparicio told the reporter—probably in jest) the
army's general slept in a pile with other men to keep warm. "Saravia
is truly idolized," wrote the reporter, a Colorado. "They think him
not only the bravest of the brave, the caudillo par excellence, but also
a man of vast military knowledge."[8] Aparicio's detractors could scoff
all they wanted, for his followers continued to rhapsodize, even in
private letters like this one written in May 1897:

> Enduring all kinds of physical trials, he keeps vigil while
> others sleep, not surrendering to the rigors of the weather,
> exhaustion, or any other material need. In the fight, he's
> everywhere at once, seeing everything, not still for an in-
> stant. In sum, he is worthy to be our general.[9]

In camp, on the march, and during the fighting, Aparicio's column
developed a sense of group identity rooted in comradeship and in a
mutual enthusiasm for their leader. Long war memoirs like Ponce's
The Revolution of 1897: Intimate Impressions, Scenes, and Episodes
(1898) and Herrera's *For the Patria* (1898) are full of anecdotes
reminiscent of high-spirited young men establishing the dynamics of
group interaction on any outdoors adventure. The army assigned new
nicknames to its members, for example, and maintained elaborate
running jokes mystifying to the uninitiated. Certain whistled tunes
were on everyone's lips. Above all, the army agreed about the splen-
dors of its affable general. Ponce describes a brief rest during which
his group lay on the grass in a large circle, each man resting his head
on the knees of the next in a sort of daisy chain that included General
Saravia as one of its links, and he frequently calls Aparicio the army's
"father."[10]

The wider and more enduring charisma of Aparicio Saravia was
that which extended beyond the few thousand men who composed
the Saravista army—and beyond Saravia's own death—to make him
one of the most popular Uruguayan heroes of the twentieth century.
"Let us carry out the orders of Aparicio!" exhorted an undaunted
Blanco publication after the collapse of the last patriada in 1904, and

three generations later, the party's newspapers and election paraphernalia continued to display Saravia's image, and Blanco poets and songwriters gave evidence of the feelings that the image could still evoke. Somehow, "Aparicio Saravia [had] incarnated the sacred image of the Patria," at least for those with the will to believe. To see how he could plausibly do so, we must view him in the context of the nativist discourse of turn-of-the-century Uruguay.[11]

Admittedly, his image elicited a wide variety of responses among Blancos. In the figure of Aparicio Saravia, rural borderlanders saw the best of themselves—the peerless horseman, the courageous lancer, the sharp-eyed tracker and guide, and the consummate "gaucho" who did not hesitate to throw a lasso in the presence of a highly expert and notoriously critical audience. The young doctores, for their part, saw an "authentic" emblem of national identity: "the bravest among the brave, the Bayard of our nationality, . . . the father of his soldiers, the best of the sons of this land, the greatest of its citizens, the most beloved and admired of all the Orientales." Those less enthused by nativist imagery might call him "a Cid Campeador who had never trod the chambers of the king or attended the noble jousts of the court." But in any case, Aparicio's rustic associations were always inescapable, and his enemies also made the most of them. Duvimioso Terra, a doctoral member of the Buenos Aires war committee, quickly quarreled with Saravia during the war and rushed into print with an angry description of "the rustic citizen, [who] according to a chronicle recently published in *El nacional,* often wanders alone through the wilderness of El Cordobés, sleeping at the feet of his horse." Terra's open letter of protest, published first in several newspapers and later as a pamphlet, accuses Aparicio of uncouth manners and of inept generalship due to his obsession with a trivial, local rivalry with Muniz. "According to his own words, he only knows how to lead lance charges," fumed the sorely insulted Terra, "with a lance in one hand and a knife in the other." As for Acevedo Díaz, his public praise of Aparicio was measured, indeed, for one so given to purple prose. In his description, Saravia is sincere, generous, and appropriately modest, but also distinctly "raw" and "campesino" (a word with the supercilious nuance of English *peasant*) and there is a studied ambiguity in the celebrated orator's description of Aparicio calmly drinking mate amid the droning bullets, before handing the mate gourd to an aide, hefting his lance, and galloping off toward the thick of the fight.[12]

Those who wanted to discredit Aparicio as a Blanco leader also seized on another, quite obvious, political vulnerability. "The countryman Saravia," announced a former Municista legislator in the political diary that he published annually, "is a genuinely Brazilian personage." Duvimioso Terra (not without Rio Grandense connections of his own) carefully used the original Portuguese spelling, Saraiva, in his furious and almost interminable public letter of self-justification, and Justino Muniz referred to him routinely as "the Portuguese Aparicio." This critique undercut Aparicio's status as a symbol of Uruguayan national authenticity and played on the supercilious Montevidean attitude toward borderland "hicks" with Portuguese accents. Javier de Viana tried to defend Aparicio by pointing out that Aparicio's use of *rompido* for *roto* ("breaked" for "broken") actually reflected his Rio Grandense background, since *rompido* is standard usage in Portuguese. Of course, some of Saravia's soldiers (many of whom were Luso-Uruguayans like him) surely felt a thrill of identification on hearing the same Portuguese locutions that made the Montevideans wince. If Aparicio's constant affirmations of Uruguayan nationality during the Brazilian war—and his tendency to speak Spanish even there—helped blunt the jabs against him, most people who disregarded them seem to have done so because of their will to believe in the hero.[13]

Signs of his identity as a native gaucho reassured the doubters. Aparicio's country abilities (like skill at roping cattle) and country habits (like his unquenchable thirst for mate)—both amply chronicled by his eulogists—have already been mentioned. His country speech, freed by transcription of its Brazilian tinge, constituted another identifying sign, a particularly important one, since it resonated strongly with the gauchesque tradition in popular literature. Aparicio always spoke with *"sal criolla"* (creole spice), reminisced a Blanco veteran. "He understood that we puebleros liked that." Ponce described the general's "picturesque" speech as punctuated every five minutes by colorful sallies that Aparicio himself celebrated with his "frank and thunderous laughter." Nor was the appeal of "sal criolla" limited to urban people in search of rural authenticity, as one can deduce from a rural folk song, sung in later years, that lovingly dwells on Saravia's

"gauchesque expressions." The general's newspaper biographer devoted a special section to "The Sayings of Aparicio," and, concerned
that some of his readers might find Aparicio's language "too picturesque to be real," he explained that "the caudillo speaks a figurative
language, full of tropes and metaphors," precisely—though this went
without saying—like the gaucho Martín Fierro and many other characters of the period's gauchesque verse and fiction. Some of Aparicio's famous phrases show the earthy, aphoristic sagacity that
witnesses agree in attributing to him. "You can't make a good corral
with rotten posts," he said, referring to the deserters from his army.
More sonorous phrases ("the Patria means dignity on high and joy
below") usually came from the manifestos, proclamations, and letters
produced by his secretaries. Aparicio's few surviving private letters
make clear that anything he wrote would have to be substantially
"doctored" in order to meet the exacting rhetorical standards of Uruguayan public discourse at the turn of the century.[14]

Articles of "typical costume" constituted other important signs of
nativist identity, and descriptions of Aparicio written during the 1897
war seldom omit details of his dress. The general's "gaucho" apparel
was of fine wool and silk, hardly rustic in the sense of "crude," but it
conveyed a cultural affiliation much like that signaled by snake-skin
cowboy boots in the twentieth-century United States. "I like the General," wrote Carlos Roxlo in issue number six of *The Echo of War*.
"He dresses as a countryman, but dresses well, with black poncho
and jingling spurs of fine silver." (Aparicio's poncho had been the
color of the Uruguayan flag until he dyed it black in mourning for
Chiquito's death in 1897.) "The general's clothes are attractive, and
he carries them well," wrote Herrera after first seeing Aparicio, and
proceeded to describe his broad-brimmed hat with its famous divisa
(embroidered with the slogan "For the Patria"), his black jacket and
pants, his high patent-leather boots and spurs, his fringed silk poncho, and his neckerchief fastened with a golden clasp in the form of
crossed Uruguayan flags. "I can still see him there," Herrera effused,
"he who saved the honor of the Orientales." After the war, visions of
a Saravia clad in chiripá and toeless boots for his daily activities
became an obligatory topic of conversation in Montevidean political
clubs, producing horror in some and delight in others.[15]

Party merges with nation in the Uruguayan insurgent discourse of the 1890s, and, for true believers, Aparicio "incarnated" both: nation, through his embodiment of nativist definitions of national identity; party, because of his role as Blanco caudillo in a reenactment of the patriadas. "I felt as if I were taking part in a legendary episode, one that transported me to another epoch," wrote Abdón Arósteguy of the day when Saravia's army of several hundred crossed the border from Brazil: "It had the same effect on me as the heroic invasions of Artigas that I'd learned about in school." In fact, the day chosen was 5 March, anniversary of the day in 1870 when Blanco general Timoteo Aparicio (in whose honor, incidentally, Aparicio's younger brother Timoteo Saravia was named) had begun the last major patriada, sometimes called the Revolution of the Lances. The army's habit of calling Saravia "General Aparicio" contributed to the blending of his name with that of the earlier caudillo. Herrera says that the figure of the caudillo and the scenes of fighting with lances brought history-book images to his imagination, as well. Oral tradition, for its part, eventually provided Aparicio with a suitable hero legend linking him to the Revolution of the Lances, and if there is no convincing evidence that he really ran away at the age of fourteen to join the montonera of a tough war captain with a taste for lance charges—as the legend goes—the notion is far from incredible.[16]

Aparicio did, after all, know something about lance charges, and thus he could easily represent the party's warlike past in the eyes of his eager young followers. Whenever one of them bewailed the overwhelmingly superior resources of the government forces, Aparicio minimized the importance of the insurgents' lack of guns: "If we have to, we'll fight as men did before, with knives and lances, or aren't Orientals up to that anymore?" On the eve of the battle of Cerros Blancos, Aparicio bought a cartload of knotty cane to make famous *tacuara* lances, a stock element of the patriada myth, and, laying aside his own silver-trimmed weapon, he put on a sturdy glove and demonstrated the handling of a tacuara for the army. No one, it seems, was really eager to use the things, or at least, so Aparicio's jocular approach to the demonstration and Herrera's dubious description of it appear to indicate. Certainly, the lance's value as a symbol of the old patriadas outweighed its advantages as a weapon for the new ones. One Blanco commander topped his flag staff with an ornate lance head that had once belonged to a famous Blanco martyr of the 1860s, and Ponce describes how an old veteran tearfully kissed the lance head his father had carried during the wars of independence when the insurgents surrendered their arms at the end of the 1897 war.[17] The chroniclers of 1897 also gave special attention to another grizzled veteran, Fortunato Jara, a septuagenarian who had fought in the party's "legendary struggles" since before the Guerra Grande. Fortunato Jara received cheers from the admiring younger men before the battle of Cerros Blancos, died there leading them in a charge, and then received the unusual honor of an official wake when he was laid out, surrounded by candles, on the counter of a nearby country store. Old Jara, one might think, provided as apt a patriarchal figure as the army could desire, and Herrera (who specifies Jara's age as seventy-seven but later makes him eighty for good measure) provides a roll call of gray-haired colonels who constituted other living links with patriadas past.[18]

Yet it was the much younger Aparicio whom the insurgents insisted on calling "father," a final clue for us to consider in exploring his charisma as a caudillo. First, witness Ponce's description of the tearful farewells at the end of the campaign, "the scene becoming most tender when a poor, and not so young, soldier went to embrace the General, and after doing so, called out in a voice broken by sobs, LONG LIVE OUR FATHER, GENERAL SARAVIA, and all present instantly took up the chorus." Borderlanders assigned the battlefield an important place in the relationship between fathers and sons. The elder sons of Gumercindo, Aparicio, Chiquito, and Basilicio all went to war with their fathers, though (perhaps significantly) none played an important role. In 1897, Basilicio's son Carlos—a Blanco—nevertheless accompanied his father's Colorado contingent, but he did refuse to wear a red divisa. Angelo Dourado told many battlefield stories of fathers and sons in *Volunteers for Martyrdom*. In one, a father captures the enemy who killed his son and forces the killer to take his son's place; another father meets his son (who is fighting on the opposite side) in battle, with tragic results; a third father hears of his son's death elsewhere on the field, but refuses to leave his post. (A story similar to the last was told of Aparicio when his eldest son lost a leg in 1897.) These stories have various implications, but all reveal a clash of loyalties, the tension between allegiance to kin and allegiance to something larger. At issue, once again, is collective identity.[19]

The fact that a man older than Aparicio (for that is clearly Ponce's implication in the scene recounted above) called the general "father" demands further explanation, too. We learn from Ponce that Aparicio's two flesh-and-blood sons with the army did not belong to his inner circle (that is, share his campfire). Does this indicate a kind of cognitive dissonance among the competing formulations of paternity? Did the general's status as "father" of his soldiers lose credibility if his biological sons were too much in evidence? Ponce seems to reveal this principle of mutual exclusivity when he says Aparicio left the army after the war to attend his wounded son and "become a father again." Thus, the evidence suggests the pattern of group psychology that Sigmund Freud believed common in creating an extraordinary esprit de corps in certain armies. The soldiers' belief in the leader's paternal love makes them, by analogy, brothers. One recalls the anecdotal insistence of Blanco chroniclers on Aparicio's refusal to eat scarce food, his late-night vigils over the sleeping army, his frequent expressions of affection for his men. If Aparicio Saravia's charisma came partly from his ability to incarnate cherished signs of Blanco heritage and values, it also came partly from this extension of kinship feelings to embrace the whole Blanco "family."[20]

Aparicio's followers considered family to be a natural locus of primary loyalty and blood commitment, and those who promoted the imagined communities of party and nation often made use of familial metaphors precisely for that reason. Aparicio vindicated the honor of the party, in the eyes of his followers, because he led them in responding to Colorado "insults" with masculine violence in a manner analogous to the defense of family honor. As we have seen, this analogy lay at the heart of the myth of the patriada, as invoked by Acevedo Díaz in his incessant appeals to vindicate Blanco "virility." Family likewise formed a necessary frame of reference for *Fratricidal Struggle and Reconciliation,* the drama of consensual values presided over by the characters of doña Leonor and Colonel Valiente, in which women stoically bore their personal losses while the men disputed the question of which group, beyond the family, should receive their primary loyalty. Aparicio's offer to mortgage his property—the patrimony of his children—to buy arms for the revolution was often used to represent an impressive transcendence of narrow interests. A Blanco publication of 1905 provides an explicit articulation of the idea:

"Aparicio Saravia was the father of a family who sacrificed his own domestic happiness for the cause of his party and for the supreme general interest of his beloved Patria." The drama of Saravia, like the drama of doña Leonor and her daughters, turned on the personal cost of living up to socially-sanctioned ideals.[21]

In real life, as in the play, families divided by civil war had to choose among competing definitions of primary loyalty. In 1897, not only Aparicio's cousin Cesáreo, but also his older brother Basilicio fought against him. Once, when the forces commanded by Aparicio and Basilicio were camped on opposite sides of the Río Negro, the brothers exchanged a number of letters. Sometimes angry, even bitter, but also affectionate, the letters repeatedly invoke the figures of the two men's parents and appeal to various conceptions of family loyalty. Basilicio's letters criticize his brother's conduct as irresponsible because, by starting the war, Aparicio wasted the patrimony of his own children and despoiled the property "fertilized by the honest sweat" of other hardworking Uruguayan fathers. Aparicio's letters, on the other hand, emphasize a moral conscience that transcends personal interests, but they, too, seek legitimation in the idea of family by tracing this transcendent conscience to "the august virtues" of him who bequeathed the name Saravia to the brothers. Competing constructions of family loyalty occur again when Aparicio invokes the image of Chiquito, pledging loyalty to the cause of the fallen, and Basilicio replies that both he and Aparicio should think about providing for Chiquito's orphans. Finally, Aparicio invokes the redeeming power of sacrifice, and Basilicio asks him to forget the "literary falderal and theatrical gestures that sent our countrymen to die on the battlefields of years gone by, stupefied by the incense of metaphors."[22]

Following their first appearance in a Montevideo newspaper, these six letters have been much rehearsed in biographies such as the 1942 *Life of Aparicio Saravia* by the Argentine author Manuel Gálvez—who reads Aparicio as an idealistic don Quixote and Basilicio as a mundane Sancho Panza. One must keep in mind that the two brothers did not personally compose these texts, although they approved the drafts (penned by various doctoral personages) and did care about their contents. Justino Muniz reportedly found Basilicio with tears streaming down his face after reading Aparicio's first letter. We may fairly suppose that the brothers paid much closer attention to the passages relating to family than to those relating to such matters (interjected almost certainly by doctoral hands) as administrative history or the foreign debt, and we may guess, too, that the exchange was so protracted partly because of the ghost authors' enthusiasm for the rhetorical forum that it provided. The attention subsequently devoted to these letters confirms the dramatic potential of a "personal" exchange between the two brothers at war with each other—a situation in which conflicting definitions of primary loyalty naturally arose.[23]

And whatever its origins, the exchange drew on a widely-shared rhetorical repertory, providing a final example of the tension between overlapping claims of kin, party, and nation. Here perhaps, is the last piece of the puzzle of Saravia's charisma. Saravia personified the party's heritage and values, its rural nativism and the self-sacrificial cult of patriadas, an identity dear to some, antithetical to others, but always at issue, always in tension with the competing claims of other collective identities. This tension, I believe, generated the emotional charge that made the last of the gaucho caudillos electrifying to wizened veterans of a hundred borderland skirmishes and to the patrician youth of Montevideo, alike.

Aparicio Saravia's mystique only increased when he became a martyr, the ultimate symbol of self-transcendence and mystical union with the group. Abdón Arósteguy (who was also the author of *Julián Giménez,* one of the popular nativist dramas presented by traveling circuses during the 1890s) explicitly indicated the political function of Blanco traditionalism. Only a party that "made a cult of, and identified itself with its tradition" had any hope of maintaining cohesion during its long history of proscription. As for Aparicio Saravia, he was a guiding beacon, a model, explained Arósteguy in the party's illustrated magazine. Saravia had been no "vulgar caudillo" who attracted a following through "terror," through "personal interests or connections," or even through "personal prestige." Instead, Saravia inspired his followers by providing an example of native hardiness and disposition to self-sacrifice. The campaign of 1897 gave his followers plenty of opportunity to display these virtues in themselves, too.[24]

16

MARCH 1897-SEPTEMBER 1904

B lanco insurgents faced much hardship on the long forced marches of the last patriadas. Confronted by well-armed regular troops, they pushed across the rolling grass-covered hills for endless hours at a steady, bone-jolting trot. Simply staying ahead of the enemy and avoiding being cornered was a major triumph for a montonera in turn-of-the-century Uruguay because the country's railroad and telegraph system had so speeded the deployment of government troops. Aparicio Saravia's insurgents could shake off a pursuing government force and march seventy or eighty miles without rest, only to find the same force waiting for them, rested, rearmed, and reinforced. And there were few places to hide on the open plains of the Uruguayan countryside. Only the Río Negro and the Brazilian border offered the insurgents any tactical advantage: the Río Negro with its wide bottom land, many parts of which became a watery maze in the winter; the border, with its opportunities as a haven and a source of supplies. Fortunately for the Blancos, Aparicio knew both areas intimately. They were places he had roamed all his life, places where he had recently waged war as a Maragato. The point of maximum advantage was precisely the intersection of the Río Negro with the border—a warren of thickets, hillocks, and watercourses where the imaginary line dividing Brazil from Uruguay was impossible to patrol effectively.[1]

It was to this old hideaway of bandits and montoneras that Aparicio had retreated when his "armed demonstration" fizzled in December 1896, and here he appeared again with a montonera numbering four hundred or so in March 1897. Here Aparicio personally passed out white divisas on the day of the invasion to all who did not already have them. Here Abdón Arósteguy (after declaiming a proclamation in Aparicio's name) envisioned himself reenacting scenes of patriotic history. Here the invaders wept and embraced each other, as they would do again upon laying down their arms at the end of the war. The war committee of Buenos Aires had helped Aparicio to acquire some guns and ammunition, but his horsemen were still no better armed than Gumercindo's Maragatos had been. The officers and doctores all had pistols or rifles, but overall, the army's motley array of guns—mostly Remingtons and Winchesters with half the effective range of the army's Mausers—gave it little firepower. Most of the men who eventually joined the revolution had no guns at all, and those who did have firearms lacked an adequate supply of bullets because the large variety of weapons carried by the insurgent volunteers made acquisition of ammunition a logistical nightmare.[2]

Two other insurgent armies organized by the war committee in Buenos Aires were scheduled to invade from the south and west at the same time, and all were to converge on the middle of the country to join forces. As Aparicio waited for confirmation of the other invasions, his montonera lingered in its Río Negro hideaway, sleeping in the woods along the river during the days and making forays at night through what proved to be an almost deserted countryside, where it encountered no opposition but also few recruits to augment its modest ranks and, worst of all, no horses for desperately needed remounts. Municista influence appears to have deprived Aparicio of strong local support among the divided Blancos of Cerro Largo. Only when the army moved further south along the Río Negro toward the Saravias' own neighborhood—where Chiquito had his popular following—did its numbers multiply. Then, when Aparicio had a column of about two thousand (more than he had ever directed in battle before), he felt strong enough to face Muniz. Two weeks after crossing the border, he camped on Muniz's estancia and soon got his fight.[3]

The battle of Arbolito took its name from the single thorny tree on the battlefield. Aparicio appears to have spread his battle line too thin at Arbolito, and it proved a mistake, too, to leave no reserves. Of course, the most brilliant tactics might not have sufficed to overcome the government force's superior firepower, yet nothing seems to have been handled right. At the outset, some of the Municista Blancos bridled at the thought of fighting alongside Colorados (present among the officers of the regular army contingent) against an army wearing white divisas. In a parley, Arósteguy tried to win over some of the disgruntled Municistas for the revolution, but the talks failed when Chiquito Saravia's men refused to cease fire, and these potential insurgent reinforcements left the field. Chiquito Saravia had (in his own words) "an itch to fight" Justino Muniz. Despite various charges by the insurgent lancers, the better armed forces under Muniz gradually pushed forward during several hours of shooting, and the fifty-nine-year-old caudillo himself led the final advance. Perhaps Chiquito had in mind to equal his brother's reputation as a lancer by suddenly turning the tide of battle with a desperate show of valor. Seeing a defeat in the offing, he hefted his huge lance, called for all who dared to follow, and galloped toward the advancing Municista line. About seventy riders began this counter attack, twenty made it halfway, three reached the enemy line, and none of those three lived to boast of the exploit. One of the three was Chiquito, who lunged in the direction of Justino Muniz before going down tangled in a boleadora, lanced in the chest, shot twice, and finished with a massive saber blow to the head. The story still circulates in Cerro Largo, despite some fairly convincing testimony to the contrary, that Aparicio's brother had been drinking during the battle. However it was, Chiquito's death clinched the victory for Muniz, and the Blanco army marched all night in the direction of the Río Negro, suffering considerable desertion.[4]

Arbolito was the first of Aparicio's famous defeats, but hardly the last. In fact, Aparicio was not present at the only significant victory that the Blancos won during the 1897 war, an engagement fought at Tres Arboles by the insurgent force that had invaded from the south. The victors of Tres Arboles and the losers of Arbolito met at an inauspicious rendezvous a few days afterward. (The third insurgent force had invaded from the west, but it was fraught with dissension from the beginning and soon disintegrated.) Aparicio, humiliated and grieving for Chiquito, scarcely seems to have noticed the arrival of the newcomers, and a number of status-conscious officers and punctilious doctoral types were sorely offended, at this time, by his breaches of etiquette toward them. Duvimioso Terra, later one of Aparicio's most vicious critics, arrived with the victors of Tres Arboles but soon became enraged by Aparicio's slights and left. Abdón Arósteguy had left the army in a similar huff immediately after Arbolito. Eduardo Acevedo Díaz's stay with the army had not yet begun, but it would not last long. In general, the revolution's doctores wanted a taste of the campaign but did not feel compelled to stay for the duration. As a whole, the army expanded and contracted considerably during the six months of the war, but never was it impressively large, even for Uruguay. The wet winter months of June, July, and August would bring flood waters to borderland streams and rivers, a circumstance helpful to the insurgents in shaking their pursuers, but the cold winds and rains also discouraged volunteers. Aparicio promised his fan club of young elite Montevideans that the army would swell with old veterans come spring.[5]

In the meantime Aparicio tried to keep the Río Negro between him and Muniz, moving north along the far bank toward his newly acquired estancias in the districts of Tacuarembó and Rivera, staying where his knowledge of the ground gave his army its only advantage. When a government force threatened to corner him there, his army fought the battle of Cerros Blancos, the second largest engagement of the war, and escaped intact only because of a famous charge led by Aparicio himself against a government force that threatened to cut off their retreat. (It was here that Florencio Sánchez and hundreds of other deserters fled across the border into Brazil, leaving Aparicio to regale his remaining followers with parables about rotten posts not making good corrals.) Aparicio decided to stay close to the border for a while, marching his army west toward the Uruguay River, in the hope of an arms shipment of the sort that the Rio Grandense insurgents received there in 1893, but no such shipment arrived, and the insurgents returned empty handed after skirmishing fruitlessly with some ironclad river cruisers.[6]

Three months after Aparicio's invasion, his army returned to its hideaway where the Río Negro intersects the border, only to find government forces waiting for them. The battle that followed took a particularly heavy toll on the Montevideans, and the rebels began for the first time to entertain government propositions of peace. A truce was called, and while Basilicio Saravia and his close followers were greeted effusively by Aparicio in the revolutionary camp, negotiations began. Highly unpopular Colorado president Idiarte Borda negotiated from political rather than military weakness. The war had destroyed huge amounts of rural property—thousands of fence posts for fire wood, scores of cattle for one day's meat—and the climate of uncertainty had been terrible for investment, as witnessed most starkly by the Montevideo stock market's plunge at the time of Aparicio's initial armed demonstration. When the negotiations stalled, "peace at all cost" demonstrations in Montevideo brought twenty thousand people into the street to clamor against President Borda.[7]

Aparicio's main sticking point in the protracted discussions was his demand for local Blanco control (of the kind Justino Muniz had exercised) in eight of Uruguay's nineteen administrative districts. The government offered him four, with Justino Muniz to preside over one of them, and Aparicio refused. At that juncture the truce expired, and the insurgents moved south once more through the neighborhood of his estancia at El Cordobés, their number swelling to about twenty-five hundred. Then a young retail clerk assassinated Borda, the post-Borda government hurriedly offered the Blancos six districts, all to be controlled by Saravia, and peace was at hand. Somehow, Aparicio had emerged from the war with direct control over a third of the national territory of the Uruguayan republic.[8]

Thus, the peace agreement reaffirmed the territorial formula of power sharing that some Blancos had supported and others had opposed before the war, but in the warm glow of their first victory over the Colorados in forty years, that rift was temporarily forgotten. The new pact took its inspiration directly from the agreement that had ended the preceding patriada in 1872, a circumstance that added to its "historic" luster in the eyes of many tradition-minded Blancos. From an administrative point of view, it meant that in the designated districts the political chief and the police force would be Blancos, effectively establishing the nucleus of a permanent army under Saravia's command. Aparicio's Brazilian connections made the 1897 pact especially menacing to the central government since Cerro Largo and Rivera, two of the three Uruguayan districts bordering on Brazil, came under Blanco control. After his old Federalist comrades had let him down in 1896, Aparicio had made peace with the Júlio de Castilhos and the Rio Grandense Republicans, so the Blancos could now strengthen their armed forces still further through unhindered informal importations of weapons from across the border. Blancos celebrated the party's new pride in an illustrated magazine called (roughly) *White Dawn,* that adorned its weekly cover with portraits of "A Parade of Veterans" and vigorously propagated the myth of the patriada. Meanwhile, the Blanco militia received formal organization and published a roster of its officers, including almost one hundred and fifty colonels and lieutenant colonels, but only one general.[9]

With dizzying speed, Aparicio Saravia had become Blanco party's undisputed "national caudillo." An angry Florencio Sánchez lampooned the fawning attitude of his former "co-religionaries" toward Saravia: "If he threatens the government, we reach for our weapons, if he smiles we nod our heads, when he speaks seriously we become grave, and we burst out laughing in unison if he utters some gaucho drollery." Indeed, public attention to Aparicio had suddenly become overwhelming. Immediately uncomfortable wearing the laurels of victory, Aparicio had ridden north to Bagé after the armistice, accompanied only by his wounded son and a small escort, while many of his officers received a hero's welcome in Melo and other towns. Soon after Aparicio returned to his estancia at El Cordobés, letters and gifts began to arrive from all over the country, flattering him and requesting favors. Admirers sent white dogs, cats, and chickens, bottles of wine, fancy boleadoras, the sword wielded by the most famous Blanco martyr of the 1860s, and the lance that had belonged to the caudillo Timoteo Aparicio, as well as some fancy pedigreed cattle of the kind increasingly common in the southern part of the country. For a couple of years, Aparicio continued to live at El Cordobés, where he began to rebuild herds decimated by the war and even introduced a number of the agronomic innovations so notably lacking before. His remote residence forced Montevidean doctores to take a long ride on horseback if they wanted to talk to him, and many went away wide-eyed with stories of the rustic borderlander who had become the second most powerful man in Uruguay—as when one found him personally driving an ox cart full of rocks to construct an extra room on his house for his eldest son, the amputee. El Cordobés became a famous name in Montevideo, both as the estancia of the elusive general and as an internal fault line in Uruguayan sovereignty: the stream dividing the Colorado-controlled district of Durazno from Blanco-controlled Cerro Largo, where contrabandists operated totally in the open and, according to what one local told a visitor, the "government did not rule."[10]

So many traveled to see the reclusive Saravia, and the cost of the requisite hospitality became so onerous, that Aparicio transferred his household to Melo (where guests could stay in hotels) in 1899. The move was not entirely a matter of economic self-defense, because Aparicio also seems to have wanted a change. After moving his household to Melo in the last year of the nineteenth century, he modified his style of clothing completely, and, without ever abandoning his country bonhomie, he sought to acquire more urban polish. The "gaucho" garb that had attracted such attention in 1897 disappeared permanently into a trunk. Indeed, Aparicio's refusal to put aside his new starched collar even during the later campaign of 1904 suggests an almost desperate bid for a certain kind of respectability. He filled the house he had rented in Melo with the sort of overstuffed furniture appropriate to his new status, and began to read more, especially military history. He enjoyed his new life (quite suddenly his girth swelled like that of his father and a number of his brothers), but Aparicio's lifetime of rural habits could not be put aside as quickly as his gaucho apparel. As the second most influential political leader in Uruguay, Aparicio was clearly out of his depth, a perfect study in indecision. The emissaries who made the trip from Montevideo to get his direction on some matter of dispute almost invariably left Melo frustrated, some enigmatic parting jest ringing in their ears. "The doctores are the ones who should decide those things," said Aparicio, and continued to refuse all invitations to go to Montevideo. On more than one occasion, he agreed to appear at mass rallies of Blanco supporters, only to back out at the last minute. Invited by the president to view a military parade from the balcony of the government house, he alleged that heights made him dizzy. Told that the Montevidean public would pay money to see his face, he laughed his famous laugh. When his old bullet wound from Passo Fundo began to bother him, he considered traveling to Europe for x-rays. Would that finally get him to Montevideo? No indeed, he would sail from Rio Grande.[11]

In 1902, a new Colorado president took office and began to challenge Aparicio's control of a third of the country. This was José Batlle y Ordóñez, the great reformer who would eventually transform Uruguayan politics, making one of the most revolution-wracked Spanish American republics into one synonymous with democratic government. Just as Saravia represented the predominantly rural Uruguay of the nineteenth century, Batlle represented the overwhelmingly urban Uruguay of the twentieth, and he was determined to carry out a "reconquest" of the national territory and put an end to the country's divided sovereignty. Renewed Blanco factionalism made his job easier after 1900. Certain Blancos—chief among them, Eduardo Acevedo Díaz—let it be known that they were unimpressed by the pact of 1897 and might collaborate with Batlle in spite of Saravia's opposition. In 1903, Batlle attempted to assign control of two Blanco districts to these dissident Blancos, and Saravia mobilized his army in response. Less than a week later, fifteen thousand horsemen had converged on a point in the middle of Uruguay, and in the presence of reporters from as far away as Buenos Aires, Aparicio and his staff reviewed a mounted multitude that passed at a canter shouting vivas for the general. At one point a rider broke ranks and galloped in front of Saravia, frenetically waving his hat and shouting "Long live the gauchos!" Aparicio smiled and, for the first time that day, respectfully doffed his own hat. The show of force convinced Batlle to back down in 1903, but the next year a second challenge to Aparicio's control of Blanco districts led to another mobilization, and this time the government was ready to fight.[12]

The ensuing Uruguayan civil war of 1904 was larger, longer, and grimmer than the insurgency of 1897. The government's use of newly acquired automatic weapons now made the insurgents' lance charges totally obsolete, but the Blanco army also had more resources than in 1897. In most respects, 1904 was a repetition of the earlier war on a larger scale. Again the revolutionaries lost every major battle and had to content themselves with the more poignant glory of repeatedly surviving their close scrapes. They ranged a bit more widely, marauding more in the southern part of the country than they had dared do seven years earlier. As before, their chief strategic objective was simply to continue the war until an exhausted government came to terms, and, as the war dragged on, achievement of that goal did not appear impossible. After nine months of fighting, Saravia once again took his army west along the border to the Uruguay River in search of an arms shipment, and on this occasion he found the arms waiting for him. Now, the insurgents could boast three artillery pieces of their own.[13]

No one knows what difference they might have made in the long run. As Saravia's army made its way back east along the border toward the Río Negro, a government force met it, a pitched battle began, and just as had happened to Gumercindo ten years earlier, Aparicio was shot as he surveyed the battlefield. The insurgent army fled across the border in panic, and Uruguay's last patriada ended utterly with the death of its caudillo in a borderland estancia house several days later. "This is a Saravista army," explained one of the Blanco officers helpless to contain the disintegration of his forces. "With Saravia gone, nobody can keep it together."[14]

17
APOTHEOSIS AND OBLIVION

Now for the final twist. Aparicio Saravia was not more memorable than his brother, Gumercindo. Unlike Aparicio, Gumercindo seldom lost a battle. He maneuvered over a broader area of a larger country and became the hero of a more terrible and harder fought war. The devotion of his soldiers and the popular enthusiasm that he evoked were not less than in Aparicio's career. Yet, as Gumercindo's image becomes increasingly obscure and irrelevant in the late twentieth century, Aparicio's image—not the starched-collar Saravia of 1904 but the bearded gaucho of 1897—is still emblazoned on the covers of periodical publications and electoral paraphernalia. What explains the contrasting posthumous careers of these two heroes on horseback?

To begin with, while Uruguay's durable Blanco party has assiduously cultivated the memory of Aparicio, the politics of Rio Grande do Sul has lost any association with the memory of Gumercindo, and the cult of Rio Grandense traditionalism has never made him a central figure. Unlike the Blancos, the Federalist party had been called into existence only a year before the 1893 war, and, for well over half a century now, no political party has claimed a Federalist political lineage in Rio Grande do Sul. The traditionalist cult of "gaúchismo"— formally organized in hundreds of local clubs that emphasize estancia nostalgia, folk dance, and tributes to the Farrapos—constitutes the one setting in which Gumercindo is occasionally remembered today, but historical conditions did not favor the apotheosis of this hero. The

Rio Grandense traditionalist movement began only a few months after that 1893 war, apparently as an attempt to forget all about it. In the traditionalist movement's first phase, it seems to have functioned as a common ground where Federalists and Republicans could ritualize and commemorate—despite the ravages of the recent war—a shared "gaúcho" identity conducive to social stability and the cultural hegemony of the dominant class. Because nativist traditionalism had been promoted mostly by the Federalists during the war, they could view the Republican embrace of nativism as a kind of moral victory, making the permanence of Republican rule (unbroken until the 1930s) easier for them to accept. Symptomatically, it was only in the twentieth century that the word *gaúcho* began to be used as a general name for all Rio Grandenses. But the image of Gumercindo obviously had no place in this circle of good feelings, and the specter of brutal vendettas and mass throat-cutting made the whole war best forgotten in the process of healing. The nostalgic vision of Rio Grandense nativist traditionalism then inspired new devotees in the 1920s and 1950s, and the late twentieth-century movement has maintained institutional continuity for almost half a century, drawing inspiration, in many respects, from the gauchesque nativism of the Río de la Plata. This formal cultivation of "gaúchismo" clearly corresponds to what has been called the "invention of tradition."[1]

On the other hand, Rio Grandense regionalism must compete with Brazilian nationalism as a formulation of primary identity. This tension has long existed (for example, in the late nineteenth century, Silveira Martins is supposed to have been called Rio Grandense first, Brazilian second) though the strength of Brazilian identity among Rio Grandenses has usually been underestimated by other Brazilians. For at least a century, the superior resources and international priority of the national state have made it steadily ascendant in people's minds. In fact, the "gaúcho" title seems to have been adopted as a general name for Rio Grandenses only after it became popular in Rio de Janeiro, suggesting that, in an important way, the regionalist identity of modern "gaúchos" arises only in relation to the rest of Brazil. With neither an ongoing party tradition nor the primary force of nationalist associations to lend importance to the figure of Gumercindo, and in view of the negative associations of the 1893 war, it is hardly surprising that the harmlessly swashbuckling Bento Gonçalves should have proved more attractive a hero for twentieth-century Rio Grandense traditionalists. Today, the equestrian statue of Gonçalves is Porto Alegre's most imposing by far and the Farrapo colors have reappeared on the state flag of Rio Grande do Sul.[2]

In sum, Gumercindo has been less remembered than Aparicio because his image resonated less in the social institutions of collective memory. The party that might have glorified his memory soon disappeared, and the traditionalist movement has generally excluded him for the reason just described. His image does not speak in any satisfying way to people's sense of Brazilian national identity. Aparicio's legend, as we have seen, took an entirely different trajectory. Postcards of Aparicio Saravia on a rearing charger (or with his figure substituted for Napoleon's in a battle scene copied from a European painting) made their appearance soon after his rise, and commemorative postcards continued to circulate after his death. A steady rhythm of partisan biographies has continued over the course of the twentieth century, his statue was put up in the 1950s, and during the military dictatorship of the 1980s the government made his estancia house at El Cordobés into one of the world's least accessible historical museums. Meanwhile, Uruguayan folksingers wrote songs about Aparicio that the military government found subversive enough to ban from air play.

The contrasting fates of Aparicio's and Gumercindo's legends can, of course, prove nothing about a more general contrast between Spanish America and Brazil, but their story does suggest an explanation of why the history of Spanish America is more filled with heroes on horseback. First, the manner in which Spanish America became independent—involving long and difficult wars well exemplified in Uruguay—contrasts with Brazilian independence. Brazilian independence occurred with a minimum of disruption, allowing a Portuguese prince to remain on the throne of a united country, in possession of a serviceable army and bureaucracy, as in Rio Grande do Sul. Local strongmen had always been on the scene in both Spanish America and Brazil, but in the aftermath of independence the governmental weakness and political disorganization prevalent in the fragmented Spanish American republics opened space for local strongmen to move into larger roles as guarantors of the social order at a national level. While Brazil went simultaneously through a stormy period of its own, the disruptions there pale by comparison with the Spanish American experience, and the imperial government never ceded its role as guarantor to any caudilho. Therefore, the political fragmentation of Spanish America contributed directly to the multiplication of heroes like Artigas, Rivera, Lavalleja, and Oribe in Uruguay, while Rio Grande do Sul, with its breakaway Farrapo republic and its famous caudilho Bento Gonçalves, is atypical in Brazil.

Over the course of the nineteenth century and into the twentieth, local strongmen continued to dominate the countryside of both Spanish America and Brazil, while a profusion of Spanish American civil wars or "revolutions" continued, for decades, to provide small-time caudillos greater opportunity for military glory and career advancement than enjoyed by Brazilian coronéis who, after the 1840s, had to be content to remain small (albeit occasionally uncooperative or independent-minded) local enforcers of the Brazilian imperial state. Brazilian coronéis like Gumercindo might inspire awe through their displays of force and ruthlessness, but the situations to which they applied violence rarely had overtones of patriotic glory. The Federalist revolt of 1893, like all similar events in Brazilian history, was ultimately put down. Spanish American caudillos, on the other hand, often succeeded in overthrowing national governments and—since history is written by winners—their share of patriotic glories expanded accordingly. As a result, the figure of the caudillo became an omnipresent element of Spanish American history and public life. The Blanco conspirators of 1896 never considered making their bid for power without a hero on horseback to raise the countryside.

In Brazil, the national state weathered the stormy consolidation of republican rule and recaptured its air of inexorable stability in the twentieth century, but in Spanish America, even after the export boom of the late nineteenth century allowed the process of state consolidation to slow the rhythm of civil wars, the impact of past experience remained embodied in political discourse. The inculcation of national identities gained momentum through an extension of public education and an accompanying proliferation of literary nationalism. For Uruguayans, heroes on horseback like Aparicio remained emblems of collective identity—part of the imaginative landscape of politics—long after they had finally disappeared forever. After all, each republic must have its patriot heroes and its equestrian statues, for these (along with anthems, flags, and so on) are conventional ingredients in the tried-and-true recipe for cooking up a national identity. One might say that heroes on horseback proliferated in the pages of Spanish American history, first as a result of the region's political disorganization and then as a result of its political reorganization. In Brazil, fewer such figures were available and, as the example of Gumercindo illustrates, they were usually downplayed by national historians anyway.

As for the question of caudillo charisma, the story of the Saravia brothers suggests that historians may have mistakenly invoked the mesmerizing stare of the leader rather than the yearning gaze of the followers. The mere image of the leader may be enough to inspire reverence. In fact, I believe that some Uruguayans still respond charismatically to representations of Aparicio Saravia nearly a century after his death. During my research in Uruguay, many asked me—sometimes rather resentfully—how I had become concerned with something so intimately Uruguayan. Someone told me how the military had captured a descendent of Aparicio Saravia among the Tupamaro guerrillas in the 1970s and freed him in exchange for Aparicio's archive, which had reposed ever since in army headquarters. When I went there to consult it, suspicious soldiers watched lest I make off with any of the photocopied archival documents—they didn't trust me with the originals at all, for these were relics of national identity.

After looking me over, one incredulous officer told me that until I could ride a horse, drink mate, smoke a cornhusk cigarette, and play cards like a gaucho, I would never be able to write a credible biography of the Saravias. His challenge inspired this book, but I hope that he was wrong about the main requirements for writing it.

NOTES

CAUDILLOS

1. C. Enrique Mena Segarra, *Aparicio Saravia: Las últimas patriadas* (Montevideo: Ediciones de la Banda Oriental, 1981), 153–58.

2. Nepomuceno Saravia García, *Memorias de Aparicio Saravia: Relato histórico-biográfico de su hijo Nepomuceno, ilustrado con la documentación del archivo del General* (Montevideo: Editorial Medina, 1956), 580–92.

3. Sejanes Dornelles, *Gumersindo Saravia: O guerrilheiro pampeano* (Caxias do Sul: EDCUS, 1988), 226–31.

4. For changing interpretations of caudillismo, see Domingo Faustino Sarmiento, *Facundo o civilización y barbarie* (Caracas: Biblioteca Ayacucho, 1977); Alberto Zum Felde, *Proceso histórico del Uruguay: Esquema de una sociología nacional* (Montevideo: Maximino García, [1919]); Charles E. Chapman, "The Age of the Caudillos: A Chapter in Hispanic American History," *Hispanic American Historical Review* 12 (1932): 281–300; Eric R. Wolf and Edward Hansen, "Caudillo Politics: A Structural Analysis," *Comparative Studies of Society and History* 9 (1967): 168–79; Hugh M. Hamill, *Caudillos: Dictators in Spanish America* (Norman: University of Oklahoma Press, 1992); and John Lynch, *Caudillos in Spanish America, 1800–1850* (Oxford: Clarendon Press, 1992).

5. Manuel Gálvez, *Vida de Aparicio Saravia* (Buenos Aires: Imprenta López, 1942).

6. For overviews of nineteenth-century political history, see Frank Safford, "Politics, Ideology, and Society," in *The Cambridge History of Latin America,* vol. 3 (Cambridge: Cambridge University Press, 1985); Tulio Halperín Donghi, *The Contemporary History of Latin America,* ed. and trans. John Charles Chasteen (Durham: Duke University Press, 1993); Roderick J. Barman, *Brazil: The Forging of a Nation, 1798–1852*

(Stanford: Stanford University Press, 1988); and Emilia Viotti da Costa, *The Brazilian Empire: Myths and Histories* (Chicago: University of Chicago Press, 1985).

7.   In addition to Wolf and Hansen, "Caudillo Politics"; and Lynch, *Caudillos in Spanish America;* see Tulio Halperín Donghi, *The Aftermath of Revolution in Latin America* (New York: Harper and Row, 1973); and E. Bradford Burns, *The Poverty of Progress: Latin America in the Nineteenth Century* (Berkeley: University of California Press, 1983).

8.   Charles Lindholm, *Charisma* (Cambridge: Basil Blackwell, 1990). The connection with nationalism is made through Benedict Anderson, *Imagined Communities: Reflections on the Origin and Spread of Nationalism* (London: Verso, 1983).

9.   Lindholm, *Charisma*, 22–35. For a larger theoretical context, see Michael Brint, *A Genealogy of Political Culture* (Boulder: Westview Press, 1991), esp. 117–20.

10.   My attitude toward historical narrative has been influenced by Hayden White. See, for example, "The Fictions of Factual Representation," in *The Tropics of Discourse: Essays in Cultural Criticism* (Baltimore: The Johns Hopkins University Press, 1978), 121–131.

JANUARY 1893

1.   Manuel Fonseca, *Gumersindo Saravia: El general de la libertad* (Montevideo: Editorial Florensa & Lafón, 1957), 261–71.

2.   See Rodolfo González Rissotto and Susana Rodríguez Varese de González, "Contribución al estudio de la influencia guaraní en la formación de la sociedad uruguaya," *Revista histórica* (Montevideo) 2d ser., 75 (April 1982): 199–316. On rural material culture, see Fernando O. Assunçao, *Pilchas criollas: usos y costumbres del gaucho,* 2d ed. (Montevideo: Ediciones Master Fer Ltda., 1979).

3.   Fonseca, *Gumersindo Saravia,* 265.

4.   "Revelación fidedigna," *El deber cívico* (Melo), 1 November 1892; Manoel da Costa Medeiros, *História do Herval: Descrição física e histórica.* (Porto Alegre: Escola Superior de Teologia São Lourenço de Brindes; Caxias do Sul: Universidade de Caxias do Sul; Herval: Prefeitura Municipal, 1980), 383–93.

5.   Saravia García, *Memorias,* 28–30; Mena Segarra, *Aparicio Saravia: Las últimas patriadas,* 10–19.

6.   The best introduction to the Rio Grandense politics of the period

is Joseph L. Love, *Rio Grande do Sul and Brazilian Regionalism, 1882–1930* (Stanford: Stanford University Press, 1971).

7. Fonseca, *Gumersindo Saravia,* 138–48; "Gomercindo não passou," *O correio do povo* (Porto Alegre), 23 August 1938.

8. On the political logic of patronage and clientele, see Steffen W. Schmidt, Laura Guasti, Carl H. Landé, and James C. Scott, *Friends, Followers, and Factions: A Reader in Political Clientelism* (Berkeley: University of California Press, 1977), xiii–xxxvii; Linda Lewin, *Politics and Parentela in Paraíba: A Case Study of Family-Based Oligarchy in Brazil* (Princeton: Princeton University Press, 1987); and Richard Graham, *Patronage and Politics in Nineteenth-Century Brazil* (Stanford: Stanford University Press, 1990).

9. Péricles Azambuja, *História das terras e mares do Chuí* (Porto Alegre: Escola Superior de Teologia São Lourenço de Brindes; Caxias do Sul: Universidade de Caxias do Sul, 1978), 385–93. Fonseca, *Gumersindo Saravia,* 124–37. On the figure of the coronel (comparable to the Spanish American *caudillejo, cacique,* or *gamonal*), see Victor Nunes Leal, *Coronelismo: The Municipality and Representative Government in Brazil,* trans. June Henfrey (Cambridge: Cambridge University Press, 1977), and Maria Isaura de Pereira de Queiroz, *O mandonismo local na vida política brasileira e outros ensaios* (São Paulo: Editorial Alfa-Omega, 1976).

10. Love, *Rio Grande do Sul and Brazilian Regionalism,* 22–25; Mário Teixeira de Carvalho, *Nobiliário sul-riograndense* (Porto Alegre: Livraria do Glôbo, 1937), 262–77.

11. For a detailed discussion, see Helga Iracema Langraf Piccolo, *A política rio-grandense no Segundo Império (1868–1882)* (Porto Alegre: Universidade Federal do Rio Grande do Sul, 1974).

12. Saravia García, *Memorias,* 21; Fonseca, *Gumersindo Saravia,* 49–51, 81–152.

13. On Castilhos, see Sérgio da Costa Franco, *Júlio de Castilhos e sua época* (Porto Alegre: Editôra Glôbo, 1967); Ricardo Vélez Rodríguez, *O castilhismo: Uma filosofia da República* (Porto Alegre: Escola Superior de Teologia São Lourenço de Brindes; Caxias do Sul: Universidade de Caxias do Sul, 1980); and Love, *Rio Grande do Sul and Brazilian Regionalism,* 26–25, 38–43.

14. AHRS, Correspondência do General Barreto Leite, 4 May 1892: Particulares, Lata 36, Maço 10. "No sul" and "A revolução," *O jornal do comércio* (Porto Alegre), 17 and 20 Nov. 1891; Love, *Rio Grande do*

Sul and Brazilian Regionalism, 44–48. Events at the national level are recounted in José Maria Bello, *A History of Modern Brazil, 1889–1964* (Stanford: Stanford University Press, 1966), 77–138.

15.   On the meeting at Bagé, see "Congresso de Bagé, *O jornal do comércio,* 2 and 7 April 1892; Epaminondas Villalba, *A Revolução Federalista no Rio Grande do Sul: documentos e commentários* (Rio de Janeiro, São Paulo, and Recife: Laemmert & Cia. Editôres, 1897), xxxi; Wenceslau Escobar, *Apontamentos para a história da Revolução Rio-grandense de 1893,* 2d ed. (Brasília: Editôra Universidade de Brasília, 1983), 59–60.

16.   "O Sul do Estado," *O jornal do comércio,* 2 July 1892. On the long subsequent period of Republican rule, see Love, *Rio Grande do Sul and Brazilian Regionalism,* 76–215.

17.   Saravia García, *Memorias,* 30. On Gumercindo's and Aparicio's other brothers, see José Virginio Díaz, *Historia de Saravia: Contribución al estudio del caudillaje en América* (Montevideo: A. Barreiro y Ramos, 1920), 214–25.

BORDERLANDERS

1.   See Washington Reyes Abadie, Oscar H. Bruschera, and Tabaré Melogno, *La Banda Oriental: Pradera—frontera—puerto,* 3d ed. (Montevideo: Ediciones de la Banda Oriental, 1974); and Carlos G. Rheinghantz, "Povoamento do Rio Grande de São Pedro: A contribuição da Colônia do Sacramento," in *Anais do Simpósio Comemorativo do Bicenténario da Restauração do Rio Grande (1776–1976),* vol. 2 (Rio de Janeiro: Instituto Histórico Geográfico Brasileiro, 1979), 273–81. On the imperial clash, see Dauril Alden, *Royal Government in Colonial Brazil: With Special Reference to the Administration of the Marquis of Lavradio, Viceroy, 1769–1779* (Berkeley: University of California Press, 1968).

2.   APRS, "Inventário de Bernardo José Ferreira": Cartório de Orfãos e Ausentes, Porto Alegre 1794/176; "Inventário de Bartholomeu Rodrigues da Silva": Cartório de Orfãos e Provedoria, Rio Grande 1810/77. On early Rio Grande do Sul, see [Francisco] Oliveira Viana, *Populações meridionais do Brasil,* vol. 2: *O campeador rio-grandense,* [2d ed.] (Rio de Janeiro: Paz e Terra, 1974); and Guilhermino César, *História do Rio Grande do Sul: Período colonial* (Porto Alegre: Editôra Globo, 1956); and Arthur Ferreira Filho, *História geral do Rio Grande do Sul,* 5th ed. (Porto Alegre: Editôra Globo, 1978).

3.   Fernando O. Assunçao, *El gaucho, su espacio y su tiempo* (Montevideo: Ediciones Arca, 1969), 179–85; Spencer L. Leitman, *Raízes sócio-econômicas da Guerra dos Farrapos: Um capítulo da história do Brasil no século XIX,* trans. Sarita Linhares Barsted (Rio de Janeiro: Edições Graal, 1979), 79–102; Charles Gary Lobb, "The Historical Geography of the Cattle Regions along Brazil's Southern Frontier" (Ph.D. diss., University of California, Berkeley, 1970); Charles Julian Bishko, "The Peninsular Background of Latin American Cattle Ranching," *Hispanic American Historical Review* 32 (November 1952): 491–515.

4.   Auguste de Saint-Hilaire, *Voyage à Rio Grande do Sul (Brésil)* (Orléans: H. Herluison, 1887), 156, 166, 174, 192, 205, 216, and 261–62. See also Germán Gil Villaamil, *Ensayo para una historia de Cerro Largo hasta 1930* (Montevideo: Imprenta del Palacio Legislativo, 1982), 34–35.

5.   Emilio A. Coni, *El gaucho: Argentina—Brasil—Uruguay* (Buenos Aires: Editorial Sudamericana, 1945), 75–86; González and Rodríguez, "Contribución al estudio de la influencia guaraní," 199–316.

6.   AGN, "Padrón de la segunda sección de Durazno, 1832," Libro 280, Ex Archivo General Administrativo; Francisco N. Oliveres, *Toponimia histórico-geográfica de Treinta y Tres y Cerro Largo* (Montevideo: n.p., 1938), 138; González and Rodríguez, "Contribución al estudio de la influencia guaraní," 260–61.

7.   AGN, "Padrón de la segunda sección de Durazno, 1832," Libro 280, Ex Archivo General Administrativo.

8.   AGN, "Padrón de Cerro Largo, 1836," Libro 273; and "Padrón de la segunda sección de Durazno, 1832," Libro 280, (both) Ex Archivo General Administrativo.

9.   AGNJ, "Querella—Don José Silveyra de Amaral y Don Francisco Saravia do Amaral sobre heridas de un esclavo," Letrados, Cerro Largo 1842/17.

10.   AHRS, Autos crime, Bagé 1853/3347; "Atenção," *O bageense,* 1 Nov. 1863. On slavery in the borderland, see Spencer L. Leitman, "Slave Cowboys in the Cattle Lands of Southern Brazil," *Revista de História* 51 (Jan.–Mar. 1975); and Fernando Henrique Cardoso, *Capitalismo e escravidão no Brasil meridional: O negro na sociedade escravocrata do Rio Grande do Sul,* 2d ed. (Rio de Janeiro: Paz e Terra, 1977).

11.   APRS, "Registro Paroquial de Arroio Grande, 1855–1857," Secção Extra Judiciária.

12.   On the Farrapo War, see Leitman, *Raízes sócio-econômicas;* Dé-

cio Freitas, et al. *A Revolução Farroupilha: história & interpretação* (Porto Alegre: Mercado Aberto, 1985); Walter Spalding, *A epopéia farroupilha: Pequena história da Grande Revolução acompanhada de farta documentação da época, 1835–1845* (Rio de Janeiro: Biblioteca do Exército, 1963); and Alfredo Varela, *Revoluções cisplatinas: a República Rio-Grandense* (Porto: Livraria Chardon, 1915).

13.   See José Pedro Barrán, *Apogeo y crisis del Uruguay pastoril y caudillesco, 1838–1875* (Montevideo: Ediciones de la Banda Oriental, 1974).

14.   The social importance of agregados (as opposed to hired hands) is clear in all surviving census manuscripts. In addition to those already cited, see AHRS, "Quadros da estatística territorial em 1847" and "População dos distritos," Estatística, Lata 531; and AGN, "Padrón de Salto, 1834" and "Padrón de la Villa de Florida, 1839," Ex Archivo General Administrativo, Libros 274 and 1351.

15.   APRS, "Inventário de Francisco Saraiva do Amaral": Cartório de Orfãos e Ausentes, Jaguarão 1854/321; José Monegal, *Vida de Aparicio Saravia* (Montevideo: A. Monteverde y Cía., 1942), 11–22.

16.   On rural routines, see the notebooks of Roberto J. Bouton (first entry dated 1890): *La vida rural en el Uruguay* (Montevideo: A. Monteverde y Cía., 1961); João Cezimbra Jacques, *Ensaio sobre os costumes do Rio Grande do Sul: Precedido de uma ligeira descrição física e de uma noção histórica* (Porto Alegre: Typografia de Gundlach & Cia., 1883; reprint ed., Estante Rio-grandense União de Seguros, [1979]), 45–73; and Severino de Sá Brito, *Trabalhos e costumes dos gaúchos* (Porto Alegre: Livraria do Globo, 1928; reprint ed., Estante Rio-Grandense União de Seguros, n.d.), 27–94.

17.   Luís Carlos Barbosa Lessa and Paixão Côrtes, *Aspectos da sociabilidade gaúcha* (Porto Alegre: Editôra Proletra, 1985), 43–48; Monegal, *Vida de Aparicio Saravia,* 25; Fonseca, *Gumersindo Saravia,* 85.

18.   APRS, "Inventário de Francisco Saraiva do Amaral": Cartório de Orfãos e Ausentes, Jaguarão 1854/321; and AGNJ, "Testamentaría de Manuel Pereira de la Luz," Letrados, Cerro Largo 1857/97.

19.   Bouton, *La vida rural,* 9–17; F. Maya D'Avila, *Terra e gente de Alcides Maya* (Porto Alegre: Livraria Sulina Editôra, [1969]), pp. 25–27; Mena Segarra, *Aparicio Saravia: las últimas patriadas,* 10.

20.   APRS, "Inventário de Francisco Saraiva do Amaral": Cartório de Orfãos e Ausentes, Jaguarão 1854/321. Bouton, *La vida rural,* 11–13; D'Avila, *Terra e gente,* 39–42.

21. Bouton, *La vida rural,* 101-3, 118-27.

22. Ibid., 45, 285-88.

23. Ibid., 42, 62-63; Brito, *Trabalhos e costumes,* 55-62, 86-90.

24. Barbosa Lessa and Paixão Côrtes, *Aspectos da sociabilidade gaúcha,* 43-45; Bouton, *La vida rural,* 321-25; Jacques, *Costumes do Rio Grande do Sul,* 66; José Hernández, *El gaucho Martín Fierro* (Buenos Aires: Imprenta de La Pampa, 1872), 10-14.

FEBRUARY 1893

1. Fonseca, *Gumersindo Saravia,* 269-70, 288.

2. Saravia García, *Memórias,* 28; Gil Villaamil, *Ensayo para una historía de Cerro Largo,* 16-58.

3. "Correspondencia: Zapallar," *El deber cívico,* 11 April 1893.

4. AHRS, Câmara Municipal de Bagé, 15 Oct. 1888. Inclusion: *Relatório da Câmara Municipal da Cidade de Bagé apresentado à Assambleia Legislativa Provincial* (Typografia do Independente, 1888). See also the photographic panorama taken 20 Oct. 1875 by Eduardo Wilhelmy, Biblioteca Pública de Bagé; Eurico Jacinto Salis, *História de Bagé* (Porto Alegre: Globo, 1955), 196-205; and *O Cruzeiro do Sul* and *A União Liberal* (both Bagé), 1884-86, passim. For population figures, see *O jornal do comércio* (Porto Alegre), 26 April 1889.

5. Escobar, *Apontamentos para a história da Revolução Rio-grandense,* 73-76; Carvalho, *Nobiliario,* 122-24, 222, 257-61; "Correspondencias" and "Noticias del Brasil," *El deber cívico,* 24 and 28 Jan. 1893; "Factos Graves," *O jornal do comércio,* 3 Nov. 1892.

6. *El deber cívico:* "Pasada de Gumercindo Saravia, " 27 Jan. 1893; "Los federales," 7 Feb. 1893; and "Los sucesos del Brasil," 17 Feb. 1893.

7. Fonseca, *Gumersindo Saravia,* 276-77; Escobar, *Apontamentos para a história da Revolução Rio-grandense,* 91-96.

8. José Antônio Dias Lopes, *A cidade de Dom Pedrito* (Porto Alegre: Livraria do Glôbo, 1972), 54-60; Escobar, *Apontamentos para a história da Revolução Rio-grandense,* 97.

9. This account draws on Lopes, *A cidade de Dom Pedrito.* Cf. Love, *Rio Grande do Sul and Brazilian Regionalism,* 65-66.

STATES AND NATIONS

1. Washington Reyes Abadie, *Crónica de Aparicio Saravia* (Montevideo: Ediciones El Nacional, 1989), 1:70; "Proclamação do Gen. Joca

Tavares, distribuida pela campanha a 5 de fevereiro de 1893," doc. 47 in Villalba, *Revolução Federalista*, 97–98.

2. Raymond Pebayle, "Eleveurs es agriculteurs du Rio Grande do Sul" (Ph.D. diss., Univ. of Paris, 1974), 115–21; Moisés Vellinho, *Fronteira* (Porto Alegre: Universidade Federal do Rio Grande do Sul and Editôra Globo, 1975); quotation: Alfredo Varela, *Revoluções cisplatinas: a República Rio-Grandense* (Porto: Livraria Chardon, 1915), 1:30.

3. Abadie, Bruschera, and Melogno, *La Banda Oriental: Pradera—frontera—puerto*, 12–18; Alden, *Royal Government*, 86–104, 263–67; César, *História do Rio Grande do Sul*, 51–56, 146–75; 207–9; AGN, Jefatura Política de Cerro Largo, 24 March 1869; see articles on "Cordón sanitario," in *El riverense* (Rivera), 28 November 1886–6 January 1887.

4. On the militarization of the borderland, see Fernando Uricoechea, *The Patrimonial Foundations of the Brazilian Bureaucratic State* (Berkeley: University of California Press, 1980), 128–54; Love, *Rio Grande do Sul and Brazilian Regionalism*, 15–16; AHRS, Comandos superiores da Guarda Nacional, Bagé, 1866–1886, Caixa 417. On Uruguay, *Diarios de sesiones de la Cámara de Representantes*, 1834–37, 1853–58, and 1861–73, passim; and "Por qué no tenemos Guardia Nacional?" *El deber cívico*, 28 Aug. 1894.

5. See *Presupuesto jeneral de gastos para el año de 1854* (Montevideo: Imprenta Uruguaya, 1853); *Presupuesto general del departamento de Guerra y Marina, 1869* (Montevideo: Departamento de Guerra y Marina, 1869); "Proyecto de presupuesto general de gastos, 1895–7," *Diario de sesiones de la Cámara de Representantes*, Tomo 143: 502–3; and Gil Villaamil, *Ensayo para una historía de Cerro Largo*, 83–87, 97–107. For Brazilian presence in an Uruguayan revolution, see AGN, Jefatura Política de Tacuarembó, 2 April 1870.

6. AHRS, Delegacia de polícia, Jaguarão, 27 April and 16 June 1846. First quotation: AGN, Jefatura política de Cerro Largo, 15 Jan. 1870. On Brazilian neutrality, see "Um protesto solemne," *A Pátria* (Montevideo), 3 Dec. 1881. For attitudes observed by travelers, see Nicolau Dreys (quoted), *Notícia descritiva da Província do Rio Grande do São Pedro do Sul*, 3d ed. (Porto Alegre: Instituto Estadual do Livro, 1961), 151; and Saint-Hilaire, *Voyage*, 216.

7. Quotation: AHRS, "Relatório do Presidente da Província," João Lins Vieira Cansanção de Sinumbu, 1853, 4–7. Sample criminal records: APRS, "Sumário: Reos Jerônimo Ibarra e Juan Ojeda," Autos crime,

Bagé 1851/3340; and AGNJ, "Sumario contra Victoriano Benítez y Serafín Pedro, acusados de muerte y saqueo," Letrados, Cerro Largo 1863/53. On Silveira's murder: AHRS, Delegacia de polícia, Bagé, 17 October 1870. See other reports of Rio Grandense sufferings in AHRS, "Relatório do Presidente da Província do Rio Grande do Sul," Francisco José Soares de Andrêa, 1 June 1849; and "Relatório do Vice Presidente da Província do Rio Grande do Sul," Luiz Alves Leite de Oliviera Bello, 1 Oct. 1852.

8. First quotation: AHRS, Delegacia de Polícia, Jaguarão, 2 Feb. 1865; second quotation, "Brado Riograndense," O bageense (Bagé), 23 June 1864; poems remitted from the campaign appeared in the same paper on 2 March 1865 and 2 April 1865. Third quotation: "O general Neto," O bageense, 26 May 1864.

9. First quotation: "Sete de setembro," O bageense, 16 Sept. 1866; second quotation from O Canabarro, 10 January 1895. See also "O imperador," O bageense, 2 March 1865; and Almanaque literário e estatístico do Rio Grande do Sul 1892 (Pelotas, Rio Grande, Porto Alegre: Editôres Pintos & Cia., 1892).

10. On Uruguayan incursions, see AHRS, Câmara Muncipal de Jaguarão, 13 Aug. 1834; "Relatório do Presidente da Província do Rio Grande do Sul," Antônio Rodrigues Fernandes Braga, 20 April 1835; "Relatório do Vice-Presidente da Província," Patrício Corrêa da Câmara, 2 Oct. 1851; and Delegacia de Polícia, Bagé, 19 Nov. 1870. On armed forces in Rio Grande do Sul, see AHRS, "Relatório do Presidente da Província," Jerónimo Francisco Coelho, 15 Dec. 1856. On Mauá's investments in Uruguay, see Doris Bradenbury McLaughlin, "From Batlle to Batlle: Uruguay in the Late Nineteenth Century" (Ph.D. diss., University of Michigan, 1973), 41.

11. See Sérgio da Costa Franco, "A campanha," in Rio Grande do Sul: terra e povo (Porto Alegre: Editôra Globo, 1963), 66–67; Spencer L. Leitman, "Socio-economic Roots of the Ragamuffin War: A Chapter in early Brazilian History" (Ph.D. diss., University of Texas, 1972), 93–108; De Província de São Pedro a Estado do Rio Grande do Sul: Censos do RS: 1803–1950, 60; "Censo de 1860," in Anuario estadístico de la República Oriental del Uruguay 1902–3, 1:54; and "Bienes declarados," Anuario estadístico, 1886, 356–73. Quotation: Eduardo Acevedo, Anales históricos del Uruguay (Montevideo: Barreiro y Ramos, 1933), 3:125.

12. "Anexo A: negócios do Rio da Prata," in Paulo José Soares de Souza, Relatório da repartição dos negócios estrangeiros apresentado a

assambléia geral legislativa na 3a sessão da 8a legislatura pelo repectivo ministro e secretário de estado (Rio de Janeiro: n.p., 1851); "Primer Libro de Matrimonios," 1837–1840, Iglesia Catedral, Melo; Carvalho, *Nobiliario,* 265–66.

13. For Uruguayan justices reporting in Portuguese: AGNJ, "Oficio" from Luis Barcellos, 1 Aug. 1830 (quoted); "Oficio" from Carlos Silveira (father of Silveira Martins), 3 April 1838; and "Elecciones de autoridades civiles," Letrados, Cerro Largo 1867. Quotation: AGN, Jefatura política de Cerro Largo, Nov. 1867 report. On intrusos: AGN, "Padrón de Cuadra, distrito de Tacuarembó" Ex Archivo General Administrativo, libro 273.

14. On enslavement of Uruguayan blacks, see AHRS, "Relatório do Presidente da Província do Rio Grande do Sul," 2 Oct. 1854; also AGNJ, "Rapto de una joven de color," Letrados, Cerro Largo 1858/49; APRS, "Pelo crime de reduzir pessoas livres à escravidão," Autos crime de Bagé, 1854/3361 and 1855/3368. On contracts of indenture, see "Esclavos de Rio Grande," *La constitución* (Montevideo), 6 Feb. 1853; and "Relación de las personas de color que, en calidad de peones han sido introducidos del Brasil y cuyos contratos han sido presentados a esta jefatura," addendum to *Memoria de la Jefatura Política y de Policía del Departamento de Cerro Largo correspondiente a los años de 1876–77–78* (Montevideo: La Tribuna, 1879). For reports of Brazilian and Uruguayan impressment in northern Uruguay, see AGN, Jefaturas Políticas de Cerro Largo (8 July 1865, 28 Feb. 1866, and 16 Mar. 1867), Tacuarembó (12 Mar. 1867, 18 Sept. 1867, and 17 Oct. 1868), and Salto (12 July 1866). Such press gangs also operated in Brazil: AHRS, Cámara Municipal de Bagé, 21 Sept. 1868.

15. AHRS, "Relatório do Vice Presidente da Provincia," Luiz Alves Leite de Oliviera Bello, 1 October 1852; and "Relatório do Presidente da Provincia," Conselheiro Barão de Muritiba, April 1856. On Gonçalves, see Tau Golin, *Bento Gonçalves: o herói ladrão* (Santa Maria, RS: LGR Artes Gráficas, 1983); and Gil Villaamil, *Ensayo para una historia de Cerro Largo,* 94. On Chico Bonito, see AHRS, Delegacia de Polícia, Jaguarão, April–June 1846; and AGNJ, Letrados, Cerro Largo 1829/5.

16. "Dos palabras," *La prensa* (Melo), 17 Feb. 1884; Santiago Giuffra, *Fronterizas: Paliques uruguayos–brasileros* (Montevido: El siglo ilustrado, 1900); "Cuestión vieja e interesante," *El deber cívico,* 4 Oct. 1895; and "De Artigas," *El Cerro Largo* (Melo), 2 July 1887.

17. On educational systems at mid-century, compare AHRS, "Rela-

tório do Presidente da Província do Rio Grande do Sul," José Antônio Pimenta Bueno, October 1850; and Uruguay, *Presupuesto jeneral de gastos para el año de 1854* (Montevideo: Imprenta uruguaya, 1853). On school reform in Cerro Largo, see "La enseñanza en Cerro Largo" and "Instrucción pública," *El deber cívico*, 28 July 1896 and 1 Jan. 1897; and Saviniano Pérez, *Cartilla geográfica con notícias históricas y datos estadísticos del departamento de Cerro Largo* (Melo: Tipografía del Deber Cívico, 1902), 70–763. A school-centered, rural "fiesta patria" is described in "Correspondencia en Sierra de Ríos," *El deber cívico*, 18 July 1893.

18. On reactions to the reform, see "Instrucción pública," *El Cerro Largo*, 16 April 1887; "Instrucción pública," *El Partido Colorado* (Melo), 17 March 1894; Carlos Carbajal, *La penetración luso-brasileña en el Uruguay* (Montevideo: n.p., 1948), 105–6. On the special border schools, see "Las escuelas fronterizas," *El deber cívico*, 8 Jan. 1897; and *Diario de sesiones* (Reps), vol. 143, 420–52. For "p-e-rr-o, cachorro," see "Cuestión vieja e interesante," *El deber cívico*, 4 Oct. 1895. Quotation from essay by Sara Lestido: "Homenaje," *El deber cívico*, 23 October 1894.

19. Fonseca, *Gumersindo Saravia*, 53–80; Dornelles, *Gumersindo Saraiva*, 25–27.

20. Gumercindo's nationality as declared in legal documents also varied according to the immediate situation: Fonseca, *Gumersindo Saravia*, 77–78.

21. In 1800, Spanish official Félix de Azara made this comparison: *Memoria sobre el estado rural del Río de la Plata y otros informes* (Buenos Aires: Editorial Bajel, 1943), 3–25. See also Saint-Hilaire, *Voyage*, 156 and 236; and Medeiros, *História do Herval*, 84–86.

22. "Gumercindo Saravia," *El deber cívico*, 3 July 1896. On Santana and Rivera, see William Henry Koebel, *The Great South Land: The River Plate and Southern Brazil Today* (New York: Dodd, Mead, and Co., 1920), 192–94. On preference for Brazilian towns, see Uruguay, *Memoria de la Jefatura Política y de Policía de Artigas*, 1888–89, 14–15; and Carbajal, *La penetración luso-brasileña*, 109–10.

23. On the development of the press, see Gil Villaamil, *Ensayo para una historia de Cerro Largo*, 136; and the collection entitled "World's Columbian Exposition: Brazilian Newspapers—State of Rio Grande do Sul," in the Biblioteca Pública of Porto Alegre. See also Hélio Vianna, *Contribuição à história da imprensa brasileira (1812–1869)* (Rio de Ja-

neiro: Imprensa Nacional, 1945); and Nelson Werneck Sodré, *Historía da Imprensa no Brasil* (Rio de Janeiro: Editôra Civilização Brasileira, 1966). On the mail, "Horario," *La prensa* (Melo), 31 Dec. 1882.

24. AHRS, "Estatística judicial dos juizados de paz," Lata 531, Maço 1, 1846; "Continuamos," *El Cerro Largo* (Melo), 18 Sept. 1886; and, more generally, Thomas Flory, *Judge and Jury in Imperial Brazil, 1808–1871: Social Control and Political Stability in the New State* (Austin: University of Texas Press, 1981). On Brazilian attitudes toward Uruguayan justice, see "Juizes Letrados," *A Pátria*, 5 Jan. and 17 Oct. 1883.

25. AHRS, "Relatório do Presidente da Província do Rio Grande do Sul," Patrício Corrêa da Câmara, 2 Oct. 1851; "Relatório do Presidente da Província," Angelo Moniz da Silva Ferraz, 4 May 1859; and "Sessões do jury," *O Cruzeiro do Sul*, 8 June 1884, and *A União Liberal*, 23 Dec. 1887. Also APRS, Autos crime, Bagé 1849/3327; and AGNJ, Letrados, Cerro Largo 1831/32, 1831/34, and 1837/18; and *O bageense*, 1883–1884, passim. (Contrary to the general pattern, notaries had transnational validity: AHRS, Secção Extra Judiciária, Primeiro Tabelionato de Jaguarão, 23 March 1832.)

26. Uruguay, *Memoria de la Jefatura Política y de Policía de Artigas*, 1888–1889, 85–98; and *Memoria del Ministerio de Hacienda, 1889–1890*, 176–7. See also "Nemencio Escobar," *O Cruzeiro do Sul*, 12 Feb. 1885; and AHRS, "Relatório do Vice Presidente da Província," Luiz Alves Leite de Oliveira Bello, 1 Oct. 1852, Addendum 4.

MARCH 1893

1. Love, *Rio Grande do Sul and Brazilian Regionalism*, 59–64; Escobar, *Apontamentos para a história da Revolução Rio-grandense*, 98–103.

2. "Manifesto dos principais chefes federalistas," doc. 1 in Villalba, *Revolução Federalista*, 3–5. On pro-insurgent sympathies, see *Las noticias* (Rivera), March 1893; the Brazilian war was very good for business in northern Uruguay: "El director de aduanas," *Las noticias*, 12 May 1893; "Campos y ganados," *El deber cívico*, 6 April 1894.

3. "Sección telegráfica," *El deber cívico*, 21 March 1893.

4. "Del Brasil," *El deber cívico*, 28 March 1893; Escobar, *Apontamentos para a história da Revolução Rio-grandense*, 103.

5. "Correspondencia: 5a sección," *El deber cívico*, 7 April 1893.

6. Letter from Aparicio Saravia to Cándida Díaz, 2 April 1893, collection of Diego Saravia, Cerro Largo.

7. Photograph in the Museu Dom Diogo de Souza, Bagé. "Adios verano," *El deber cívico*, 4 April 1893.

8. Villalba, *Revolução Federalista*, xii. Quotations: "Sección especial," *El deber cívico*, 9 Jan. 1893; and Angelo Dourado, *Voluntários do martírio: Fatos e episódios da guerra civil* (Porto Alegre: Martins Livreiro, 1979), 164 (first published 1896). On Latorre and Macedo, see "Desfile de veteranos," *La alborada* (Montevideo), 15 Mar. 1899; and Dourado, *Voluntários do martírio*, 164.

9. "Los revolucionarios brasileños en Montevideo," *El deber cívico*, 27 April 1894; "En el campamento revolucionario," *El día*, 22 Sept. 1897; Mena Segarra says there was only one woman with Saravia's force in 1897, while many accompanied the government troops: *Aparicio Saravia: Las últimas patriadas*, 71.

10. "Salteadores" and "Boatos alarmantes," *O jornal do comércio*, 3 Aug., 8 Aug., and 13 Sept. 1892, and many other reports in the second half of 1893; also "Los sucesos del Brasil," *El deber cívico*, 17 Feb. 1893; "Banditismo," *O Canabarro*, 21 Nov. 1895; Love, *Rio Grande do Sul and Brazilian Regionalism*, 59–61; and Medeiros, *História do Herval*, 152–65.

HARD TIMES

1. See John Charles Chasteen, "Background to Civil War: The Process of Land Tenure in Brazil's Southern Borderland, 1801–1893," *Hispanic American Historical Review* 71 (1991), 737–60. On the climate of violence, see Love, *Rio Grande do Sul and Brazilian Regionalism*, 54–59.

2. An 1894 property map of Bagé is preserved in the Museu Dom Diogo de Souza, Bagé. Similar information can be gleaned from the registry of "salidas fiscales" in the Banco Hipotecario del Uruguay. For comparative perspective, see Jonathan Brown, *A Socioeconomic History of Argentina, 1776–1860* (Cambridge: Cambridge University Press, 1979), 146–62; and María Sáenz Quesada, *Los estancieros* (Buenos Aires: Editorial de Belgrano, 1980), 246–48.

3. "Bagé ha trinta anos," *Correio mercantil*, 6 August 1887. Census figures as follows:

For Cerro Largo:

| 1860 | 17,475 | (National Census 1860) |
| 1908 | 73,519 | (National Census 1908, includes Treinta y Tres) |

For the Rio Grande Frontier:

1858	37,541	(Compiled from parochial lists, missing districts 3 and 4 of Bagé.)
1900	101,343	(National Census 1900, includes Bagé, Cacimbinhas, Piratini, Cangussu, Herval, Arroio Grande, and Jaguarão.)

Fundação de Economia e Estatística, *Censos do RS, 1803–1950*, pp. 66, 109; *Anuario estadístico de la República Oriental del Uruguay*, 1902–3 and 1908.

4. On the "pobrerío rural," see José Pedro Barrán and Benjamín Nahum, *Historía social de las revoluciones de 1897 y 1904*, vol. 4, 1972, 21–47. Signs of increasing rural poverty multiplied in *El deber cívico* during the fall and winter of 1893. Although the Cerro Largo cattle market improved by early 1895 ("Bueno para los ganaderos," 18 Jan. 1895) poverty did not decrease ("Los limosneros," 12 Mar. 1895). Cf. the 1860s, when the police chief counted ten beggars in all of Cerro Largo: "Anexo Número 12," in *Memoria que el Ministro de Estado en el Departamento de Gobierno presenta a la Honorable Asamblea Jeneral Legislativa en 1861* (Montevideo: Imprenta de la viuda de Jaime Hernández, 1861), 63. On rural-urban migration, see Juan Rial, *La población uruguaya y el crecimiento económico social entre 1850 y 1930: Cambio demográfico y urbanización en un pequeño país* (Montevideo: Centro de Informaciones y Estudios Sociales del Uruguay, 1981); also "Por las calles," *El deber cívico*, 23 May 1893. Quotation: "Morreu de fome," *Cruzeiro do Sul*, 8 June 1884.

5. On fencing in Uruguay, see Raúl Jacob, *Consequencias sociales del alambramiento (1872–1880)* (Montevideo: Ediciones de la Banda Oriental, 1969); José Pedro Barrán and Benjamín Nahum, *Historía rural del Uruguay moderno, 1851–1885*, vol. 1, 1967, 536–37; and "Cuadros estadísticos de la contribución directa de los departamentos de campaña," in *Contribuyentes de la contribución directa* (Montevideo: Contaduría del Estado, 1877–1880). On the apparently slower process in Brazil, see Franco, "A campanha," 70–71; and Brito, *Trabalhos e costumes*, 25. Usufruct rights were imperiled but not immediately canceled by enclosure; see "José Antônio da Costa ao público," *O Cruzeiro do Sul*, 15 Feb. 1885. The chief public issue was how fences affected freedom of transit: "Estrada tapada," *O Cruzeiro do Sul*, 22 May 1884; "Sobre desvíos de caminos," *La voz de Rivera*, 2 Aug. 1885; "Cortes de alambres," *El ciudadano* (Melo), 11 March 1887.

6. Francisco J. Ros, *La feria de Melo: Reflexiones económicas sobre los departamentos de Cerro Largo, Trienta y Tres, Rocha, Minas, y Maldonado* (Montevideo: Tipografía de El Nacional, 1902), 15–16; Barrán and Nahum, *Historía social de las revoluciones de 1897 y 1904*, 34–35. Ad from *El independiente* (Melo), Oct.–Dec., 1867.

7. AGNJ, "Causa contra Rufino Silva por abijeato," Letrados, Cerro Largo 1893/103. See censuses of Cerro Largo (1890), Durazno (1892), and Treinta y Tres (1895), in the *Anuario estadístico de la República Oriental del Uruguay* (1889), 718–27; (1894), 711–14 and 724–28. For Rio Grande do Sul, a slave census from the time of emancipation appears in AHRS, "Relatório do Presidente da Provincia," José Júlio de Albuquerque Barros, 19 September 1885.

8. AHRS, Autos crime, Bagé 1849/3329; AGNJ, Letrados, Cerro Largo 1826/3, 1831/8 and 1832/6. See the pardon urged by local landowners for a number of prisoners for abigeato: AGN, Jefatura Política de Cerro Largo (José Arredondo), 3 Sept. 1865. First quotation: "Correspondência de Autoridades Militares, 1821," cited in Sérgio da Costa Franco, *Origens de Jaguarão (1790–1833)* (Porto Alegre: Escola Superior de Teologia São Lourenço de Brindes; Caxias do Sul: Universidade de Caxias do Sul, 1980), 82; second quotation: "Furto de gado," *União Liberal,* 27 October 1886. See also Assunçao, *El gaucho,* 186–87.

9. Barrán and Nahum, *Historía social de las revoluciones de 1897 y 1904*, 37–38. Generalizations are based on twenty cases in Cerro Largo during 1893 (AGN, Letrados, Cerro Largo 1893/3, 4, 7, 10, 19, 54–6, 68, 83, 87, 92–6, 99, 102, 103, 147); and on twenty cases in the Brazilian municípios of Bagé, Herval, and Jaguarão, 1888–92 (APRS, Autos crime, Bagé 1888–91/ 4306, 4310, 4317, 4338, 4344, 4360, 4362, 4363, 4381, 4383, 4400; Jaguarão, 1889–91/ 2757A, 2733, 2744, 2747, 2768, 2762; Herval, 1889–90/532, 536, 542. Prosecutions for animal theft in Cerro Largo rose from nineteen in 1886–1888 to fifty-nine in 1889–1891: "Jefaturas de Campaña," *Anuario estadístico de la República Oriental del Uruguay,* 1886–1891. First quotation: "D. Pedrito," *O Cruzeiro do Sul,* 25 May 1884; second quotation: "Correspondencia," *El deber cívico,* 9 May 1893.

10. AGN, "Causa contra Presentación Pereira y Felisbino Antonio Gularte por abijeato," Letrados, Cerro Largo 1893/93; "Causa contra Antonio Tavares por abijeato," 1893/83; "Causa contra Tomás Silva y Clarimundo González por abijeato," 1893/56; "Causa contra Fernando Viera y Justiniano Tavarez por homicidio y abijeato," 1893/87.

11. Ros, *La feria de Melo,* 10–11 and passim.

12. AGNJ, "Testamentaría de doña Propícia da Rosa," Letrados, Cerro Largo 1880/167; "Testamentaría de don Ciséreo Saravia," 1894/184; "Testamentaría de don Francisco Saravia," 1894/212. Barrán and Nahum, *Historía social de las revoluciones de 1897 y 1904,* 86.

13. *Anuario estadístico de la República Oriental del Uruguay,* (1894) [*sic*], 711–14. On the rise of fatteners like Silveira, see Barrán and Nahum, *Historia rural del Uruguay moderno,* vol. 2, *La crisis económica, 1886–1894* (Montevideo: Ediciones de la Banda Oriental, 1971), 206–11. On the borderland's economic conservatism, see vol. 3: *Recuperación y dependencia, 1895–1904* (Montevideo: Ediciones de la Banda Oriental, 1975), 191–203; Germán W. Rama, "Dependencia y segmentación en el Uruguay del siglo XIX," *Revista paraguaya de sociología* 16 (1979): 54–56; and Carbajal, *La Penetración luso-brasileña,* 155–56.

14. See *El deber cívico:* "Ramón E. Silveira," 5 April 1895; "Venta de ganado," 17 May 1895; "La exposición de Cerro Largo," 4 Aug. 1895; "Progreso ganadero," 19 Nov. 1895; "De tres islas," 17 Mar. 1896; "Exposición ganadera," 1 May 1896; "Manifesto," 22 May 1896; "Ramón E. Silveira," 16 June 1896.

15. AGN, "Sumario contra Domingo José dos Santos por la muerte de Tertuliano Pifania," Letrados, Cerro Largo 1873/106. The situation of an agregado's agregado was precarious indeed. See also "Causa contra Lorenzo Justiniano Martínez por abijeato," Letrados, Cerro Largo 1896/29.

16. Monegal, *Vida de Aparicio Saravia,* 19–20.

17. APRS, "Inventario de Manuel Amaro da Silveira," Cartório de Orfãos e Ausentes, Jaguarão, 1824/76. On the eve of the 1893 war, Bagé probate inventories showed a mean of just 336 per heir: APRS, 1 Cartório de Orfãos e Ausentes, inv. 544–640; 1 Cartório Civel e Crime, inv. 136–168 (incomplete documents excluded). The average size of 1,914 hectares for the properties subdivided in Bagé, 1887–1892, is close to the average of 1,899 hectares per landowner in the Saravias' neighborhood, as shown by the Uruguayan agricultural census of 1900: *Anuario estadístico de la República Oriental del Uruguay,* 1900.

18. AGNJ, "Testamentaría de María Sensata Saravia," Letrados, Cerro Largo 1897/135; APRS, "Inventario de Manuel Saraiva do Amaral," Cartório de Orfãos e Ausentes, Herval 1897/261; "Registro Paroquial," Secção Extra Judiciária, Herval, 1854–57; Robert Wilton Wilcox, "Cattle Ranching on the Brazilian Frontier: Tradition and In-

novation in Mato Grosso, 1870–1940" (Ph.D. diss., New York University, 1992), 151.

19. "Suicídio," *O jornal do comércio,* 2 April 1892. In Uruguay there were eighty-five lawyers, seventy in Montevideo: "Profesiones, industrias, y ramos de comercio," *Anuario estadístico de la República Oriental 1889,* 662; in Porto Alegre, 44 lawyers: "Advocacia," *O jornal do comércio,* 20 March 1892. See also Censo del Departamento de Cerro Largo (executed 31 August 1890), in *Anuario estadístico de la República Oriental del Uruguay* 1889 [*sic*], 718–23.

20. Lucía Sala de Touron et al., *La evolución económica de la Banda Oriental* (Montevideo: Ediciones Pueblos Unidos, 1967): 12, 81–120, 121–29, 157; and Dreys, *Notícia descritiva,* 164–66. On the importance of the Pelotas market in Uruguay, see *El estanciero* (Melo): "La exportación de ganado en pié para el Brasil," 22 May 1886; "El último mono," 26 May 1886; "Exportación de ganado," 23 June 1886; and "Temores infundados," 30 June 1886; see also *El Cerro Largo* (Melo): "El impuesto de exportación," 21 Nov. 1885; and "La exportación de ganados," 2 April 1887.

21. For estimates of cattle illegally exported from Uruguay, see Barrán and Nahum, *Historia rural,* vol. 2: *La crisis económica, 1886–1894,* 125–28. On the Farrapos, see Spencer Leitman, *Raízes sócio-econômicas,* 123–47. On the Brazilian–Uruguayan Treaty of 1851, see Mario Dotta, Duaner Freire, and Nelson Rodríguez, *El Uruguay ganadero: de la explotación primitiva a la crisis actual* (Montevideo: Ediciones de la Banda Oriental, 1972), 50–52; and Gil Villaamil, *Ensayo para una historia de Cerro Largo,* 119.

22. AGN, Jefatura Política de Cerro Largo, Joaquín Suárez, 27 Nov. 1866, and Nicomedes Castro, 15 Jan. 1870; AGNJ, "Sumario contra don Manuel Amaro da Silveira y el Sub-Receptor de San Servando por extracción de ganado," Letrados, Cerro Largo 1843/1; APRS, "Sumário por contrabando," Autos crime, Herval 1871/498. Quotation: AGNJ, "Sumario contra don Felixberto Barcelo por extracción de ganado," Letrados, Cerro Largo 1843/11. On Mauá's men, see "Conflito na fronteira," *União Liberal,* 27 Feb. 1886.

23. AGNJ, "Causa contra Don Manuel Viera Carrillo y Don Santiago Varela por contrabando," Letrados, Cerro Largo 1843/7; APRS, "Contrabando," Autos crime, Bagé 1848/3323. See articles on "Contrabando," in *União Liberal,* 6 March and 16 June 1887, 22 February, 23 March, 17 April, 18 May, and 18 March 1888.

24.   AHRS, Camara Muncipal de Bagé, 26 Feb. 1853 (Caixa 103); *Memoria de la Jefatura Política y de Policía del Departamento de Cerro Largo correspondiente a los años de 1876–77–78* (Montevideo: La Tribuna, 1879). See also Oscar Mourat, *La crisis comercial en la cuenca del Plata (1880–1920)* (Montevideo: Ediciones de la Banda Oriental, 1973), 67–68; Gil Villaamil, *Ensayo para una historia de Cerro Largo,* 119; and Franco, "A campanha," 70.

25.   "El contrabando," *El deber cívico,* 4 Aug. 1896. On the anti-contraband crusade in Cerro Largo, see *El deber cívico:* "Cartas cambiadas," 20 Jan. 1893; "Un asunto de actualidad," 12 June 1894; "El contrabando," 15 June 1894; "Revelaciones de un remitido," 3 July 1894; "Detalles de una manifestación fracasada," 6 July 1894; "Sección especial," 10 July 1894; and "Servicio de policias de la frontera," 30 Oct. 1894. Also, *El Partido Colorado* (Melo): "Los verdaderos contrabandistas," 14 Oct. 1893; "Sobre contrabando, 28 Oct. 1893; and "De la frontera," 17 Jan. 1894. For Brazilian perspectives, see "O contrabando," *O Canabarro* (Rivera), 17 Oct. 1895 and 13 Sept. 1896; "A campanha e suas necessidades," *A Pátria* (Montevideo), 28 August, 6 Sept, 10 Sept, 1887; "O contrabando e a tarifa especial," *O Brasil* (Montevideo), 20 Feb 1890; and "Processos de contrabando," *O jornal do comércio,* 6 Aug. 1890.

26.   Uruguay, *Memoria de la Jefatura Política y de Policía de Rivera,* 1895 (Montevideo: Tip. Litografía Oriental, 1896), 19–23; *O jornal do comércio:* "Imposto de gado" (7 Feb. 1892) and "A vida (3 May 1892); *A Pátria* (Montevideo): "Exportação de gados" (18 Sept. 1883) and "O privilégio na questão de exportação de gados" (23 Jan. 1885). See also Pedro Cosio, *Aduanas de fronteras: Estudio presentado por el subtesorero de la aduana al Ministro de Hacienda* (Montevideo: A. Barreiro y Ramos, 1905), and *Diario de sesiones de la Cámara de Representantes* (1888), 95:81–94, 95:236–71.

27.   See Sandra Jatahy Pesavento, *República velha gaúcha: Charqueadas—frigoríficos—criadores* (Porto Alegre: Editôra Movimento, 1980), 36–39, 124–51; Love, *Rio Grande do Sul and Brazilian Regionalism,* 54–55; Barrán and Nahum, *Historia rural,* vol. 2, *La crisis económica, 1886–1894,* 33–48 and 117–44; vol. 3, *Recuperación y dependencia, 1895–1904,* 45–48; and vol. 5, *La prosperidad frágil, 1905–1914,* 66–67, 147–49. Also, "La tarifa de exportación para los ganados de Cerro Largo," *El telégrafo marítimo* (Montevideo), 12 Feb. 1885; "Mejoraríamos," *El Cerro Largo,* 10 Oct. 1885; and *Diario de sesiones de la*

Cámara de Representantes (1888), 95:274–301. On early emancipation, "Viva o abolicionismo," *Cruzeiro do Sul,* 11 Sept. 1884.

28. AGNJ, "Causa contra Terencio and Cesário Sarabia por Contrabando," Letrados, Cerro Largo 1892/137; Fonseca, *Gumersindo Saravia,* 82–84.

29. "Imposto de gado," *O jornal do comércio,* 7 Feb 1892.

APRIL–OCTOBER 1893

1. "Los sucesos de Río Grande," *El deber cívico,* 11 April 1893.

2. Escobar, *Apontamentos para a história da Revolução Rio-grandense,* 106–33. For Republican strength in the western borderland, see AHRS, Papers of Barros Cassals, 1892 passim, Particulares, Lata 36, Maço 10.

3. Escobar, *Apontamentos para a história da Revolução Rio-grandense,* 117–18.

4. Love, *Rio Grande do Sul and Brazilian Regionalism,* 65–66; Escobar, *Apontamentos para a história da Revolução Rio-grandense,* 119; Mena Segarra, *Aparicio Saravia: las últimas patriadas,* 20.

5. *El deber cívico:* "Sección especial," 9 May 1893; and "Ultima hora," 16 May 1893. Also, Escobar, *Apontamentos para a história da Revolução Rio-grandense,* 119–24.

6. Fonseca, *Gumersindo Saravia,* 297–98.

7. See *El deber cívico:* "Párrafos de una carta," 30 May 1893; "La revolución federal," 6 June 1893; "Correspondencia: Aceguá," 30 June; 4 July; 7 July, and 18 July 1893; Escobar, *Apontamentos para a história da Revolução Rio-grandense,* 126–49; and "Sobre la prisión del general Tavares," *El Partido Colorado,* 12 Aug. 1893.

8. Letter from Aparicio Saravia to Cándida Díaz, 26 June 1893, collection of Diego Saravia, Cerro Largo. See also Villalba, *Revolução Federalista,* pp. lxv–lxvi; and Escobar, *Apontamentos para a história da Revolução Rio-grandense,* 151–53. For a version more sympathetic to Salgado, see Antônio Augusto de Carvalho, *Apontamentos sobre a revolução no Rio Grande do Sul* (Montevideo: El Siglo Ilustrado, 1895), 12–14.

9. Angelo Dourado, *Voluntários do martírio,* 17–18.

10. "Ultima hora," *El deber cívico,* 5 Sept. 1893; Escobar, *A Revolução Rio-grandense,* 153–58.

11. Escobar, *A Revolução Rio-grandense,* 157–58; Fonseca, *Gumersindo Saravia,* 313; Dourado, *Voluntários do martírio,* 22–26; letter

from Aparicio Saravia to Cándida Díaz, 31 August 1893, collection of Diego Saravia, Cerro Largo.

12. Carvalho, *Apontamentos*, 31; Escobar, *Apontamentos para a história da Revolução Rio-grandense*, 158–65; Dourado, *Voluntários do martírio*, 57; and Love, *Rio Grande do Sul and Brazilian Regionalism*, 66–69.

STRONGMEN

1. Dourado, *Voluntários do martírio*, 272.

2. Halperín Donghi, *Contemporary History of Latin America*, 77–79.

3. See Sílvio R. Duncan Baretta and John Markoff, "Civilization and Barbarism: Cattle Frontiers in Latin America," *Comparative Studies in Society and History* 20 (1978): 587–620. On the death of Cándido Saravia, see AGN, Jefatura Política de Cerro Largo, 31 Dec. 1876. Quotation: Lessa and Côrtes, *Aspectos da sociabilidade gaúcha*, 15.

4. Mena Segarra, *Aparicio Saravia: las últimas patriadas*, 68; and Justino Zavala Muniz, *Crónica de Muniz* (Montevideo: El Siglo Ilustrado, 1921), 163–74. For comparative perspective, see Robert L. O'Connell, *Of Arms and Men: A History of War, Weapons, and Aggression* (Oxford: Oxford University Press, 1989), 40–41, 84–93.

5. Bouton, *La vida rural*, 293 and 434; Robert Crawford, *South American Sketches* (London: Longman's, Green, and Co., 1898), 41–42.

6. Lessa and Côrtes, *Aspectos da sociabilidade gaúcha*, 22; Saravia García, *Memorias*, 22; Monegal, *Vida de Aparicio Saravia*, 34–38.

7. Zavala Muniz, *Crónica de Muniz*, 113–14. For a general treatment, see John Charles Chasteen, "Violence for Show: Knife Dueling on a Nineteenth-Century Cattle Frontier," in *The Problem of Order in Changing Societies: Essays on Crime and Policing in Argentina and Uruguay*, ed. Lyman L. Johnson (Albuquerque: University of New Mexico Press, 1990).

8. Eduardo Acevedo Díaz, "El primer suplicio," in *Los mejores cuentos camperos del siglo XIX*, ed. Diego Pérez Pintos (Montevideo: Ediciones de la Banda Oriental, 1966), 15–20. See also AHRS, "Relação dos escravos fugidos para o Estado Oriental pertencentes a diversas pessoas desta província, 1850," Lata 531, Maço 1; APRS, Autos crime, Piratini 1834/1078 and Bagé 1853/3347; and AGNJ, Letrados, Cerro Largo 1839/22 (quoted).

9. John Charles Chasteen, "Trouble Between Men and Women: Machismo on Nineteenth-Century Estancias," in *The Middle Period in Latin American History: Essays on Values and Attitudes in the 17th–19th Centuries*, ed. Mark D. Szuchman (New York: Lynne Rienner Publishers, 1989).

10. AGNJ, "Sumario contra Ignacio Muñoz por haber forzado a Juana María Sarabia," Letrados, Cerro Largo 1861/35; Monegal, *Vida de Aparicio Saravia,* 44.

11. AGNJ, "Doña Cecilia Saravia contra don Agustín Abreu por separación de bienes," Letrados, Cerro Largo 1896/177; Monegal, *Vida de Aparicio Saravia,* 36; and Fonseca, *Gumersindo Saravia,* 70 (quoted).

12. Fonseca, *Gumersindo Saravia,* 269; Monegal, *Vida de Aparicio Saravia,* 43–45.

13. AGN, Jefatura Política de Cerro Largo, 16 May 1872; and correspondencia pasiva, Fondo Ministerio de Gobierno, 24 March 1853, and 7, 8, and 15 June 1853 (Caja 1004), and 15 Feb. 1859 (Caja 1095); AGNJ, "Elecciones de Alcalde Ordinario, Defensor de Menores, Jueces de Paz, y Tenientes Alcaldes de este departamento," Letrados, Cerro Largo 1855/1.

14. AGN, Jefatura Política de Cerro Largo, 24 October 1878. *O jornal do comércio* (Pelotas), 15 Sept. 1878; Fonseca, *Gumersindo Saravia,* 81–94, 101; Mena Segarra, *Aparicio Saravia: las últimas patriadas,* 13.

15. Fonseca, *Gumersindo Saravia,* 95–105.

16. APRS, "Inventários de Gomercindo Saraiva and Francisco Saraiva," Cartório de Orfãos and Ausentes, Santa Vitória do Palmar 1895/1925 and 1897; Cartório do crime, "Sumários," Santa Vitória do Palmar 1888/1105, 1890/1121.

17. APRS, Cartório do Crime, "Sumários," Santa Vitória do Palmar 1890/1123, 1891/1141, 1891/1142.

18. Mena Segarra, *Aparicio Saravia: las últimas patriadas,* 10–11; Fonseca, *Gumersindo Saravia,* 58–59.

19. AGNJ, "Testamentaría de Propícia de la Rosa," Letrados, Cerro Largo 1880/167; "Testamentaría de Francisco Saravia de Amaral," 1894/special collection; "Sucesión de Aparicio Saravia," 1904/special collection. Escribanía del Juzgado Ordinario (Melo), 27 April, 16 May, 17 May 1866. See also Fonseca, *Gumersindo Saravia,* 128–29.

20. Gálvez, *Vida de Aparicio Saravia,* 116.

JANUARY–AUGUST 1894

1. Dourado, *Voluntários do martírio*, 152; Escobar, *Apontamentos para a história da Revolução Rio-grandense*, 195–202.

2. Fonseca, *Gumersindo Saravia*, 381–88; Escobar, *Apontamentos para a história da Revolução Rio-grandense*, 249–66.

3. Dourado, *Voluntários do martírio*, 178–80; Fonseca, *Gumersindo Saravia*, 427–28.

4. Escobar, *Apontamentos para a história da Revolução Rio-grandense*, 202–32; Love, *Rio Grande do Sul and Brazilian Regionalism*, 68–69; Dourado, *Voluntários do martírio*, 63; and Fonseca, *Gumersindo Saravia*, 437–45.

5. Love, *Rio Grande do Sul and Brazilian Regionalism*, 69–70; Escobar, *Apontamentos para a história da Revolução Rio-grandense*, 271–81; Mena Segarra, *Aparicio Saravia: las últimas patriadas*, 24–25.

6. Escobar, *Apontamentos para a história da Revolução Rio-grandense*, 282–83; *El deber cívico:* "Rio Grande," 28 Sept. 1894; "Ultimos momentos de Saraiva," 25 Sept. 1894.

7. Love, *Rio Grande do Sul and Brazilian Regionalism*, 66–68; Escobar, *Apontamentos para a história da Revolução Rio-grandense*, 167–93; *El deber cívico:* "La revolución federal," 1 Dec. 1893; "La revolución federal," 27 February 1894; "La verdad sobre los sucesos del sitio de Bagé," 13 March 1894.

8. Letter from Aparicio Saravia to Cándida Díaz, 20 November 1894, collection of Diego Saravia, Cerro Largo: "llo no pensaba embolberme mas en la rebolucion pero como esabido que los tiranos desenterraron alfinado y lo anecho pedasos me obliga atomar armas en bengansa de su cadaber" [*sic*]. See also Saravia García, *Memorias*, 29.

THE WILL TO BELIEVE

1. This chapter has been influenced by Melissa M. Bullard, "The Magnificent Lorenzo de Medici: Between Myth and History," in *Politics and Culture in Early Modern Europe: Essays in Honour of H. G. Koenigsberger*, ed. Phyllis Mack and Margaret C. Jacob (Cambridge: Cambridge University Press, 1987), 25–58. *El deber cívico:* "Guayabas," 1 May; "Noticias de Saraiva," 18 May 1894; "Asuntos brasileros," 17 August 1894; "Sobre Saraiva," 14 Sept. 1894; "Sobre Saraiva," 18 Sept. 1894; "Todavía Saraiva," 21 Sept. 1894. Quotation: AHRS, Delegacia de Polícia, Santa Vitória do Palmar, 11 Sept. 1893.

2.   *El deber cívico:* "Correspondência: Aceguá," 18 July 1893; "Los revolucionarios brasileros en Montevideo," 27 April 1894; and "Saraiva," 6–13 Nov. 1894.

3.   Francisco Ricardo Rudiger, "A imprensa: fonte e agente da Revolução de 1893"(unpublished paper presented in the Museu Dom Diogo de Souza, Bagé, November 1983), 2–4. In 1891, Rio Grande do Sul had the highest literacy rate in Brazil: Love, *Rio Grande do Sul and Brazilian Regionalism,* 19–20.

4.   "Ferocidade humana," *O jornal do comércio,* 15 Dec. 1892; See also "Assassinato e linchamento" (from Minas Gerais), *Folha nova* (Porto Alegre), 1 Jan. 1893; "Selvageria" (from Rio), *Diario do Rio Grande,* 14 Jan. 1893; "Horrível" (from the U.S.), *O jornal do comércio,* 18 April 1891; "Fato bárbaro" (from Recife), *O jornal do comércio,* 13 March 1891; "Jack o estripador," *O jornal do comércio,* 14 May 1891.

5.   Germano Hasslocher, *A verdade sobre a Revolução* (Porto Alegre: Livraria Americana, 1894), 10. See also "Horroroso," *Folha do sul* (Bagé), 15 Jan. 1893; "Proclamação do Gen. Joca Tavares, distribuida pela campanha a 5 de fevereiro de 1893," doc. 47, in Villalba, *Revolução Federalista,* 97–98; "A invasão," *El deber cívico,* 2 May 1893; Escobar, *Apontamentos para a história da Revolução Rio-grandense,* 286–87; Love, *Rio Grande do Sul and Brazilian Regionalism,* 58–59.

6.   AHRS, Delegacia de Polícia, Bagé, 17 March 1893; Euclides B. de Moura, *O vandalismo no Rio Grande do Sul* (Pelotas: Livraria Universal, 1892), 66–73. See also the Republican press accounts in Gustavo Morritz, *Acontecimentos políticos no Rio Grande do Sul,* 89–90–91 (Porto Alegre: Tip. Thurmann, 1939.

7.   Dourado, *Voluntários do martírio,* 17, 36.

8.   Dourado, *Voluntários do martírio,* 3–4.

9.   For a contemporary emphasis on the generational contrast, see "Atualidade política," *O jornal do comércio,* 7–18 June 1890.

10.   Dourado, *Voluntários do martírio,* 6–10, 133–34; Hasslocher, *A verdade sobre a Revolução,* 56–61.

11.   J. Simões Lopes Neto, *Cancioneiro guasca,* 2d ed. (Rio de Janeiro: Editôra Globo, 1960), 141. See also "A face desconhecida de Gomercindo Saraiva, *Correio do povo,* 10 July 1938; Apolinário Porto Alegre, *Cancioneiro da Revolução de 1835* (Porto Alegre: Companhia União de Seguros, 1981), 39; and Dourado, *Voluntários do martírio,* 14.

12. Quotations: Fonseca, *Gumersindo Saravia,* 155–57, 268, 291. See also Gálvez, *Vida de Aparicio Saravia,* 39; and *El deber cívico:* "La revolución federalista," 8 May 1894; "Noticias de Saraiva," 18 May 1894; and "Sucesos del Brasil," 1 June 1894.

13. Dornelles, *Gumersindo Saraiva: O guerrilheiro pampeano,* 77–79.

14. *Correio do povo:* "A face desconhecida de Gomercindo Saraiva," 10 July 1938 and 4 August 1938 (quoted); also "Gomercindo não passou," 23 August 1938.

15. Fonseca, *Gumersindo Saravia,* 74, 543.

16. *El deber cívico:* "De Rio Grande," 6 July 1894; "La revolución riograndense," 20 July 1894; "Asuntos del Brasil," 27 July 1894; and "Asuntos brasileros," 17 Aug. 1894. "Gumercindo Saraiva," *El deber cívico,* 8 June 1894; "A face desconhecida de Gomercindo Saraiva," *Correio do povo,* 10 July 1938; Dourado, *Voluntários do martírio,* 87–99.

17. See poems dedicated to "O gaúcho, *O paladino* (Porto Alegre), 15 Jan. 1893. Fonseca, *Gumersindo Saravia,* 324.

18. Archivo Aparicio Saravia (Estado Mayor del Ejercito, Montevideo), letter from I. Ramasso to José Saravia, 30 June 1894.

19. "Cartas rio-grandenses," *O jornal do comércio,* 3 March 1889, 19 March 1889, 9 April 1889, and 8 Nov. 1891.

20. "Cartas de Silvério," *O Canabarro,* 14 May, 28 June, and 13 Aug. 1896.

21. *Homenagem aos heróis da Revolução de 1893* (Rivera: Tipografia d'O Maragato, 1901) 55–56; "Telegr. de Gumercindo Saraiva ao. mar. Floriano Peixoto consitando-o a deixar o poder," doc. 121, in Villalba, *Revolução Federalista,* 236; Amaro da Silveira's "Ordem do dia," *O Canabarro,* 17 Sept. 1895.

22. "Funeral," *El deber cívico,* 12 Feb. 1895; Fonseca, *Gumersindo Saravia,* 538–39 (quoted). For the negotiations ending the war, see Love, *Rio Grande do Sul and Brazilian Regionalism,* 71–72; and Escobar, *Apontamentos para a história da Revolução Rio-grandense,* 334–40.

23. Bouton, *La vida rural,* 439. Quotations in *O Canabarro:* "Ahí vem," 7 Mar. 1895; and "10 de agosto," 9 Aug. 1896. On Saldanha da Gama, see Love, *Rio Grande do Sul and Brazilian Regionalism,* 70–71; and Escobar, *Apontamentos para a história da Revolução Rio-grandense,* 307–34.

24. Letter from Aparicio Saravia to Cándida Díaz, undated fragment, collection of Diego Saravia, Cerro Largo.

OCTOBER 1895

1. "Un interview con Aparicio Saravia en las costas del Quebracho," *El deber cívico*, 12 Nov. 1895.

2. Mena Segarra, *Aparicio Saravia: las últimas patriadas*, 30.

3. See Enrique Méndez Vives, *El Uruguay de la modernización, 1876–1904*, 3d ed. (Montevideo: Ediciones de la Banda Oriental, 1977).

4. *El deber cívico:* "Crónica social," 17 April 1894; "Luz, más luz!," 1 Jan. 1895; and "Breve descripción de Melo," 25 June 1895. See also Uruguay, *Diario de sesiones de la Cámara de Representantes* (1895), 139:256–58 and 143:398–99; and Gil Villaamil, *Ensayo para una historia de Cerro Largo*, 131–48.

5. AGNJ, "Sucesión de don Aparicio Saravia," 1904/special collection; Díaz, *Historia de Saravia*, 228; and Saravia García, *Memorias*, 21. For the tax evaluation of Saravia's land, see "Contribución Inmobiliaria," *El deber cívico*, 13 July 1894.

6. José Virginio Díaz, *Los Saravia: Una familia de Guerreros (Apuntes rápidos para una biografía)* (Montevideo: La Razón, 1903), 87–94.

7. "El tostado de Francisco Saravia versus el potrillo oscuro de Muniz," *El deber cívico*, 15 Nov. 1895. On Muniz, see Zavala Muniz, *Crónica de Muniz*.

8. AGNJ, "Varios ciudadanos en queja contra el presidente de la mesa receptora de votos de la 9a sección por falsificación de votos," Letrados, Cerro Largo 1887/172; "Resabios de antaño," *El ciudadano* (Melo), 15 Mar. 1887; *El deber cívico:* "Triunfo espléndido," 30 Nov. 1887; "Nuestro boletín último," 13 Dec. 1887; "Escrutinio verdadero," 7 Feb. 1888; "Apéndice al escrutinio verdadero," 10 Feb. 1888; and "Reincidencia criminal," 22 Feb. 1888.

9. "Nuestras fuerzas," *El eco nacionalista* (Melo), 9 Oct. 1890.

10. AGN, "Interesantes apuntes biográficos de los Coroneles, árbitros y señores del departamento de Cerro Largo," Papeles de José Gabriel Palomeque (1860–1863), II, Caja 372; AGNJ, "Comandante General del Departamento," Letrados, Cerro Largo 1849/21; Gil Villaamil, *Ensayo para una historia de Cerro Largo*, 51–72.

11. Zavala Muniz, *Crónica de Muniz*, 32–39.

THE MYTH OF THE PATRIADA

1. On myth, see Roland Barthes, *Mythologies* (New York: Hill and Wang, 1972). Barthes' ideas have been applied to Mexico by Ilene O'Malley, *The Myth of the Revolution: Hero Cults and the Institutionalization of the Mexican State, 1920–1940* (New York: Greenwood Press, 1987).

2. Alvaro Barros Lémez, *La obra cuentística de Javier de Viana* (Montevideo: Libros del Astillero, 1985) 15–20, 128–30. Javier de Viana (1868–1926) was quite prolific and published partisan fiction in the newspapers throughout his life. See Renie Sum Scott, *Javier de Viana: un narrador del 900* (Montevideo: Ediciones de la Banda Oriental, 1986).

3. "Sangre Vieja" (dated October 1896), in Javier de Viana, *Gurí y otras novelas* (Biblioteca Rodó de Literatura e Historia: Autores Uruguayos; Montevideo: Claudio García y Cía., 1945), 130–31.

4. See Juan Pivel Devoto, *Historia de los partidos políticos en el Uruguay,* 2 vols. (Montevideo: Claudio García & Cía, 1942). On the cult of self-sacrifice, see Mena Segarra, *Aparicio Saravia: las últimas patriadas,* 69; and (for its connection to nationalism) Benedict Anderson, *Imagined Communities: Reflections on the Origin and Spread of Nationalism* (London: Verso, 1983), 129–40.

5. Pivel Devoto, *Historia de los partidos políticos,* 1:81–84; Díaz, *Los Saravia,* 42–43, 83–84; Gálvez, *Vida de Aparicio Saravia,* 148; Fonseca, *Gumersindo Saravia,* 176; Bouton, *La vida rural,* 105–6.

6. Juana de Ibarbourou, "La Guerra," in *Chico Carlo* (Buenos Aires: Editorial Sudamericana, 1944); Saravia García, *Memorias,* 54.

7. Antonio N. Pereira, *La lucha fratricida y la conciliación: boceto histórico-dramático* (Montevideo: El Siglo Ilustrado, 1897), 7–17.

8. Letter from Cándida Díaz to Aparicio Saravia, 4 October 1897, collection of Diego Saravia, Cerro Largo; Fonseca, *Gumersindo Saravia,* 549–50.

9. Eduardo Acevedo Díaz (1851–1924) became well known in southern Spanish America, though his reputation has not endured as well as Viana's. *Ismael,* the first of Acevedo's novels about the patriadas, appeared in 1888. See Eduardo Acevedo Díaz (h.), *La vida de batalla de Eduardo Acevedo Díaz* (Buenos Aires: El Ateneo, 1941), esp. documentary appendix: "Discurso pronunciado en Minas," 16 May 1896 (quoted); "Discurso pronunciado en Migues," 14 April 1896 (quoted); "Discurso pronunciado en el Club Pantaleón Pérez," 21 July 1896; "Dis-

curso pronunciado en San José," 8 Sept. 1896; Dourado, *Voluntários do martírio*, 56.

10. First quotation: Barros Lémez, *La obra cuentística*, 126–27; second quotation: Viana, "31 de Marzo," in *Campo* (Biblioteca Rodó de Literatura e Historia: Autores Uruguayos; Montevideo: Claudio García y Cía., 1945), 166–87.

11. Barrán, *Apogeo y crisis del Uruguay pastoril y caudillesco, 1838–1875*, 20–40; Mena Segarra, *Aparicio Saravia: las últimas patriadas*, 5.

12. The articles by Coronel are in *El deber cívico*: "La nación y el gobierno," 19 May 1893; "Los comicios de 1893," 15 Dec. 1893; "Refutación histórica," 11 and 14 Sept. 1894; and "Gumercindo Saraiva," 28 Sept. 1894. See also Antonio D. Lussich, *Los tres gauchos orientales*, Colección de clásicos uruguayos, no. 56 (Montevideo: Ministerio de Instrucción y Previsión Social, 1964). On the print media and national identities, see Anderson, *Imagined Communities*, 29–49.

13. Pereira, *La lucha fratricida y la conciliación*, 18–30.

14. Florencio Sánchez, "Carta 2: No creo en ustedes," in *El caudillaje criminal en Sud América / Cartas de un flojo / Diálogos de actualidad* (Montevideo: Ediciones del Río de la Plata, 1962), 31–34. Sánchez (1875–1910) is a leading figure in the history of theater in both Uruguay and Argentina. See Fernando García Esteban, *Vida de Florencio Sánchez* (Montevideo: Editorial Alfa, 1970).

15. See Javier de Viana, *Con divisa blanca* (Montevideo: Ediciones de la Plaza, 1979). Quotation: "El fraude electoral," *El nacional* (Montevideo), 1 Dec. 1896.

16. See previous chapter, "Hard Times."

17. Pivel Devoto, *Historia de los partidos políticos*, 287–337; and *El deber cívico*: "Cisma en el Partido Blanco," 5 Aug. 1887; and "La desorganización del Partido Nacional," 27 Sept. 1887.

MARCH–DECEMBER 1896

1. *El deber cívico*: "Inauguración del club Cnel. Dionisio Coronel," 17 Mar. 1896; and "Telegráfica," 20 Nov. 1896; and Mena Segarra, *Aparicio Saravia: las últimas patriadas*, 34.

2. "La revolución de los comícios," *La alborada* (Montevideo), 2d ser. (1898), 7:50–51.

3. "La revolución de los comícios," *La alborada*, 2d ser. (1898), 8:63–64.

4.   "Comisario de la 9a sección," *El deber cívico,* 10 Nov. 1896; Quotation: AGN, letter from Francisco J. Ros to Gumercindo Collazo, 24 Aug. 1896, Particulares, caja 182. See also Mena Segarra, *Aparicio Saravia: las últimas patriadas,* 46–50; "Rumores," *El deber cívico,* 7 Aug. 1896.

5.   "Silveira Martins," *O Canabarro,* 3 Dec. 1896. On the Muñoz family, see Arturo Ardao and Julio Castro, "Sesenta años de revolución: vida de Basilio Muñoz," in *Cuadernos de Marcha* (Montevideo), Dec. 1971.

6.   "La revolución de los comicios," *La alborada,* 2d ser. (1898), 9:73–75, 12:110–12, 13:122–24.

7.   "Narración sobre las campañas del 96 y 97 por el entonces Comandante Basilio Muñoz (h)," *La revista uruguaya: órgano del Partido Nacional* (1905), 11:14–18; 12:12–13.

8.   Saravia García, *Memorias,* 48–49; "La revolución de los comicios," *La alborada,* 2d ser. (1898), 21:217–20; Gálvez, *Vida de Aparicio Saravia,* 151.

9.   See *La revolución oriental de 1896: La campaña de Saravia* (Bagé: n.p., 1897) and (for the quotation) *Crónica de la insurrección: sus orígenes, sus comienzos, su marcha, y su derrota* (Montevideo: La Razón, 1896), 19–52.

10.   AGNJ, "Antecedentes relativos al incendio de la casa comercial de don José Zavala," Letrados, Cerro Largo 1896/100; Zavala Muniz, *Crónica de Muniz,* 225–53; and *El deber cívico:* "Incendio," 27 November 1896; "Efectos de la pacificación," 29 Dec. 1896; Mena Segarra, *Aparicio Saravia: las últimas patriadas,* 20; and Bouton, *La vida rural,* 288.

11.   "Chico Saravia en Buenos Aires," *El deber cívico,* 29 Dec. 1896; Archivo Aparicio Saravia, letters to Aparicio Saravia from Abdón Arósteguy (8 Jan. 1897) and Eduardo Acevedo Díaz (13 Feb. 1897).

12.   "Circo Vázquez," *El deber cívico,* 15 Jan. 1897; Zavala Muniz, *Crónica de Muniz,* 131–41.

A COUNTRYMAN IN REBELLION

1.   On the gauchesque tradition, see Lauro Ayestarán, *La primitiva poesía gauchesca en el Uruguay,* vol. 1: *1812–1838* (Montevideo: El Siglo Ilustrado, 1950); Adolfo Prieto, *El discurso criollista en la formación de la Argentina moderna* (Buenos Aires: Editorial Sudamericana,

1988); and Nicolas Shumway, *The Invention of Argentina* (Berkeley: University of California Press, 1991). Quotation: Díaz, *Los Saravia*, 44.

2.   See *Crónica de la insurrección*, 8 (quoted), and *El eco de la guerra: episódios de la presente campaña con ilustraciones de los principales jefes que actúan en ésta; biografías, episodios, anécdotas, sacrificios, rasgos de heroísmo, etc.* (Montevideo: La Nueva Central, 1897).

3.   On the hegemony of urban elite language see Angel Rama, *La ciudad letrada* (Hanover, N.H.: Ediciones del Norte, 1984); and Richard Graham, *Patronage and Politics in Nineteenth–Century Brazil* (Stanford: Stanford University Press, 1990).

4.   Archivo Aparicio Saravia, letter from Carlos Roxlo to Aparicio Saravia, 2 April 1897. First quotation: Luis Ponce de León, *La revolución del 97: escenas y episodios de los combates, las marchas, y los campamentos* (Montevideo: Arca Editorial, 1978 [1st ed. 1898]), 15.

5.   See Luis Alberto de Herrera, *Ventajas e inconvenientes en nuestro país del aumento del número de personas que adquieren título para ejercer profesiones liberales* (Montevideo: Marcos Martínez, 1902); quotation: J. Ariel Madeiro López, *La revolución de 1897* (Montevideo: Ediciones de la Banda Oriental, 1980), 147.

6.   Luis Alberto de Herrera, *Por la patria*, 2 vols. (Montevideo: Cámara de Representantes, 1990 [1st ed. 1898]), 2:261; Ponce, *La revolución del 97*, 96, 118.

7.   Luis R. Ponce de León, *Aparicio Saravia, héroe de la libertad electoral: escrito con la base fundamental de cartas y documentos del archivo de Luis Ponce de León, abanderado en 1897 y secretario del general en 1903 y 1904* (Montevideo: Barreiro y Ramos, 1956), 18; Ponce de León, *La revolución del 97*, 117. On the exclusion of "interests" from insurgent rhetoric, see John Charles Chasteen, "Fighting Words: The Discourse of Insurgency in Latin American History," *Latin American Research Review* 28 (November 1993).

8.   "En el campamento revolucionario: recuerdos e impresiones," *El día*, 20 Sept. 1897. First quotation: "Del diario de Carlos Roxlo," *El eco de la guerra* (July 1897), 6:83.

9.   Ponce de León, *Aparicio Saravia: héroe de la libertad electoral*, 26.

10.   Ponce de León, *La revolución del 97*, 94–104.

11.   "Aparicio Saravia," *La revista uruguaya* (1905), 11:4–8.

12.   Eduardo Acevedo Díaz, *Arroyo Blanco: rememoración en el Club Nacional* (Montevideo: El Nacional, 1898), 15–16, 26–29. First quotation: Ponce de León, *La revolución del 97*, 9; second: Alberto

Palomeque, *El año fecundo (1897–1898)* (Montevideo: A. Barreiro y Ramos, 1898), 76–80; third: Duvimioso Terra, *La revolución de 1897* (Montevideo: El Siglo, 1898), 10. See also Herrera, *Por la patria*, 40–41.

13. Palomeque, *El año fecundo*, 23–27; Viana, *Con divisa blanca*, 60, 109; Dourado, *Voluntários do martírio*, 46.

14. First quotation: "La caída de Aparicio Saravia," *La revista Uruguaya* (1905), 3:8–9; second: Ponce de León, *La revolución del 97*, 76; third: Museo Histórico Nacional, "Milonga a Aparicio Saravia," cinta 10, cara B, no. 6; fourth: Díaz, *Los Saravia*, 41–42; fifth: Herrera, *Por la patria*, 219; sixth: Saravia García, *Memorias*, 88.

15. "Del diario de Carlos Roxlo," *El eco de la guerra* (July 1897), 6:83; Herrera, *Por la patria*, 2:39–40; Díaz, *Historia de Saravia*, 254–55.

16. Abdón Arósteguy, "Narración sobre la revolución de 97," *La revista uruguaya* (1906), 19:10–12; Herrera, *Por la patria*, 2:41; Monegal, *Vida de Aparicio Saravia*, 25–30; Gálvez, *Vida de Aparicio Saravia*, 26.

17. Herrera, *Por la patria*, 2:37 (quoted) and 2:167; "Narración del Comandante Apolinario Vélez sobre la expedición revolucionaria del norte en el 97," *La revista uruguaya* (1905), 8:11; Ponce de León, *La revolución del 97*, 152–53.

18. Ponce de León, *La revolución del 97*, 58–59; Herrera, *Por la patria*, 2:190–97.

19. Ponce de León, *La revolución del 97*, 149–52; Díaz, *Los Saravia*, 46; Dourado, *Voluntários do martírio*, 24–45; Saravia García, *Memorias*, 222.

20. Ponce de León, *La revolución del 97*, 149; Sigmund Freud, "Psicología de las masas y análisis del yo," in *Obras completas*, (Madrid: Amorrotu Editores, 1974).

21. "Aparicio Saravia: recuerdo al mártir," *La revista uruguaya* (1905), 9:8–9. Aparicio's offer of his land titles to buy arms is paralleled by a similar story in which Gumercindo offers personally to repay a man's debts in order to recruit him for the revolution: Fonseca, *Gumersindo Saravia*, 266.

22. Díaz, *Los Saravia*, 47–69.

23. Gálvez, *Vida de Aparicio Saravia*, 197–98; Saravia García, *Memorias*, 84–93. Herrera identifies the ghost authors: *Por la patria*, 2:164–65.

24. "Aparicio Saravia," *La revista uruguaya* (1905), 11:4–7. See also Raúl H. Castagnino, *Circo, teatro gauchesco, y tango* (Buenos Aires: Instituto Nacional de Estudios de Teatro, 1981), 79–106.

MARCH 1897–SEPTEMBER 1904

1. For complete background on the war, see Madeiro López, *La Revolución de 1897*.

2. Norberto Acevedo Díaz, *Invasión del General Aparicio Saravia: Arbolito, diario de campaña* (Montevideo: n.p., 1897), 6–9; Mena Segarra, *Aparicio Saravia: las últimas patriadas*, 87–91; Ponce de León, *La revolución del 97*, 150; Gálvez, *Vida de Aparicio Saravia*, 164.

3. Acevedo Díaz, *Invasión del General Aparicio Saravia*, 10–20.

4. [Abdón Arósteguy], *Memorias de un soldado raso* (Buenos Aires: Galileo, 1897), 45–57; Zavala Muniz, *Crónica de Muniz*, 275; Díaz, *Los Saravia*, 89–94.

5. Terra, *La revolución de 97*, 13–19; [Arosteguy], *Memorias de un soldado raso*, 63; Herrera, *Por la patria*, 2:230.

6. Mena Segarra, *Aparicio Saravia: la últimas patriadas*, 52–54.

7. Madeiro López, *La revolución de 1897*, 147–59.

8. Ibid., 159–68.

9. Sergio Muñoz Miranda, *Escalafón militar del partido blanco* (Montevideo: n.p., 1902). For the "Parade of Veterans," see, for example, *La alborada* (1898), 39. See also Mena Segarra, *Aparicio Saravia: las últimas patriadas*, 38.

10. Florencio Sánchez, "Carta 3: Idolos gauchos," *El caudillaje criminal en Sud América* (Montevideo: Ediciones del Rio de la Plata, 1962), 35–38; Díaz, *Los Saravia*, 42; Díaz, *Historia de Saravia*, 178; Mena Segarra, *Aparicio Saravia: las últimas patriadas*, 110–11; Monegal, *Vida de Aparicio Saravia*, 432–34.

11. Mena Segarra, *Aparicio Saravia: las últimas patriadas*, 104–5, 112–15; Gálvez, *Vida de Aparicio Saravia*, 233–34; Díaz, *Historia de Saravia*, 198–200.

12. Barrán and Nahum, *Historia social de las revoluciones de 1897 y 1904*, 84. On Batlle, see Milton I. Vanger, *José Batlle y Ordóñez of Uruguay: The Creator of His Times, 1902–1907* (Cambridge: Harvard University Press, 1963), and Vanger, *The Model Country: José Batlle y Ordóñez of Uruguay, 1907–1915* (Hanover, N.H.: University Press of New England, 1980).

13.   Mena Segarra, *Aparicio Saravia: las últimas patriadas,* 135–53.

14.   Saravia García, *Memorias,* 587.

APOTHEOSIS AND OBLIVION

1.   See Eric Hobsbawm and Terence Ranger, *The Invention of Tradition* (Cambridge: Cambridge University Press, 1983); Tau Golin, *A ideologia do gauchismo* (Porto Alegre: Tchê, 1983); Luís Carlos Barbosa Lessa, *Nativismo: um fenômeno social gaúcho* (Coleção Universidade Livre; Porto Alegre: L&PM Editores, 1985); Luís Barbosa Lessa and Paixão Côrtes, *Danças e andanças da tradição gaúcha* (Porto Alegre: Editôra Garatuja, 1975).

2.   On usage of the term *gaúcho,* see Lessa, *Nativismo: um fenômeno social gaúcho,* 46.

GLOSSARY

POLITICAL ADVERSARIES OF THE 1890s

Republicans—Rio Grandense ruling party

Federalists—Rio Grandense opposition and insurgent party

Colorados—Uruguayan ruling party

Blancos—Uruguayan opposition and insurgent party

SPANISH/PORTUGUESE TERMS

agregado—social dependent of the landowner, paying no rent

boleadora/boleadeiras—three tethered stones used as tool and weapon

caudillo/coronel—local or regional political leader

chacra/chácara—small agricultural plot

chiripá—loose breech cloth

comisario/delegado—local police chief

comisariato/delegacia—office of the local police chief

cuchilla/coxilha—long, low ridges of Uruguay and Rio Grande do Sul

degüello/degola—execution by throat cutting

divisa—party insignia worn on the hat

doctor/bacharel—doctor of laws (doctorcito is a diminutive form)

estancia/estância—ranch

estanciero/estancieiro—rancher

facón/facão—long knife carried by rural males

Farrapos—Rio Grandense rebels, 1835–1845

gaucho/gaúcho—cowboy of the southern plains

guerra gaucha—the light-cavalry warfare of a *montonera*

mate/chimarrão—Paraguayan tea

Maragatos—followers of Gumercindo, 1893–1895

mestizo/mestiço—mixed race (usually Indian and European)

montonera—a party of mounted guerrillas (*montoneros*)

patriada—an Uruguayan insurgency

patrón/patrão—land owner and "boss"
puebleros—Uruguayanism for "city folks"
puestero/posteiro—worker at an estancia outpost

BIBLIOGRAPHY

PRINCIPAL ARCHIVAL COLLECTIONS

Archivo General de la Nación (AGN), Montevideo
Archivo General de la Nación, Sección Judicial (AGNJ), Montevideo
Arquivo Histórico do Rio Grande do Sul (AHRS), Porto Alegre
Arquivo Público do Rio Grande do Sul (APRS), Porto Alegre

NEWSPAPERS

La alborada (Montevideo)
O bagéense (Bagé)
O Canabarro (Rivera)
El Cerro Largo (Melo)
El ciudadano (Melo)
Correio do povo (Porto Alegre)
O cruzeiro do sul (Bagé)
El deber cívico (Melo)
El eco nacionalista (Melo)
El estanciero (Melo)
O jornal do commércio (Porto Alegre)
El nacional (Melo)
Las noticias (Rivera)
El Partido Colorado (Melo)
A Pátria (Montevideo)
La prensa (Melo)
A restauração (Rivera)
A União Liberal (Bagé)
La voz de Rivera (Rivera)

PUBLISHED PRIMARY SOURCES

Almanaque literário e estatístico do Rio Grande do Sul 1892. Pelotas, Rio Grande, Porto Alegre: Editôres Pintos & Cia., 1892.

Anuario estadístico de la República Oriental del Uruguay. Contribuyentes de la contribución directa. Montevideo: Contaduría del Estado, 1877–1880.

Crónica de la insurrección: sus origenes, sus comienzos, su marcha, y su derrota. Montevideo: La Razón, 1896.

De Província de São Pedro a Estado do Rio Grande do Sul: Censos do RS: 1803–1950

Diarios de sesiones de la Cámara de Representantes (Uruguay)

El eco de la guerra: episódios de la presente campaña con ilustraciones de los principales jefes que actúan en ésta; biografías, episodios, anécdotas, sacrificios, rasgos de heroísmo, etc. Montevideo: La Nueva Central, 1897.

Homenagem aos heróis da Revolução de 1893. Rivera: Tipografia d'O Maragato, 1901.

Memoria de la Jefatura Política y de Policía de Artigas, 1888–89. Montevideo: Tip. Litografía Oriental, 1890.

Memoria de la Jefatura Política y de Policía de Rivera, 1895. Montevideo: Tip. Litografía Oriental, 1896.

Memoria de la Jefatura Política y de Policía del Departamento de Cerro Largo correspondiente a los años de 1876–77–78. Montevideo: La Tribuna, 1879.

Memoria del Ministerio de Hacienda, 1889–1890 (Uruguay).

Memoria que el Ministro de Estado en el Departamento de Gobierno presenta a la Honorable Asamblea Jeneral Legislativa en 1861. Montevideo: Imprenta de la viuda de Jaime Hernández, 1861.

Memorias de un soldado raso. Buenos Aires: Galileo, 1897.

Presupuesto general del departamento de Guerra y Marina, 1869. Montevideo: Departamento de Guerra y Marina, 1869.

Presupuesto jeneral de gastos para el año de 1854. Montevideo: Imprenta Uruguaya, 1853.

Relatório da Câmara Municipal da Cidade de Bagé apresentado à Assembleia Legislativa Provincial. Typographia do Independente, 1888.

Relatório da repartição dos negócios estrangeiros apresentado a assambléia geral legislativa na 3a sessão da 8a legislatura pelo repectivo ministro e secretário de estado. Rio de Janeiro: n.p., 1851.

La revolución oriental de 1896: La campaña de Saravia. Bagé: n.p., 1897.

SECONDARY SOURCES

Acevedo, Eduardo. *Anales históricos del Uruguay.* 6 vols. Montevideo: Barreiro y Ramos, 1933.

Acevedo Díaz, Eduardo. "El primer suplicio." In *Los mejores cuentos camperos del siglo XIX,* ed. Diego Pérez Pintos, 15–20. Montevideo: Ediciones de la Banda Oriental, 1966.

Acevedo Díaz, Eduardo (h.). *La vida de batalla de Eduardo Acevedo Díaz.* Buenos Aires: El Ateneo, 1941.

Acevedo Díaz, Norberto. *Invasión del General Aparicio Saravia: Arbolito, diario de campaña.* Montevideo: n.p., 1897.

Alden, Dauril. *Royal Government in Colonial Brazil: With Special Reference to the Administration of the Marquis of Lavradio, Viceroy, 1769–1779.* Berkeley: University of California Press, 1968.

Alonso Eloy, Rosa, Lucía Sala de Touron, Nelson de la Torre, and Julio Carlos Rodríguez. *La oligarquía oriental en la Cisplatina.* Montevideo: Ediciones Pueblos Unidos, 1970.

Amaral, Anselmo F. *Os campos neutrais.* Porto Alegre: n.p., 1972.

Anderson, Benedict. *Imagined Communities: Reflections on the Origin and Spread of Nationalism.* London: Verso, 1983.

Arósteguy, Abdón. "Narración sobre la Revolución del 97." *La revista uruguaya* (Mercedes, Uruguay), 1905.

Assunçao, Fernando O. *El gaucho, su espacio y su tiempo.* Montevideo: Ediciones Arca, 1969.

———. *Pilchas criollas: Usos y costumbres del gaucho.* 2d ed. Montevideo: Ediciones Master Fer Ltda., 1979.

Ayestarán, Lauro. *La primitiva poesía gauchesca en el Uruguay,* vol. 1: *1812–1838.* Montevideo: Imprenta El Siglo Ilustrado, 1950.

Azambuja, Péricles. *História das terras e mares do Chuí.* Porto Alegre: Escola Superior de Teologia São Lourenço de Brindes; Caxias do Sul: Universidade de Caxias do Sul, 1978.

Azara, Félix de. *Memoria sobre el estado rural del Río de la Plata y otros informes.* Buenos Aires: Editorial Bajel, 1943.

Bagé. *Relatório da Câmara Municipal da Cidade de Bagé apresentado à Assambleia Legislativa Provincial.* Bagé: Typografia do Independente, 1888.

Bakos, Margaret Marchiori. *RS: Escravismo & abolição.* Série Documenta no. 13. Porto Alegre: Mercado Aberto, 1982.

Baretta, Silvio Rogério Duncan. "Political Violence and Regime Change: A Study of the 1893 Civil War in Southern Brazil." Ph.D. diss., University of Pittsburgh, 1985.

Baretta, Silvio Rogério Duncan, and John Markoff. "Civilization and Barbarism: Cattle Frontiers in Latin America." *Comparative Studies in Society and History* 20 (1978): 587–620.

Barman, Roderick J. *Brazil: The Forging of a Nation, 1798–1852.* Stanford: Stanford University Press, 1988.

Barrán, José Pedro. *Apogeo y crisis del Uruguay pastoril y caudillesco, 1838–1875.* Montevideo: Ediciones de la Banda Oriental, 1974.

Barrán, José Pedro, and Benjamín Nahum. *Historia rural del Uruguay moderno.* 5 vols. Montevideo: Ediciones de la Banda Oriental, 1967–1977.

_____. "Proletariado ganadero, caudillismo, y guerras civiles en el Uruguay del Novecientos." *Nova americana* 2 (1979): 169–94.

Barrios Pintos, Aníbal. *De las vaquerías al alambrado: contribución a la historia rural uruguaya.* Montevideo: Ediciones del Nuevo Mundo, 1967.

_____. *Rivera en el ayer: de la crónica a la historia.* Montevideo: Editorial Minas, 1963.

Barros Lémez, Alvaro. *La obra cuentística de Javier de Viana.* Montevideo: Libros del Astillero, 1985.

Barthes, Roland. *Mythologies.* New York: Hill and Wang, 1972.

Bell, Stephen. "Early Industrialization in the South Atlantic: Political Influences on the *charqueadas* of Rio Grande do Sul before 1860." *Journal of Historical Geography* 19 (1993):399–411.

Bello, José Maria. *A History of Modern Brazil, 1889–1964.* Stanford: Stanford University Press, 1966.

Bishko, Charles Julian. "The Peninsular Background of Latin American Cattle Ranching." *Hispanic American Historical Review* 32 (November 1952): 491–515.

Bouton, Roberto J. *La vida rural en el Uruguay.* Montevideo: A. Monteverde y Cía, 1961.

Brazil. Fundação de Economia e Estatística. *De Província de São Pedro a Estado de Rio Grande do Sul—Censos do RS, 1803–1950.* Porto Alegre: Fundação de Economia e Estatística, 1981.

Brint, Michael. *A Genealogy of Political Culture.* Boulder: Westview Press, 1991.

Brito, Severino de Sá. *Trabalhos e costumes dos gaúchos.* Porto Alegre: Livraria do Globo, 1928; reprint ed., Estante Rio-Grandense União de Seguros, n.d.

Bullard, Melissa M. "The Magnificent Lorenzo de Medici: Between Myth and History." In *Politics and Culture in Early Modern Europe: Essays in Honour of H. G. Koenigsberger,* ed. Phyllis Mack and Margaret C. Jacob. Cambridge: Cambridge University Press, 1987.

Burns, E. Bradford. *The Poverty of Progress: Latin America in the Nineteenth Century.* Berkeley: University of California Press, 1983.

Caggiani, Ivo. *Santana do Livramento: 150 años de história.* 2 vols. Santana: Associação Santanense Pro-Ensino Superior, 1983.

Carbajal, Carlos. *La penetración luso-brasileña en el Uruguay.* Montevideo: n.p., 1948.

Cardoso, Fernando Henrique. *Capitalismo e escravidão no Brasil meridional: O negro na sociedade escravocrata do Rio Grande do Sul.* 2d ed. Rio de Janeiro: Paz e Terra, 1977.

Carvalho, Antônio Augusto de. *Apontamentos sobre a revolução no Rio Grande do Sul.* Montevideo: El Siglo Ilustrado, 1895.

Carvalho, Mário Teixeira de. *Nobiliário sul-riograndense.* Porto Alegre: Livraria do Glôbo, 1937.

Castagnino, Raúl H. *Circo, teatro gauchesco, y tango.* Buenos Aires: Instituto Nacional de Estudios de Teatro, 1981.

Castellanos, Alfredo R. *Aparicio Saravia: El caudillo e su tiempo.* Montevideo: Arca Editorial, 1976.

————. *La Cisplatina, la independencia, y la república caudillesca, 1820–1838.* Historia Uruguaya, no. 3. Montevideo: Ediciones de la Banda Oriental, 1974.

César, Guilhermino. *O contrabando no sul do Brasil.* Porto Alegre: Escola Superior de Teologia São Lourenço de Brindes; Caxias do Sul: Universidade de Caxias do Sul, 1978.

————. *História do Rio Grande do Sul: Período colonial.* Porto Alegre: Editôra Globo, 1956.

Chapman, Charles E. "The Age of the Caudillos: A Chapter in Hispanic American History." *Hispanic American Historical Review* 12 (1932): 281–300.

Chasteen, John Charles. "Background to Civil War: The Process of Land Tenure in Brazil's Southern Borderland, 1801–1893." *Hispanic American Historical Review* 71 (1991).

———. "Fighting Words: The Discourse of Insurgency in Latin American History." *Latin American Research Review* 28 (1993).

———. "Trouble Between Men and Women: Machismo on Nineteenth-Century Estancias." In *The Middle Period in Latin American History: Essays on Values and Attitudes in the 17th–19th Centuries,* ed. Mark D. Szuchman. New York: Lynn Rienner Publishers, 1989.

———. "Violence for Show: Knife Dueling on a Nineteenth-Century Cattle Frontier." In *The Problem of Order in Changing Societies: Essays on Crime and Policing in Argentina and Uruguay,* ed. Lyman L. Johnson. Albuquerque: University of New Mexico Press, 1990.

Coni, Emilio A. *El gaucho: Argentina—Brasil—Uruguay.* Buenos Aires: Editorial Sudamericana, 1945.

Cosio, Pedro. *Aduanas de fronteras: Estudio presentado por el subtesorero de la aduana al Ministro de Hacienda.* Montevideo: A. Barreiro y Ramos, 1905.

———. *Crónica de los sucesos de Rivera.* Montevideo: Dornaleche y Reyes, 1903.

Costa, Emilia Viotti da. *The Brazilian Empire: Myths and Histories.* Chicago: University of Chicago Press, 1985.

Crawford, Robert. *South American Sketches.* London: Longman's, Green, and Co., 1898.

Crónica de la insurreción: sus origenes, sus comienzos, su marcha, y su derrota. Montevideo: La Razón, 1896.

D'Avila, F. Maya. *Terra e gente de Alcides Maya.* Porto Alegre: Livraria Sulina Editôra, [1969].

De la Torre, Nelson, Julio C. Rodríguez, and Lucía Sala de Touron. *Después de Artigas (1820–1836).* Montevideo: Ediciones Pueblos Unidos, [1972].

Díaz, José Virginio. *Historia de Saravia: Contribución al estudio del caudillaje en América.* Montevideo: A. Barreiro y Ramos, 1920.

———. *Los Saravia: Una familia de Guerreros (Apuntes rápidos para una biografía).* Montevideo: La Razón, 1903.

Dornelles, Sejanes. *Gumersindo Saraiva: O guerrilheiro pampeano.* Caxias do Sul: EDCUS, 1988.

Dotta, Mario, Duaner Freire, and Nelson Rodríguez. *El Uruguay gana-*

dero: de la explotación primitiva a la crisis actual. Montevideo: Ediciones de la Banda Oriental, 1972.

Dourado, Angelo. *Voluntários do martírio: Fatos e episodios da guerra civil.* Porto Alegre: Martins Livreiro, 1979. First published 1896.

Dreys, Nicolau. *Notícia descritiva da Província do Rio Grande do São Pedro do Sul.* 3d ed. Porto Alegre: Instituto Estadual do Livro, 1961.

Escobar, Wenceslau. *Apontamentos para a história da Revolução Rio-grandense de 1893.* 2d ed. Brasília: Editôra Universidade de Brasília, 1983.

Faoro, Raymundo. *Os donos do poder: Formação do patronato político brasileiro.* Rio de Janeiro: Editôra Globo, 1958.

Fernandes, Florestán. *The Negro in Brazilian Society.* New York: Atheneum, 1971.

Ferreira Filho, Arthur. *História geral do Rio Grande do Sul.* 5th ed. Porto Alegre: Editôra Globo, 1978.

Flory, Thomas. *Judge and Jury in Imperial Brazil, 1808–1871: Social Control and Political Stability in the New State.* Austin: University of Texas Press, 1981.

Fonseca, Pedro C. Dutra. *RS: economia & conflitos políticos na República Velha.* Porto Alegre: Mercado Aberto, 1983.

Franco, Sérgio da Costa. *Júlio de Castilhos e sua época.* Porto Alegre: Editôra Globo, 1967.

_____. *Origens de Jaguarão (1790–1833).* Porto Alegre: Escola Superior de Teologia São Lourenço de Brindes; Caxias do Sul: Universidade de Caxias do Sul, 1980.

_____. "A campanha." In *Rio Grande do Sul: terra e povo.* Porto Alegre: Editôra Globo, 1963.

_____. "O sentido histórico da Revolução de 1893." In *Fundamentos da cultura rio-grandense,* 5:193–216. Porto Alegre: Faculdade de Filosofia da Universidade do Rio Grande do Sul, 1957–62.

Freitas, Décio. *O capitalismo pastoril.* Coleção Temas Gaúchos. Porto Alegre: Escola Superior de Teologia São Lourenço de Brindes; Caxias do Sul: Universidade de Caxias do Sul, 1980.

Freitas, Décio, et al. *A Revolução Farroupilha: história & interpretação.* Porto Alegre: Mercado Aberto, 1985.

Gálvez, Manuel. *Vida de Aparicio Saravia.* Buenos Aires: Imprenta López, 1942.

García Esteban, Fernando. *Vida de Florencio Sánchez.* Montevideo: Editorial Alfa, 1970.

Gil Villaamil, Germán. *Ensayo para una historia de Cerro Largo hasta 1930.* Montevideo: Imprenta del Palacio Legislativo, 1982.

Giuffra, Santiago A. *Fronterizas: Paliques uruguayos–brasileros.* Montevideo: El siglo ilustrado, 1900.

Golín, Tau. *Bento Gonçalves: O héroi ladrão.* Santa Maria, RS: LGR Artes Gráficas, 1983.

_____. *A ideologia do gauchismo.* Porto Alegre: Tchê, 1983.

Gonzaga, Sergius. "As mentiras sobre o gaúcho: primeiras contribuições da literatura." In *RS: cultura & ideologia,* Décio Freitas, et al. Porto Alegre: Mercardo Aberto, 1980.

González, Julio César. "Apuntes bio–bibliograficos." In Félix de Azara, *Memoria sobre el estado rural del Río de la Plata y otros informes,* pp. vii–cxiv. Buenos Aires: Editorial Bajel, 1943.

González, Ramón P. *Aparicio Saravia en la Revolución de 1904.* Montevideo: Editorial Florenza y Lafón, 1949.

González Rissotto, Rodolfo, and Susana Rodríguez Varese de González. "Contribución al estudio de la influencia guaraní en la formación de la sociedad uruguaya." *Revista histórica* (Montevideo) 2d ser., 75 (April 1982): 199–316.

Goulart, Jorge Salis. *A formação do Rio Grande do Sul.* 3d ed. Porto Alegre: Escola Superior de Teologia São Lourenço de Brindes, Martins Livreiro; Caxias do Sul: Universidade de Caxias do Sul, 1978.

Goycochêa, Luís Felipe de Castilhos. *Gumercindo Saraiva na guerra dos maragatos.* Rio de Janeiro: Editôra Alba, 1943.

Graham, Richard. *Patronage and Politics in Nineteenth-Century Brazil.* Stanford: Stanford University Press, 1990.

Halperín Donghi, Tulio. *The Aftermath of Revolution in Latin America.* New York: Harper and Row, 1973.

_____. *The Contemporary History of Latin America,* ed. and trans. John Charles Chasteen. Durham: Duke University Press, 1993.

Hamill, Hugh M. *Caudillos: Dictators in Spanish America.* Norman: University of Oklahoma Press, 1992.

Hasslocher, Germano. *A verdade sobre a Revolução.* 2d ed. Porto Alegre: Livraria Americana, 1894.

Hernández, José. *El gaucho Martín Fierro.* Buenos Aires: Imprenta de La Pampa, 1872.

Herrera, Luis Alberto de. *Por la patria.* 2 vols. Montevideo: Cámara de Representantes, 1990.

_____. *Ventajas e inconvenientes en nuestro país del aumento del número de personas que adquieren título para ejercer profesiones liberales.* Montevideo: Marcos Martínez, 1902.

Hidalgo, Bartolomé. *Obra completa.* With a prologue and notes by Walter Rela. Montevideo: Editorial Ciencias, [1979].

Hobsbawm, Eric, and Terence Ranger. *The Invention of Tradition.* Cambridge: Cambridge University Press, 1983.

Holanda, Sérgio Buharque de., gen. ed. *História geral da civilização brasileira.* 2d ed. vol. 2: *O Brasil monárquico* (part 2). São Paulo: Difusão Européia do Livro, 1967.

Homenagem aos heróis da Revolução de 1893. Rivera: Tipografia d'O Maragato, 1901.

Ibarbourou, Juana de. *Chico Carlo.* Buenos Aires: Editorial Sudamericana, 1944.

Isabelle, Arsenio. *Viaje a Argentina, Uruguay, y Brasil en 1830.* Buenos Aires: Editorial Americana, 1943.

Jacob, Raúl. *Consequencias sociales del alambramiento (1872–1880).* Montevideo: Ediciones de la Banda Oriental, 1969.

Jacques, João Cezimbra. *Ensaio sobre os costumes do Rio Grande do Sul: Precedido de uma ligeira descrição física e uma noção histórica.* Porto Alegre: Typografia de Gundlach & Cia., 1883; reprint ed., Estante Rio-grandense União de Seguros, [1979].

Koebel, William Henry. *The Great South Land: The River Plate and Southern Brazil Today.* New York: Dodd, Mead, and Co., 1920.

Leal, Victor Nunes. *Coronelismo: The Municipality and Representative Government in Brazil,* trans. June Henfrey. Cambridge: Cambridge University Press, 1977.

Leitman, Spencer L. "Negros Farrapos: Hipocrisia racial no sul do Brasil no seculo XIX." In *A Revolução Farroupilha: Historia & interpretação,* ed. José Hildebrando Dacanal, pp. 61–78. Série Documenta, no. 20. Porto Alegre: Mercado Aberto, 1985.

_____. *Raízes sócio-económicas da Guerra dos Farrapos: Um capítulo da história do Brasil no século XIX,* trans. Sarita Linhares Barsted. Rio de Janeiro: Edições Graal, 1979.

_____. "Slave Cowboys in the Cattle Lands of Southern Brazil." *Revista de História* 51 (Jan.–Mar. 1975).

Lessa, Luís Carlos Barbosa. *Nativismo: um fenômeno social gaúcho.* Coleção Universidade Livre. Porto Alegre: L&PM Editores, 1985.

Lessa, Luís Carlos Barbosa, and Paixão Côrtes. *Aspectos da sociabilidade gaúcha.* Porto Alegre: Editôra Proletra, 1985.

_____. *Danças e andanças da tradição gaúcha.* Porto Alegre: Editôra Garatuja, 1975.

Lewin, Linda. *Politics and Parentela in Paraíba: A Case Study of Family-Based Oligarchy in Brazil.* Princeton: Princeton University Press, 1987.

Lindholm, Charles. *Charisma.* Cambridge: Basil Blackwell, 1990.

Lobb, Charles Gary. "The Historical Geography of the Cattle Regions along Brazil's Southern Frontier." Ph.D. diss., University of California, Berkeley, 1970.

Lopes, José Antonio Dias. *A Cidade de Dom Pedrito.* Porto Alegre: Livraria do Glôbo, 1972.

Lopes Neto, João Simões. *Cancioneiro guasca.* 2d ed. Rio de Janeiro: Editôra Glôbo, 1960.

_____. *Contas gaúchescos e lendas do sul.* 2d ed. Rio de Janeiro: Editora Glôbo, 1959.

Love, Joseph L. *Rio Grande do Sul and Brazilian Regionalism, 1882–1930.* Stanford: Stanford University Press, 1971.

Luna, Félix. *Los caudillos.* Buenos Aires: Editorial Jorge Alvarez, 1966.

Lussich, Antonio D. *Los tres gauchos orientales,* Colección de clásicos uruguayos, no. 56. Montevideo: Ministerio de Instrucción y Previsión Social, 1964.

Lynch, John. *Caudillos in Spanish America, 1800–1850.* Oxford: Clarendon Press, 1992.

McLaughlin, Doris B., and Carlos Panizza Pons, eds. "El puerto de Montevido y el abastecimiento rio-grandense; informes consulares ingleses sobre comercio y contrabando fronterizo (1878–1901)." In *Fuentes para la história social y económica del Río de la Plata,* No. 11. Montevideo: 1971.

Madeiro López, J. Ariel. *La revolución de 1897.* Montevideo: Ediciones de la Banda Oriental, 1980.

Magalhães, Manoel Antonio de. "Almanack da Vila de Porto Alegre, 1808." In *O capitalismo pastoril,* ed. Décio Freitas, pp. 76–102 Porto Alegre: Escola Superior de Teologia São Lourenço de Brindes; Caxias do Sul: Universidade de Caxias do Sul, 1980.

Mariante, Hélio Moro. *A idade do couro no Continente d'El Rey.* 2d ed. Porto Alegre: Edições IGTF, 1979.

Maya, Alcides. *Tapera (cenários gaúchos).* 2d ed. Rio de Janeiro: F. Briguiet, 1962. [First published 1910.]

Medeiros, Laudelino. "As cidades." In *Rio Grande do Sul: terra e povo.* Porto Alegre: Editôra Glôbo, 1963.

Medeiros, Manoel da Costa. *História do Herval: Descrição física e histórica.* Porto Alegre: Escola Superior de Teologia São Lourenço de Brindes; Caxias do Sul: Universidade de Caxias do Sul; Herval: Prefeitura Municipal, 1980.

Mello, Tancredo Fernandes de. *O município do Santa Vitória do Palmar: estudo histórico, physico, e político—notas estadísticas.* Porto Alegre: Livraria Americana, 1911.

Mena Segarra, C. Enrique. *Aparicio Saravia: Las últimas patriadas.* Historia Uruguaya: Segunda serie—Los hombres, no. 12. Montevideo: Ediciones de la Banda Oriental, 1981.

Méndez Vives, Enrique. *El Uruguay de la modernización, 1876–1904.* 3d ed. Montevideo: Ediciones de la Banda Oriental, 1977.

Meyer, Augusto. *Cancioneiro gaúcho.* Rio de Janeiro: Editôra Globo, 1957.

Monegal, José. *Vida de Aparicio Saravia.* Montevideo: A. Monteverde y Cía., 1942.

Moura, Euclides B. de. *O vandalismo no Rio Grande do Sul.* Pelotas: Livraria Universal, 1892.

Mourat, Oscar. *La crisis comercial en la cuenca del Plata (1880–1920).* Montevideo: Ediciones de la Banda Oriental, 1973.

Muniz Carbalho, Segundo. *Coronel don Angel Muniz, un caudillo y un idealista, 1823–1892.* Montevideo: Ministerio de Educación y Cultura, [1978].

Muñoz Miranda, Sergio. *Escalafón militar del partido blanco.* Montevideo: n.p., 1902.

Nunes, Zeno Cardoso, and Rui Cardoso Nunes. *Dicionário de regionalismos do Rio Grande do Sul.* Porto Alegre: Martins Livreiro, 1984.

Oliveira Viana, [Francisco]. *Populações meridionais do Brasil.* Vol. 2: *O campeador rio-grandense.* [2d ed.] Rio de Janeiro: Paz e Terra, 1974.

Oliveres, Francisco N. *Toponimia histórico-geográfica de Treinta y Tres y Cerro Largo.* Montevideo: n.p., 1938.

O'Malley, Ilene. *The Myth of the Revolution: Hero Cults and the Institutionalization of the Mexican State, 1920–1940.* New York: Greenwood Press, 1987.

Onody, Oliver. *A inflação brasileira (1820–1958).* Rio de Janeiro, n.p., 1960.

Palomeque, Alberto. *El año fecundo (1897–1898).* Montevideo: A. Barreiro y Ramos, 1898.

Payró, Roberto J. *Crónica de la revolución oriental de 1903.* Montevideo: Ediciones de la Banda Oriental, 1967.

Pebayle, Raymond. "Eleveurs et agriculteurs du Rio Grande do Sul." Ph.D. diss., University of Paris, 1974.

Pereira, Antonio N. *La lucha fratricida y la conciliación: boceto histórico-dramático.* Montevideo: El Siglo Ilustrado, 1897.

Pérez, Saviniano. *Cartilla geográfica con noticias históricas y datos estadísticos del departamento de Cerro Largo.* Melo: Tipografía del Deber Cívico, 1902.

———. *Cerro Largo—Centenario.* Montevideo: Editorial Gutenberg, 1930.

Péristiany, Jean G., ed. *Honour and Shame: The Values of Mediterranean Society.* Chicago: University of Chicago Press, 1966.

Pesavento, Sandra Jatahy. *República velha gaúcha: Charqueadas—frigoríficos—criadores.* Porto Alegre: Editôra Movimento, 1980.

Piccolo, Helga Iracema Langraf. *A política rio-grandense no Segundo Império (1868–1882).* Porto Alegre: Universidade Federal do Rio Grande do Sul, 1974.

Pitt-Rivers, Julian. *The Fate of Schecham or the Politics of Sex: Essays in the Anthropology of the Mediterranean.* Cambridge Studies and Papers in Social Anthropology, no. 19. Cambridge: Cambridge University Press, 1977.

Pivel Devoto, Juan. *Historia de los partidos políticos en el Uruguay.* 2 vols. Montevideo: Claudio García & Cía, 1942.

Ponce de León, Luis. *La revolución del 97: impresiones íntimas, escenas y episodios.* Montevideo: Imprenta Artística de Dornaleche y Reyes, 1898. Abridged 2d ed.: Arca Editorial, 1978.

Ponce de León, Luis R. *Aparicio Saravia, héroe de la libertad electoral: escrito con la base fundamental de cartas y documentos del archivo de Luis Ponce de León, abanderado en 1897 y secretario del general en 1903 y 1904.* Montevideo: Barreiro y Ramos, 1956.

Porto, Aurelio. *História das missões orientais do Uruguai*. Rio de Janeiro: Imprensa Nacional, 1943.

Porto Alegre, Apolinário. *Cancioneiro da Revolução de 1835*. Porto Alegre: Companhia União de Seguros, 1981.

Porto Alegre, Aquiles. *Homens ilustres do Rio Grande do Sul*. 2d ed. Porto Alegre: Estante Rio Grandense União de Seguros, n.d.

Prieto, Adolfo. *El discurso criollista en la formación de la Argentina moderna*. Buenos Aires: Editorial Sudamericana, 1988.

Queiroz, Maria Isaura Pereira de. *O mandonismo local na vida política brasileira e outros ensaios*. São Paulo: Editorial Alfa-Omega, 1976.

Rama, Angel. *La ciudad letrada*. Hanover, N.H.: Ediciones del Norte, 1984.

Rama, Germán W. "Dependencia y segmentación en el Uruguay del siglo XIX." *Revista paraguaya de sociología* 16 (1979): 31–70.

Reyes Abadie, Washington. *Aparicio Saravia y el proceso político-social del Uruguay*. Montevideo: Ediciones del Río de la Plata, 1963.

Reyes Abadie, Washington, Oscar H. Bruschera, and Tabaré Melogno. *La Banda Oriental: Pradera—frontera—puerto*. 3d ed. Montevideo: Ediciones de la Banda Oriental, 1974.

_____. *Crónica de Aparicio Saravia*. 2 vols. Montevideo: Ediciones El Nacional, 1989.

Rheinghantz, Carlos G. "Povoamento do Rio Grande de São Pedro: A contribuição da Colônia do Sacramento." In *Anais do Simpósio Comemorativo do Bicentenário da Restauração do Rio Grande (1776–1976)*, 2:11–527. Rio de Janeiro: Instituto Histórico-Geográfico Brasileiro, 1979.

Rial, Juan. *La población uruguaya y el crecimiento económico social entre 1850 y 1930: Cambio demográfico y urbanización en un pequeño país*. Montevideo: Centro de Informaciones y Estudios Sociales del Uruguay, 1981.

_____ and Jaime Klaczko. *Uruguay: El país urbano*. Montevideo: Ediciones de la Banda Oriental, 1981.

Roche, Jean. "As bases físicas da ocupação do solo no Rio Grande do Sul." In *Tres estudos rio-grandenses*. Porto Alegre: Universidade do Rio Grande do Sul, 1966.

Rodríguez Villamil, Silvia. *Las mentalidades dominantes en Montevideo (1850–1900): I. La mentalidad criolla tradicional*. Montevideo: Ediciones de la Banda Oriental, 1968.

Rona, Pedro. *El dialecto "fronterizo" del norte del Uruguay.* Montevideo: Universidad de la República, 1959.

Ros, Francisco J. *La feria de Melo: Reflexiones económicas sobre los departamentos de Cerro Largo, Treinta y Tres, Rocha, Minas, y Maldonado.* Montevideo: Tipografía de El Nacional, 1902.

Rudiger, Francisco Ricardo. "A imprensa: fonte e agente da Revolução de 1893." Unpublished paper presented in the Museu Dom Diogo de Souza, Bagé, November 1983.

Sáenz Quesada, María. *Los estancieros.* Buenos Aires: Editorial de Belgrano, 1980.

Saint–Hilaire, Auguste de. *Viagem ao Rio Grande do Sul (1820–1821),* trans. Leonam de Azeredo Penna. Belo Horizonte: Livraria Itatiaia Editôra Ltda., 1974.

———. *Voyage a Rio Grande do Sul (Bresil).* Orleans: H. Herluison, 1887.

Safford, Frank. "Politics, Ideology, and Society." In *The Cambridge History of Latin America,* vol. 3. Cambridge: Cambridge University Press, 1985.

———. "Social Aspects of Politics in Nineteenth-Century Spanish America: New Granada, 1825–1850." *Journal of Social History 5* (Spring 1972): 344–70.

Sala de Touron, Lucía; de la Torre, Nelson; and Rodríguez, Julio C. *Artigas y su revolución agraria, 1811–1820.* Mexico City: Siglo Veintiuno Editores, 1978.

Salis, Eurico Jacinto. *História de Bagé.* Porto Alegre: Globo, 1955.

Salteraín de Herrera, Eduardo. *Lavalleja: La redención patria.* Montevideo: n.p., [1957].

Sampognaro, Virgilio. *Descripción geográfica de la frontera Uruguay–Brasil.* Montevideo: El Siglo Ilustrado, 1930.

Sánchez, Florencio. *El caudillaje criminal en Sud América / Cartas de un flojo / Diálogos de actualidad.* Montevideo: Ediciones del Rio de la Plata, 1962.

———. "M'hijo el doctor." In *El teatro del uruguayo Florencio Sánchez: Tres de sus mejores obras,* pp. 11–120. Buenos Aires: Editorial Tor, 1917.

Saravia García, Nepomuceno. *Memorias de Aparicio Saravia: Relato histórico-biográfico de su hijo Nepomuceno ilustrado con la documentación del archivo del General.* Montevideo: Editorial Medina, 1956.

Sarmiento, Domingo Faustino. *Facundo o civilización y barbarie.* Caracas: Biblioteca Ayacucho, 1977.

Schmidt, Steffen W., Laura Guasti, Carl H. Landé, and James C. Scott. *Friends, Followers, and Factions: A Reader in Political Clientelism.* Berkeley: University of California Press, 1977.

Scobie, James R. *Revolution on the Pampas: A Social History of Argentine Wheat.* Austin: University of Texas Press, 1964.

Scott, Renie Sum. *Javier de Viana: un narrador del 900.* Montevideo: Ediciones de la Banda Oriental, 1986.

Shumway, Nicolas. *The Invention of Argentina.* Berkeley: University of California Press, 1991.

Slatta, Richard W. *Gauchos and the Vanishing Frontier.* Lincoln: University of Nebraska Press, 1983.

_____. "Gaúcho and Gaucho: Comparative Socio-economic and Demographic Change in Rio Grande do Sul and Buenos Aires Province, 1869–1920." *Estudos ibero-americanos* 6 (1980): 191–202.

Sodré, Nelson Werneck. *História da Imprensa no Brasil.* Rio de Janeiro: Editôra Civilização Brasileira, 1966.

Spalding, Walter. *A epopéia farroupilha: Pequena história da Grande Revolução acompanhada de farta documentação da época, 1835–1845.* Rio de Janeiro: Biblioteca do Exército, 1963.

Street, John. *Artigas and the Emancipation of Uruguay.* Cambridge: Cambridge University Press, 1959.

Taborda, Tarciso Antonio Costa. *Bagé e a Revolução Farroupilha.* Bagé: n.p., 1985.

Terra, Duvimioso. *La revolución de 1897.* Montevideo: El Siglo, 1898.

Uricoechea, Fernando. *The Patrimonial Foundations of the Brazilian Bureaucratic State.* Berkeley: University of California Press, 1980.

Vanger, Milton I. *José Batlle y Ordóñez of Uruguay: The Creator of His Times, 1902–1907.* Cambridge: Harvard University Press, 1963.

_____. *The Model Country: José Batlle y Ordóñez of Uruguay, 1907–1915.* Hanover, N.H.: University Press of New England, 1980.

Varela, Alfredo. *Revoluções cisplatinas: a República Rio-Grandense.* 2 vols. Porto: Livraria Chardon, 1915.

Vélez Rodríguez, Ricardo. *Castilhismo: uma filosofia da República.* Porto Alegre: Escola Superior de Teologia São Lourenço de Brindes; Caxias do Sul: Universidade de Caxias do Sul, 1980.

Vellinho, Moisés. *Fronteira*. Porto Alegre: Universidade Federal do Rio Grande do Sul and Editôra Globo, 1975.

Viana, Javier de. *Campo*. Biblioteca Rodó de Literatura e Historia: Autores Uruguayos. Montevideo: Claudio García y Cía., 1945.

_____. *Con divisa blanca*. Montevideo: Ediciones de la Plaza, 1979.

_____. *Gurí y otras novelas*. Biblioteca Rodó de Literatura e Historia: Autores Uruguayos. Montevideo: Claudio García y Cía., 1945.

Vianna, Hélio. *Contribuição a história da imprensa brasileira (1812–1869)*. Rio de Janeiro: Imprensa Nacional, 1945.

Villalba, Epaminondas. *A Revolução Federalista no Rio Grande do Sul: documentos e commentários*. Rio de Janeiro, São Paulo, and Recife: Laemmert & Cia. Editôres, 1897.

White, Hayden. "The Fictions of Factual Representation." In *The Tropics of Discourse: Essays in Cultural Criticism*. Baltimore: The Johns Hopkins University Press, 1978.

Wiederspahn, Henrique Oscar. *Bento Gonçalves e as guerras de Artigas*. Porto Alegre: Escola Superior São Lourenço de Brindes; Caxias do Sul: Universidade de Caxias do Sul, 1979.

Wilcox, Robert Wilton. "Cattle Ranching on the Brazilian Frontier: Tradition and Innovation in Mato Grosso, 1870–1940." Ph.D. diss., New York University, 1992.

Wolf, Eric R., and Edward Hansen, "Caudillo Politics: A Structural Analysis." *Comparative Studies of Society and History* 9 (1967): 168–79.

Xavier, Paulo. "A estancia." In *Rio Grande do Sul: terra e povo*. Porto Alegre: Editora Globo, 1963.

Zavala Muniz, Justino. *Crónica de Muniz*. Montevideo: El Siglo Ilustrado, 1921.

Zum Felde, Alberto. *Proceso histórico del Uruguay: Esquema de una sociología nacional*. Biblioteca de Autores Uruguayos. Montevideo: Maximino García, [1919].

INDEX